WALKING ----→
CHICAGO

Walking Chicago: 35 Tours of the Windy City's Dynamic Neighborhoods and Famous Lakeshore

Second edition, second printing 2020

Copyright © 2020 by Robert Loerzel
Copyright © 2008 by Ryan Ver Berkmoes

Distributed by Publishers Group West
Manufactured in the United States of America

Managing editor: Amber Kaye Henderson
Cover design: Scott McGrew
Cartography: Steve Jones and Scott McGrew; map data: Robert Loerzel and OpenStreetMap
Interior design: Lora Westberg; typesetting: Annie Long
Photos: © Robert Loerzel, except as noted on page
Proofreader: Emily C. Beaumont
Indexer: Rich Carlson

Library of Congress Cataloging-in-Publication Data

Names: Loerzel, Robert, 1966– author. | Ver Berkmoes, Ryan, 1960– | Walking Chicago. Wilderness Press.
Title: Walking Chicago : 35 tours of the Windy City's dynamic neighborhoods and famous lakeshore / Robert Loerzel.
Description: Second Edition. | Birmingham, Alabama : Wilderness Press, 2020. | "Distributed by Publishers Group West"—T.p. verso.
Identifiers: LCCN 2019055249 (print) | LCCN 2019055250 (ebook) | ISBN 978-0-89997-697-6 (pbk.) | ISBN 978-0-89997-698-3 (ebook)
Subjects: LCSH: Chicago (Ill.)—Tours. | Walking—Illinois—Chicago—Guidebooks. Chicago (Ill.)—Description and travel. | Chicago (Ill.)—Guidebooks.
Classification: LCC F548.18 .P36 2020 (print) | LCC F548.18 (ebook) | DDC 917.73/1104—dc23
LC record available at lccn.loc.gov/2019055249
LC ebook record available at lccn.loc.gov/2019055250

Published by **WILDERNESS PRESS** . .
An imprint of AdventureKEEN
2204 First Ave. S., Ste. 102
Birmingham, AL 35233
800-443-7227, fax 205-326-1012

Visit wildernesspress.com for a complete list of our books and for ordering information. Contact us at our website, at facebook.com/wildernesspress1967, or at twitter.com/wilderness1967 with questions or comments. To find out more about who we are and what we're doing, visit blog.wildernesspress.com.

Cover photo: Chicago Riverwalk (*see Walk 8, page 46*)

SAFETY NOTICE Although Wilderness Press and the author have made every attempt to ensure that the information in this book is accurate at press time, they are not responsible for any loss, damage, injury, or inconvenience that may occur to anyone while using this book. You are responsible for your own safety and health while following the walking trips described here. Always check local conditions, know your own limitations, and consult a map.

For the latest information about places in this book that have been affected by the coronavirus, please check the "Points of Interest" listings following each walk. For general news and updates about the coronavirus in Chicago and Illinois, check chicago.gov/coronavirus and coronavirus.illinois.gov.

WALKING - - - - - →
CHICAGO

35 Tours of the Windy City's
Dynamic Neighborhoods and Famous Lakeshore

Second Edition

Robert Loerzel

 WILDERNESS PRESS . . . *on the trail since 1967*

Acknowledgments

This book is completely new, but I used the routes in *Walking Chicago*'s 2008 edition as a starting point. That edition's author, Ryan Ver Berkmoes, deserves credit for his smart choices about where to walk in this sprawling city. My key sources were the American Institute of Architects' third edition of the *AIA Guide to Chicago*; *Encyclopedia of Chicago*, available in its entirety at encyclopedia.chicagohistory.org; the detailed descriptions and histories of parks on the Chicago Park District's website, chicagoparkdistrict.com; the Commission on Chicago Landmarks' reports; architecture critic Blair Kamin's many articles for the *Chicago Tribune*; the Chicago Architecture Center's architecture.org website; and the writings and advice of knowledgeable Chicagoans, including Pamela Bannos, Daniel Kay Hertz, Rick Kogan, Richard Lindberg, Natalie Moore, Whet Moser, Bill Savage, and Adam Selzer.

—*Robert Loerzel*

The Uptown Broadway Building (see Walk 32, page 179)

Author's Note

Walking is one of the things I like best about living in Chicago. It's how I get around every day, whether I'm heading to work, going out for coffee, shopping for groceries, or exploring a neighborhood. I ride the Chicago Transit Authority's trains and buses on many of these trips, but walking is always an essential part of the journey. Sometimes, I'll exit the L or subway a stop or two away from my destination—just so I can walk a mile or so around some part of the city.

Many of my friends use bicycles as their primary mode of transportation. In Chicago, as in many cities, cyclists and motorists quarrel about how to share the streets. Personally, I'm glad to see more people finding ways to traverse the city without driving an automobile. But instead of using either form of wheels, I'd rather just walk.

Several years ago, I decided that I should walk at least an hour every day, no matter what was happening with Chicago's notoriously erratic weather. In addition to helping me stay healthy, regular walks give me something to look forward to: either small adventures or moments of peaceful reflection. I've also gotten to know my city better—though I still have many, many streets and parks left to explore. As someone who posts frequently on Twitter and Instagram, I got into the habit of taking photos or short videos during my walks whenever a scene grabbed my attention: A blue sky with puffy white clouds. An old building with fancy terra-cotta. A rabbit hopping across someone's lawn. An amusing phrase on a store's sign. Or a manhole cover with a design I'd never seen before. People began to comment about my peripatetic postings on social media, saying things like: "You're that guy on Twitter who's always walking around Chicago." Of course, I'm hardly the only person who walks around this great city. Like me, countless other Chicagoans know that walking is one of the best ways to discover the world that's within their own city limits.

—R. L.

Walking Chicago

Numbers on this map correspond to walk numbers. A map for each tour follows the text for that walk.

Table of Contents

Introduction

Chicago isn't the only city where the streets form a grid. But the numerous right angles on the map of Chicago—where most streets run straight east and west or straight north and south—make it unusually easy to navigate. And with sidewalks just about everywhere, Chicago is something of a pedestrian's paradise.

Of course, the city isn't simply a grid of streets crisscrossing to form a crossword puzzle pattern. That would be boring. Here and there, diagonal roadways cut through those squares. And streets are interrupted by patches of green space, the forks of the Chicago River, and

One of the faces from the Schiller Theater, now on a wall along Dearborn Street (see Walk 9, page 53)

The BP Pedestrian Bridge connects Millennium Park and Maggie Daley Park (see Walk 5, page 28).

other obstacles, both natural and man-made. All of these features make the Windy City a delightful place to explore on foot.

The town became a subject of fascination in the 19th century, when it was the world's fastest-growing city. Visitors were amazed at how rapidly this crowded, lively, and noisy city rose out of the swampy prairie along Lake Michigan. Chicago stunned the world again when it was reborn after the Great Chicago Fire of 1871 destroyed a third of the city. The revived metropolis became the birthplace of the skyscraper, a center for industry, and a magnet for immigrants. Millions of people from all over flocked here to see the World's Columbian Exposition of 1893. Throughout this era, whenever people saw Chicago for the first time, they marveled at the sights and sounds of this quintessentially modern city.

More than a century later, it's no longer shocking to see skyscrapers, of course. But the traces of all that history—and the surviving architectural gems—are a key part of what makes Chicago an attractive place to inhabit or visit today. Sadly, many old buildings have been demolished over the decades to make way for new ones. Some of this change is inevitable—and occasionally, the new buildings are even wondrous to behold. But it's understandable why longtime Chicagoans feel nostalgic for the old urban landscape they once knew. As you walk around Chicago, look for clues that will help you imagine what the city used to look like in various eras.

Since the 1830s, Chicago's motto has been *Urbs in Horto,* a Latin phrase meaning "City in a Garden." Chicago lives up to that slogan with its numerous parks, including the breathtaking green spaces and beaches along Lake Michigan. Walking in Chicagoland, you're certain to encounter some wildlife. Yes, that includes those stereotypical urban creatures—pigeons and rats—but also be on the lookout for rabbits, butterflies, birds, and even an occasional deer or coyote. Humans are the main species you'll see, of course, and Chicago is a terrific place for people-watching. Don't shy away from visiting neighborhoods where most of the residents belong to ethnic or racial groups different from your own. And if you feel comfortable talking with strangers, consider chatting with some of the people you run into during your walks. In my experience, Chicagoans tend to be friendly.

Chicagoans also tend to worry about their city, even as they sing its praises. Why has the population dipped in the 21st century? Are people abandoning the Windy City because of corrupt politics, high taxes, crime, or cold winters?

All of those things may motivate some folks to seek another place to live, but Chicago is also a vibrant metropolis that attracts many young people from around the Midwest and other parts of the United States as they begin their careers. In part, these new residents are drawn by the city's rich cultural offerings: innovative restaurants acclaimed by foodies, as well as countless great places for cheap eats; a lively craft beer industry; one of the world's best live theater scenes; top-notch museums; plenty of sports, whether you're a spectator or a participant; movie theaters that value the art of cinema; concert venues of all sizes; and numerous art galleries, record shops, bookstores, and boutiques. The walks in this book include many of these cultural hot spots.

This book isn't comprehensive—think of it more as a sample of great routes that will get you started. After you try our suggested walks, keep on exploring. One of Chicago's nicknames is The City That Works, but it also seems apt to call it The City That Walks.

Note: As this book went to press in 2020, the coronavirus pandemic was threatening the future of many local businesses. If you plan to visit any of the points of interest located along these walking routes, consider calling ahead or checking their websites.

1   Michigan Avenue at the Chicago River
Where Chicago Began

Above: The skyline south of the Chicago River at Michigan Avenue

BOUNDARIES: Illinois St., St. Clair St., State St., Randolph St.
DISTANCE: 1 mile
DIFFICULTY: Easy
PARKING: Paid garages and lots, including Millennium Park's underground garage
PUBLIC TRANSIT: Any Chicago Transit Authority (CTA) train downtown and exit near State and Lake, or take a Metra train downtown

The space where Michigan Avenue crosses the Chicago River feels like the true heart of the city: a grand public space surrounded by skyscrapers, with a river running through it. Until 1920, Michigan Avenue did not extend north of the river. It lined up with a roadway of warehouses on the river's north side called Pine Street. Daniel Burnham and Edward Bennett suggested building a bridge when they wrote the *Plan of Chicago* in 1909—a famous blueprint for making the city more beautiful and livable.

Walk Description

Begin at the northeast corner of Michigan Avenue and Upper Wacker Drive—at the ❶ **DuSable Bridge**'s south end. American Indians signed a treaty in 1795 handing this land to the US government. Army Captain John Whistler arrived in 1803 and began building a garrison called Fort Dearborn. Metal plates on the sidewalk here mark the fort's outline.

Half a block east of where you're standing, on Wacker's south side, the ❷ **Chicago Architecture Center** features exhibits including a scale model of downtown. Gaze across the river at the elegant 1920s architecture—the Wrigley Building and Tribune Tower—as well as newer shiny structures: the Apple Store and Trump International Hotel & Tower. Look south at the Carbide and Carbon Building, a block south of here on Michigan's west side. The Art Deco masterpiece from 1929 is covered with black granite, green and gold terra-cotta, and bronze trim.

Look at the bridge, which has sculptural reliefs on the houses at each corner. At this corner, *Regeneration* by Henry Hering commemorates the city's rebirth after the Great Chicago Fire of 1871. An angel blows a horn above workers and a female figure holding a carpenter's square. Under her feet is a giant salamander, symbolizing fire.

Walk north on the bridge's east side. Looking east, you'll see where the river passes under bridges at Columbus Drive and Lake Shore Drive, with Lake Michigan beyond. At the bridge's north end, look at the sculpture by James Earle Fraser (who also designed the buffalo nickel). *The Discoverers* shows Louis Jolliet and Jacques Marquette, Frenchmen who explored the region in canoes, reaching Chicago on September 13, 1673.

Continue north, following the sidewalk as it bends east, pausing at Erik Blome's 2009 bust of Jean Baptiste Point du Sable, an African American trader, trapper, and farmer believed to be the first permanent resident (other than American Indians) of the place now called Chicago. This is where du Sable lived in a cabin from the 1780s until 1800.

Walk north into ❸ **Pioneer Court,** where you may see food trucks, musicians, and people selling tour tickets. The plaza includes a sculpture of Jack Brickhouse, a sportscaster who announced Cubs games for four decades. Head for the ❹ **Apple Store** at the plaza's south edge. This glass box opened in 2017, with transparent walls 14 feet high at street level, and 32 feet high on the side facing the river. Inside the light-filled space, a stepped seating area faces a big video screen. On the building's west side, walk down the steps toward the river. Then go east, taking in views of the skyline south of the river (including two of architect Jeanne Gang's undulating skyscrapers, Vista Tower and Aqua at Lakeshore East). Go up the stairs on the store's east side, returning to Pioneer Court and walking north.

Pioneer Court is an ideal spot to view the ❺ **Wrigley Building** complex, over on the west side of Michigan Avenue. Completed in 1924, it was the headquarters for the world's largest chewing gum company. Designed by Graham, Anderson, Probst & White, the structures are covered with 250,000 pieces of terra-cotta glazed with six subtly different shades of white. The south building was Chicago's tallest when it was finished in 1921, with a tower rising 398 feet—including a clock with 19-foot-diameter faces pointing all four directions. The Wrigley Building has always been illuminated at night (except for a few gaps, including World War II and nine months during the 1970s energy crisis). Wrigley Company employees moved out in 2012, and now the complex is filled with offices and retail space.

The *Chicago Tribune*'s old headquarters are at Pioneer Court's north end. But that newspaper moved out of its Gothic Revival skyscraper in 2018, when ❻ **Tribune Tower**'s new owners converted it into luxury condominiums. Tribune Tower was built in 1925, after Raymond Hood and John Mead Howells won out over 259 competitors vying for the $50,000 prize in the *Tribune*'s competition seeking a design for "the most beautiful office building in the world." The 36-story tower's crown resembles the top of a medieval cathedral. The walls inside the Michigan Avenue lobby are engraved with quotations by Thomas Jefferson, James Madison, *Tribune* publisher Colonel Robert R. McCormick, and others—words exalting freedom of the press. A statue of Revolutionary War hero Nathan Hale stands along the building's west side. Walk around Tribune Tower and its adjoining buildings—north on Michigan, then east on Illinois Street—looking at the 150 fragments of other famous buildings embedded in the walls, including pieces of the Taj Mahal, Alamo, Great Wall of China, Parthenon, White House, and Great Pyramid of Giza. McCormick began this collection in 1923, instructing his reporters to obtain pieces of noteworthy buildings "by honorable means."

Return west, crossing Michigan, then turn south. In front of the Realtor Building, an opening leads down to Lower Michigan Avenue, with a sign for the ❼ **Billy Goat Tavern.** The streets where you've been walking are actually elevated above ground level. The lower level is used for deliveries and garbage pickup (and homeless people often take shelter in these hidden depths). Walk down. At the bottom of the stairs, turn right, walking west on Hubbard Street to the Billy Goat Tavern. This is where Leo Burnett adman Don Novello used to eat, amused by the way the guys behind the counter chanted, "Cheezborger, cheezborger, cheezborger." In 1978 he wrote sketches for *Saturday Night Live* inspired by the Billy Goat, starring John Belushi, Dan Aykroyd, and Bill Murray as employees who refused to accept any orders other than "cheezborgers," chips, and Pepsi. (The actual menu isn't quite so limited.)

Open since 1964, this is the most famous of several Billy Goats. Its history goes back to 1934, when Greek immigrant William Sianis bought the Lincoln Tavern near Chicago Stadium (now the

United Center). A goat fell off a truck and wandered inside. Sianis adopted it, growing a goatee and changing his bar's name to the Billy Goat. In 1945 Wrigley Field ushers refused to let Sianis bring his goat into a World Series game, and Sianis said he'd "sue for a million"—a threat that entered legend as a curse. After Sianis's nephew Sam became the Billy Goat's owner, the Cubs let him bring a goat into the ballpark. "The curse is lifted," Sam declared in 1984. But it wasn't until 2016 that the Cubs made it to the World Series again. The Billy Goat is a popular hangout for journalists, and the walls are filled with newspaper clippings and photos of reporters and local celebrities.

Return to the stairs where you descended, going back up. Head south on Michigan Avenue's west side. Julian Martinez's sculpture of Benito Pablo Juárez, Mexico's president from 1858 to 1872, stands in the Plaza of the Americas. The statue, a gift from the Mexican consulate general, was installed here in 1999.

Continuing south, take a closer look at the fleurs-de-lis, griffins, and cornucopias on the Wrigley Building's walls. A pedestrian bridge connects the third floors of the two Wrigley structures. Renovations in 2013 removed a glass-and-metal wall below the bridge, making it easier to enter the courtyard. Higher up, a bridge connecting the 14th floors was added in 1931—so that bank offices in the two buildings could be legally considered as a single branch.

As you continue south, the sidewalk widens near the river. People often pose for photos here, while magicians, musicians, and other performers try to catch the attention of passersby. On the bridge's northwest tower, sculptor Fraser's *The Pioneers* depicts an angel protecting early settlers, including John Kinzie, a British fur trader described as Chicago's first white resident. He may also have been Chicago's first murderer, though he claimed he was acting in self-defense when he killed French trader Jean Lalime on June 17, 1812. Earlier, Kinzie had purchased his cabin from Lalime, who'd apparently bought it from du Sable.

Walk south across the river on the bridge's west side. Looking west, you'll see the river stretching toward Wolf Point, where it splits into the North Branch and South Branch. Up ahead of you, ❽ **LondonHouse Chicago** stands at the southwest corner of Michigan and Wacker. The hotel (including the LH Rooftop restaurant) opened in 2016 after renovating this 318-foot tower, which was the London Guarantee and Accident Building when it opened in 1923.

At the bridge's southwest corner, sculptor Hering's *Defense* shows the Battle of Fort Dearborn on August 15, 1812. Captain William Wells faces off with an Indian, their blades drawn. After US soldiers and civilians evacuated Fort Dearborn, 500 Potawatomi attacked, killing 67 people, including Wells, and then burning down the fort.

Walk west on the north side of Wacker. Across the river, you'll see the twin cylindrical towers of Marina City. Near Wabash Avenue, there's a statue of *Sun-Times* columnist and TV talk show host Irv "Kup" Kupcinet. Cross Wabash to see the Heald Square Monument, where George Washington is flanked by American Revolution financiers Robert Morris and Haym Salomon.

Take the crosswalk south across Wacker Drive. That round building east of the intersection is the Seventeenth Church of Christ, built in 1968 and designed by Harry Weese. Walk east across Wabash and continue east on Wacker Place. On the street's north side, the ❾ **Chicago Motor Club Building** is a 15-story Art Deco gem marked with a C logo. Built in 1928 and designed by John A. Holabird and John Wellborn Root Jr., it became a Hampton Inn in 2015. The restored lobby features a 33-foot-wide mural map and a 1928 Ford Model A.

As you approach the next corner, the ornately detailed Carbide and Carbon Building is on the south side. Formerly the Hard Rock Hotel, it reopened in 2018 as ❿ **St. Jane Hotel,** named for social reformer Jane Addams. Walk south on Michigan Avenue's west side. At 180 N. Michigan, visit the second-floor ⓫ **American Writers Museum.**

This walk ends when you reach the corner of Michigan Avenue and Randolph Street. From here, you can enter Millennium Park (Walk 5), stroll south on Michigan Avenue, or head east into the Loop (Walk 2). You can catch various CTA trains a few blocks west of here or Metra trains at Millennium Station.

The Billy Goat Tavern, on Lower Hubbard Street

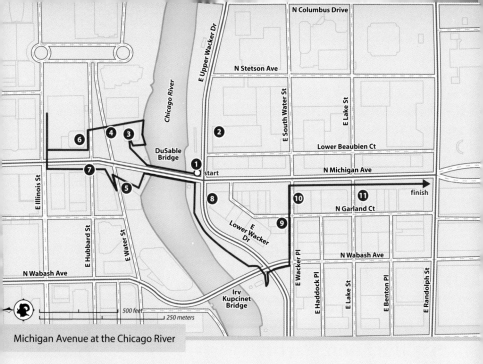

Michigan Avenue at the Chicago River

Points of Interest

1 DuSable Bridge Michigan Ave. and the Chicago River

2 Chicago Architecture Center 111 E. Wacker Dr., 312-922-3432, architecture.org

3 Pioneer Court Michigan Ave. north of the Chicago River

4 Apple Store 401 N. Michigan Ave., 312-529-9500, apple.com/retail/michiganavenue

5 Wrigley Building 400–410 N. Michigan Ave., thewrigleybuilding.com

6 Tribune Tower 435 N. Michigan Ave., tribunetower.com

7 Billy Goat Tavern 430 N. Michigan Ave., Lower Level, 312-222-1525, billygoattavern.com

8 LondonHouse Chicago 85 E. Wacker Dr., 312-357-1200, londonhousechicago.com

9 Chicago Motor Club Building–Hampton Inn Chicago Downtown 68 E. Wacker Pl., 312-419-9014, hilton.com/en/hotels/chilohx-hampton-chicago-downtown-n-loop-michigan-ave

10 St. Jane Hotel 230 N. Michigan Ave., 312-345-1000, stjanehotel.com

11 American Writers Museum 180 N. Michigan Ave., 312-374-8790, americanwritersmuseum.org

2 The Loop, Part 1
The North Loop's Civic Buildings, Stores, and Art

Above: The Chicago Theatre

BOUNDARIES: Lake St., Michigan Ave., Madison St., Wells St.
DISTANCE: 1.2 miles
DIFFICULTY: Easy
PARKING: Paid garages and lots, including Millennium Park's underground garage
PUBLIC TRANSIT: Any CTA train downtown and exit near State and Lake; take a Metra train
 downtown; any of the CTA buses running on Michigan Avenue

The Loop is the set of elevated train tracks in Chicago's central business district, but it's also what Chicagoans call downtown itself. The district was originally a mix of houses, stores, offices, factories, docks, and rail yards, but all that was reduced to ashes by the Great Chicago Fire of 1871. That disaster created a blank slate. Taller buildings went up, and Chicago became the birthplace of the skyscraper—as well as the city that invented department stores.

For much of the 20th century, the Loop was the place to go for stage shows, movies, and fancy dining. But as more people moved to the suburbs, State Street's corridor of stores was eclipsed by shopping malls. In 1979 State Street was closed off to auto traffic except for buses, taxis, and delivery vehicles. The experiment was seen as a failure, as seven department stores closed over the next 17 years. The Loop remained an important business district, but it often felt like a ghost town on evenings and weekends.

It gained new life after old theaters were renovated and reopened, starting in 1986. The city reopened State Street to traffic in 1996, with Beaux Arts–style street lamps, L entrances, and landscaping islands in the sidewalks. Millennium Park's opening in 2004 lifted the Loop's spirit. The Loop is once again a place where people want to hang out, not just go to work.

This walk covers the Loop's north end. For a longer outing, continue with Walk 3—and after that, Walk 4.

Walk Description

Start at Michigan Avenue and Randolph Street, where the ❶ **Chicago Cultural Center** is at the southwest corner. This was the city's first permanent public library when it opened in 1897. It now hosts art exhibits, concerts, and other cultural events, usually with free admission. The beautiful rooms include Preston Bradley Hall, which has the world's largest Tiffany stained glass dome. Walk west on Randolph, then turn south on Garland Court, where Chicago artist Kerry James Marshall's massive *Rush More* mural depicts 20 women who have shaped the city's culture. Marshall, who has had paintings sell for millions at auction, painted this work—his largest—for a fee of $1 in 2017.

At the end of the block, walk west on Washington, approaching the steel girders of the Loop above Wabash Avenue—a structure for elevated trains that opened in 1897. Looking south, you'll see the Loop's newest station, the Washington Street stop that debuted in 2017, with a white canopy shaped like skeletal spines. This block is Jewelers Row, where jewelry shops have been concentrated since 1912.

Continue west on Washington. Looming on your south is a 10-story-high mural of blues great Muddy Waters, clutching his guitar amid a checkered field of colors. Eduardo Kobra led a team of artists who painted it in 2016. At Washington and State Streets, look to the southwest corner at the Reliance Building, a 14-story beauty from 1895 with a shining facade of glass and white terra-cotta, designed by Daniel Burnham, John Wellborn Root, and Charles Atwood.

Turn north on State. This is the front of the ❷ **Macy's** store, which takes up an entire block. It was Marshall Field's, one of the world's leading department stores, for most of its history. Its oldest portions, designed by Atwood, were built in 1892. The store, which Macy's acquired in 2006, has a Tiffany ceiling on its fifth floor. Inside, the Walnut Room restaurant has served meals since 1907. Great clocks hang above the two corners on State—one from 1897 and the other from 1902—each made of 7.75 tons of cast bronze. The store is famous for its window displays, especially at Christmastime.

Across the street is ❸ **Block Thirty Seven.** After most of the buildings on this block were demolished in 1989, the land sat vacant for decades. Plans to develop it finally came to fruition in 2016 with this shopping center complex, which includes clothing stores, restaurants, and movie theaters.

When you reach Randolph Street, look to the west to see the marquee of the ❹ **James M. Nederlander Theatre,** which was the Oriental Theatre until 2019. Chicago's Balaban and Katz movie theater chain unveiled this lavishly decorated venue in 1926. It was created by brother architects Cornelius and George Rapp, who also designed Balaban and Katz's flagship movie palace straight north of you on State Street: the ❺ **Chicago Theatre.** Continue north on State, walking under the marquee, which has 8,915 light bulbs. Rescued from demolition plans in the 1980s, the 1921 theater is now a leading venue for concerts. Guided tours are offered at noon each day. On the sidewalk in front of the theater, a plaque is dedicated to Roger Ebert, the late *Sun-Times* film critic, who cohosted the *Sneak Previews* and *At the Movies* TV shows with the *Tribune's* Gene Siskel (and later with other critics). Across the street, the ❻ **Gene Siskel Film Center** shows a wide variety of foreign, independent, and classic movies.

Continue north to Lake Street, walk west across State, and then turn south. Gaze over at Chicago Theatre for a better view of its splendid exterior. A circle of neon lights features a C as well as the shape of the letter Y. A common symbol throughout Chicago, a Y inside a circle is known as the Chicago Municipal Device, representing the Chicago River's configuration.

As you go south, the ABC 7 Chicago studios are on your west, with large windows showing the sets where newscasts are filmed. The building was formerly the State-Lake Theatre, a vaudeville house from 1919 (another Rapp & Rapp design). Halfway down the block, turn west into the alley called Couch Place, a neatly maintained corridor with brick walls, fire escapes, murals, and classy light fixtures. This was once described as "a valley of death." Adjacent to the alley, the Nederlander Theatre stands on the site of the Iroquois Theatre, where about 600 people perished in a fire on December 30, 1903. Some jumped or fell to their deaths from fire escapes in Couch Place.

As you emerge onto Dearborn Street, look across the street at the ❼ **Goodman Theatre,** which moved here in 2000. The building's north half retains the facades of the Harris and Selwyn Theaters from 1922. Turn south on Dearborn, walking along a green building decorated with ram's heads. This was the Oliver Typewriter Company's headquarters, built in 1907. Just south of it is the Delaware Building, which was called the Bryant Block when it was built in 1872. An Italianate design with precast concrete facades, it's one of the Loop's oldest buildings. Today, the bottom two floors contain a McDonald's.

At Randolph, cross to the southwest corner—and the **❽ Richard J. Daley Center,** a steel-and-glass box containing Cook County courtrooms. Walk south along the building into Daley Plaza, where Chicago's famous 50-foot-high, 162-ton steel Pablo Picasso sculpture stands. When it was unveiled on August 15, 1967, many people didn't know what to make of it. Picasso seemed to agree when his wife, Jacqueline, told *Look* magazine, "Can't they see it's a woman's head?" Picasso smiled and remarked, "Imagine how funny it would have been if instead of a classical Cubist sculpture, I had modeled something a little bit naughty."

Walk to the plaza's southeast corner and cross to the south side of Washington. Walk west to the courtyard where Spanish artist Joan Miró's *Miró's Chicago,* which was unveiled in 1981, stands 39 feet tall with outstretched arms and something like a fork protruding from its head. Immediately west, the steeple-topped **❾ Chicago Temple** skyscraper contains the First United Methodist Church, the city's oldest congregation, founded in 1831. In the courtyard, you can view stained glass windows that tell the church's history.

Cross to the northwest corner of Washington and Clark Streets. Head north on Clark along-side the **❿ County Building,** constructed in 1911 (connecting with City Hall to the west). This wall is decorated with sculptures of robust male figures. Continue north across Randolph and stop at the **⓫ James R. Thompson Center,** an Illinois government complex that opened in 1985

The James R. Thompson Center

with a curving postmodern design by Helmut Jahn, including a vast rotunda that is 160 feet in diameter and 13 stories high. Many Chicagoans loathe the building, but it has some ardent fans. State officials put it up for sale in 2019, raising fears that it could be demolished. In front of it, that 29-foot-high white blob covered with black lines is *Monument with Standing Beast,* a 1984 fiberglass sculpture by French artist Jean Dubuffet. It includes four elements—possibly a standing animal, a tree, a portal, and an architectural form—which you can walk through and explore. Dubuffet called it a "drawing which extends . . . into space."

Go one block west on Randolph. Looking farther west, you can see the sign for the **12** **Cadillac Palace Theatre,** designed by the Rapp brothers in 1926. Turn south on La Salle Street, an urban canyon, where you'll see the Chicago Board of Trade Building five blocks ahead. Standing on the east side of La Salle with imposing columns, **13** **City Hall** was built in 1911. The entrance is flanked by sculptural reliefs representing governmental issues: playgrounds, schools, water supply, and the park system. They were created by artist John Flanagan, who also designed George Washington's portrait on the quarter.

On the west side of the street, 120 N. La Salle St. is a 40-story office building designed by Jahn in 1992. Above the entrance, a large mosaic shows a father and son flying with feathered wings. An artist from the Chicago Imagist movement, Roger Brown, created this scene, titling it *The Flight of Daedalus and Icarus.* Continue south to Washington Street, then walk west. As you pass under the L at Wells Street, the Washington Block is at the southwest corner. The five-story Italianate structure was one of the city's tallest buildings when it went up a few years after the 1871 fire.

This walk ends at Washington and Wells Streets, where you can depart via the L. Or you can continue with Walk 3.

Another Nearby Walk: The Pedway

A network of underground pedestrian passageways called the **14** **Pedway** connects many of the Loop's government buildings, stores, hotels, and transit stations. The Pedway is open Monday–Saturday, 6 a.m.–8 p.m., and Sunday, 10 a.m.–8 p.m. Enter the main east–west corridor through the steps in front of 120 N. La Salle or the stairs just inside the County Building's 118 N. Clark entrance. Walk 0.5 mile east under Daley Plaza, Block Thirty Seven, Macy's (where 22 windows from the Smith Museum of Stained Glass Windows are displayed in the corridor), and the Chicago Cultural Center; continue east through the Shops at Millennium Station and across the train platform; and arrive at the Harris Theater's lower level, where you can take stairs or an elevator up into Millennium Park.

(See tinyurl.com/thechicagopedway for a map.)

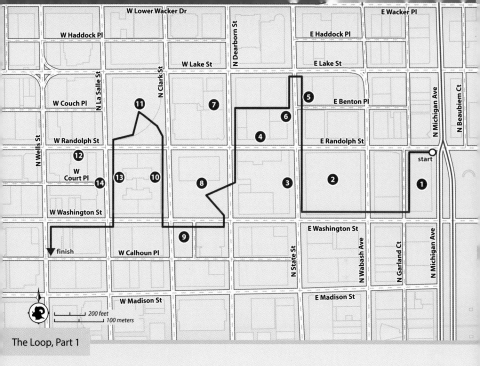

The Loop, Part 1

Points of Interest

1. **Chicago Cultural Center** 78 E. Washington St., 312-744-3316, chicagoculturalcenter.org

2. **Macy's** 111 N. State St., 312-781-1000, macys.com

3. **Block Thirty Seven** 108 N. State St., 312-261-4700, blockthirtyseven.com

4. **James M. Nederlander Theatre** 24 W. Randolph St., 312-977-1700, tinyurl.com/nederlanderchicago

5. **Chicago Theatre** 175 N. State St., 312-462-6300, thechicagotheatre.com

6. **Gene Siskel Film Center** 164 N. State St., 312-846-2800, siskelfilmcenter.org

7. **Goodman Theatre** 170 N. Dearborn St., 312-443-3800, goodmantheatre.org

8. **Richard J. Daley Center and Plaza** 50 W. Washington St., 312-603-3054, thedaleycenter.com

9. **Chicago Temple** 77 W. Washington St., 312-236-4548, chicagotemple.org

10. **County Building** 118 N. Clark St., 312-443-5500, cookcountyil.gov

11. **James R. Thompson Center** 100 W. Randolph St., 312-814-5766, tinyurl.com/jrthompsoncenter

12. **Cadillac Palace Theatre** 151 W. Randolph St., 312-977-1700, broadwayinchicago.com/theatre/cadillac-palace-theatre

13. **City Hall** 121 N. La Salle St., 312-744-5000, chicago.gov

14. **Another Nearby Walk: The Pedway** *Entrance:* 120 N. La Salle St., tinyurl.com/thechicagopedway

3 The Loop, Part 2
A Cross-Section of Downtown

Above: Riverside Plaza was originally the Chicago Daily News Building.

BOUNDARIES: Washington St., Clifton St., Van Buren St., Wabash Ave.
DISTANCE: 2.5 miles
DIFFICULTY: Easy
PARKING: Paid garages and lots
PUBLIC TRANSIT: Brown or Purple Line to Washington and Wells

On this walk, you'll cross through the middle of downtown Chicago, spanning from the impressive structures of Union Station and the Lyric Opera near the Chicago River's South Branch over to the most notable works of architecture and art in the heart of the Loop.

Walk Description

Begin at the L station at Washington and Wells Streets. Walk south on Wells, then west on Madison Street. As you cross Wacker Drive, you'll see the ❶ **Lyric Opera House** at the northwest corner. Originally the Civic Opera House when it opened in 1929, it has been the home of the Lyric Opera of Chicago since 1954. On the exterior, look for details such as sculptures of faces. Walk north up Wacker under the colonnaded portico. When you reach the end of the building, turn west, taking the Washington Street Bridge across the Chicago River's South Branch. This is downtown's oldest existing bridge, built in 1913.

After crossing the bridge, walk south on the plaza along the river's west side, in front of Riverside Plaza, an Art Deco skyscraper from 1929. Designed by Holabird & Root, it was originally the Chicago Daily News Building. That newspaper moved out of the building in 1960 and ceased publication in 1978. The building is decorated with bas-relief images of writing and printing, along with the names of prominent figures in journalism, including *Chicago Daily News* publisher Victor Lawson.

Look across to the Lyric Opera House. From this vantage, you can see how the limestone building—with its 45-story office tower and two 22-story wings—is shaped like a chair. That explains its nickname: Insull's Throne. Utilities tycoon Samuel Insull spent $20 million constructing it. The stock market crashed six days before the opera house's debut in 1929, and within a few years, Insull's opera house closed as his business empire collapsed.

Cross Madison and continue south two more blocks. Go west on Adams Street for one block, cross Canal Street, then turn south on Canal, walking alongside ❷ **Union Station** with its Corinthian columns. Built in 1925 and designed by Graham, Anderson, Probst & White, it is Chicago's last surviving intercity terminal. Halfway down the block, walk through the entrance, going down the staircase where gangsters and feds waged a gun battle in the 1987 movie *The Untouchables*. At the bottom, you'll enter the Great Hall, with a 219-foot-long barrel-vaulted skylight. Walk south, exiting onto Jackson Boulevard.

Walk east on Jackson across the river and cross Wacker. One of Chicago's most recognizable buildings is on Jackson's north side. Now named ❸ **Willis Tower,** it was originally Sears Tower, housing retailer Sears Roebuck and Company's offices. Designed by Bruce Graham and Fazlur Khan of Skidmore, Owings & Merrill, the 110-story skyscraper was the world's tallest building when it was completed in 1974, measuring in at 1,451 feet. It held that title for 25 years, but Willis Tower is no longer even in the top 10. A boxy pinnacle of black aluminum and bronze-tinted glass, it is a cluster of nine tubes supporting one another. The tubes are different heights, which disrupts the force of winds blowing against the building. Sears moved out in 1995, making way for insurance broker Willis Group Holdings to change the building's name in 2009. Visitors can pay for an elevator ride up to the Skydeck and the Ledge—glass boxes jutting out from the 103rd floor, allowing you to walk across a transparent floor and look 1,353 feet straight down.

Walk north on Franklin Street, then east on Adams Street, and south on La Salle Street, the heart of the financial district. Presiding at the southeast corner of Adams and La Salle, the Rookery was praised as "the most modern of office buildings" after it opened in 1888. Architects John Wellborn Root and Daniel Burnham mixed elements of late Roman, Venetian, Moorish, and medieval European design. Farther south, two similar buildings with classical columns face each other across La Salle Street: Bank of America and the Federal Reserve Bank Building, which includes the ❹ **Money Museum.** The ❺ **Chicago Board of Trade Building** stands south of Jackson, facing north up the middle of La Salle. This 45-story throne-shaped skyscraper, designed by the Holabird & Root firm and completed in 1930, is the epitome of Art Deco architecture, with streamlined and geometric shapes. A large clock above the main entrance is flanked by figures of men holding grain. High above them, John Storrs's faceless aluminum statue of Ceres, the Roman goddess of agriculture, stands atop the pyramid-shaped roof. Organized in 1848, the Chicago Board of Trade was the country's first grain futures exchange, famous for its trading floor, "the Pit." Now part of the CME Group, it closed most trading pits in 2015, replacing open outcry trading with online transactions.

Walk to the plaza on Jackson's south side, east of the building—where 12-foot-tall statues of two Greek goddesses stand. These figures were above the doors of an earlier Chicago Board of Trade (CBOT) Building. Walk south, passing under a portion of the CBOT complex and emerging on Van Buren Street. Walk east. When you reach Clark, look at the southeast corner. That beige triangular 27-story high-rise with narrow slits for windows is the Metropolitan Correctional Center, a federal lockup designed by Harry Weese and built in 1975. In the late 1800s, this block of Clark Street was a red-light district, including madam Carrie Watson's brothel. It was also Chicago's original Chinatown. And the building at 428 S. Clark—now occupied by a pawn shop and the Ewing Annex Hotel—was the Workingmen's Exchange, a tavern run by the famously corrupt alderman Michael "Hinky Dink" Kenna in the early 1900s.

Continue east. At the southeast corner of Van Buren and Dearborn, the curvy 17-story Old Colony Building was designed by the Holabird & Roche firm and completed in 1894. On the northeast corner, the 18-story Fisher Building—designed by D. H. Burnham & Co., built in 1896, and expanded in 1907—is covered with details depicting marine creatures. Turn north on Dearborn. The west side of this block is filled by the Monadnock Building, a turning point in skyscraper design. Its north half, completed in 1891 and designed by Burnham & Root, used load-bearing construction, relying on the strength of bricks piled on top of bricks. But when Holabird & Roche designed the south half and completed it two years later, they used a rigid steel frame to hold up the building. The exterior brick and terra-cotta aren't bearing the structure's weight there, so more ornamentation was possible.

Continue north. After crossing Jackson, you've reached the Chicago Federal Center, a trio of steel-and-glass government buildings from 1974 that epitomize the famous "less is more" philosophy of their architect, Ludwig Mies van der Rohe. Amid these boxy structures, Alexander Calder's red 53-foot-tall *Flamingo* is poised in the plaza.

Continue north. As you cross Adams, you're half a block west of the ❻ **Berghoff,** one of Chicago's oldest restaurants, a German tavern and eatery in business since 1898 (except for a few months in 2006). North of Adams on Dearborn's west side, the entrance of the Marquette Building (designed by Holabird & Roche and completed in 1895) is decorated with relief sculptures telling the story of French explorer Jacques Marquette. Stop inside the lobby to see beautiful mosaic murals, as well as an exhibit about Chicago's early skyscrapers. (You can cut west through the lobby into ❼ **Revival Food Hall,** with 15 fast-casual stalls featuring some of Chicago's best neighborhood restaurants.)

As you cross Monroe Street, look east to see the ❽ **CIBC Theatre,** which opened in 1906 as the Majestic Theatre. Half a block west, you'll see ❾ **Italian Village,** a dining spot for theatergoers that's been open since 1927.

Cross Monroe into Exelon Plaza and head for Marc Chagall's *The Four Seasons*—a mosaic with thousands of inlaid chips in more than 250 vibrant colors covering four sides of a rectangular structure. After attending the dedication in 1974, Chagall remarked, "Not bad, eh? I hope the people will like it." Explaining the theme, he said, "In my mind, the four seasons represent human life, both physical and spiritual, at its different stages." In the following years, the mosaic suffered from exposure to weather. It was restored in 1994, with a canopy added for protection. It's in the plaza for Chase Tower, a 1969 skyscraper with a tapered shape, designed by the Perkins & Will firm.

Continue north, then turn east on Madison Street. When you reach State Street, you're at an intersection that was reputedly the busiest corner in the world circa 1900, when it was crammed with cable cars, horse-drawn wagons and carriages, pedestrians, carts, and bicycles. This is also the zero point for Chicago's street-numbering system. Walk to the building at the southeast corner with an ornate rotunda, a masterpiece by Louis Sullivan that was built from 1898 to 1903. Now called the ❿ **Sullivan Center**—with a Target store as its main tenant—it was the Carson Pirie Scott & Co. store for most of its history. The ground floor is encased in dark green cast iron—a metallic skin blooming into frilly organic shapes that Sullivan found in zoology books and nature. Walk south along the building.

Cross to the south side of Monroe, then go east, passing under the canopy of the luxurious ⓫ **Palmer House,** the nation's longest continually operating hotel. Potter Palmer built a hotel here in 1871, but it burned down 13 days later in the Great Chicago Fire. A new Palmer House opened in 1875 and has been in business ever since, though it was replaced with the current structure in the 1920s. You can stop inside to eye the luxurious decor in the lobby areas and the legendary Empire Room.

At the next corner, turn south on Wabash Avenue. Hanging over the sidewalk is the neon sign for **⑫ Miller's Pub,** an old-school restaurant in business since 1935 (at this location since 1989). As you continue south, a sign at the southeast corner of Wabash and Adams marks the eastern starting point of the old US Route 66, America's most famous highway in the era before interstates.

Looking south, you can see the faded letters of an old advertisement on a wall on the east side of Wabash. LYON & HEALY, it says. EVERYTHING KNOWN IN MUSIC. This ghost sign is one of the few clues that this stretch of Wabash was known as Music Row for much of the 20th century, with businesses selling instruments, sheet music, and records. Continue south. On Wabash's east side, **⑬ Central Camera** has a classic neon sign declaring SINCE 1899. At this location since 1929, the shop is packed with photographic gear old and new.

Walk west on Jackson, where several old high-rises—relics of Music Row and former department stores—are now part of DePaul University. In the middle of the block, a corridor juts north from Jackson. This 9-foot-wide alley, called Pickwick Place, has a coffee shop in the 19-by-19-foot building at its north end. Built several years after the 1871 fire, this curious structure was Abson's English Chophouse in the late 1800s, a tiny eatery frequented by bankers, politicians, and actors. It's now the **⑭ Hero Coffee Bar.**

Continue west to Jackson and State, where DePaul has a small plaza at the southeast corner, next to DePaul Center. Designed by Holabird & Roche, this building opened in 1912 as the Rothschild & Co. store, which is why it's decorated with the letter *R*. Goldblatt's opened its flagship here in 1936, eventually selling it to the city in 1982. It now includes shops and restaurants.

This walk ends at State and Jackson. You can depart via the CTA's Red Line at Jackson or the Loop station at the Harold Washington Library. Or continue with Walk 4.

Points of Interest

① Lyric Opera House 20 N. Upper Wacker Dr., 312-827-5600, lyricopera.org

② Union Station 225 S. Canal St., 800-872-7245, chicagounionstation.com

③ Willis Tower 233 S. Wacker Dr., willistower.com; Skydeck, 312-875-9447, theskydeck.com

The Loop, Part 2

4. **Federal Reserve Bank of Chicago Money Museum** 230 S. La Salle St., 312-322-2400, chicagofed.org/education/money-museum/index

5. **Chicago Board of Trade Building** 141 W. Jackson Blvd., cmegroup.com/company/cbot.html

6. **The Berghoff** 17 W. Adams St., 312-427-3170, theberghoff.com

7. **Revival Food Hall** 125 S. Clark St., 773-999-9411, revivalfoodhall.com

8. **CIBC Theatre** 18 W. Monroe St., 312-977-1700, broadwayinchicago.com/theatre/cibc-theatre

9. **Italian Village** 71 W. Monroe St., 312-332-7005, italianvillage-chicago.com

10. **Sullivan Center and Target** 1 S. State St., 312-279-2133, target.com

11. **Palmer House** 17 E. Monroe St., 312-726-7500, palmerhousehiltonhotel.com

12. **Miller's Pub** 134 S. Wabash Ave., 312-263-4988, millerspub.com

13. **Central Camera** 230 S. Wabash Ave., 312-427-5580, centralcamera.com

14. **Hero Coffee Bar** 22 E. Jackson Blvd., 312-285-2434, herocoffeebars.com

4 The Loop, Part 3
The Artsy South Loop

Above: A train passes on L tracks in front of the former CNA Center, the Wabash Building,
and the Auditorium.

BOUNDARIES: Jackson Blvd., Michigan Ave., Dearborn St., Roosevelt Rd.
DISTANCE: 1.5 miles
DIFFICULTY: Easy
PARKING: Paid garages and lots, metered street parking
PUBLIC TRANSIT: CTA Red Line to Jackson

Books and art are two keystones of the South Loop. On this walk, you'll see Chicago's gigantic library, along with the historic district called Printers Row. Other sights include fabulous old buildings with artistic purposes, and a corridor where the numerous murals form a sprawling outdoor gallery.

Walk Description

Starting at Jackson Boulevard, walk south on State Street. On the street's west side, an area of grass in Pritzker Park is ringed by a knee-high concrete wall inscribed with famous authors' quotations. Just west of the park, you can see the sign for the Plymouth Restaurant & Bar, which has a rooftop dining space. South of the park, L trains run on the Loop above Van Buren Street. And south of that, the ❶ **Harold Washington Library Center** dominates the scene. Walk south on State Street toward the library.

One of the country's largest public library buildings—with 972,000 square feet of space—it's named after Chicago's first African American mayor, who pushed for its construction just months before he died in 1987. It opened in 1991, replacing the old central library (now the Chicago Cultural Center), which had closed in 1975. Architect Thomas Beeby's bulky postmodern building has dramatic arched five-story-high windows. Designed by sculptor Raymond Kaskey, 12-foot-high barn owls lean forward on the roof's four corners, amid a green metallic structure. Each owl clutches loose papers in one foot, with the talons of its other foot raised and ready to strike. An even bigger bird is above the main entrance facing State Street—a great horned owl, 20 feet high with a 20-foot wingspan, weighing 3 tons. Clutching an open book, it looks ready to take flight. In addition to the countless shelves filled with books, the library is filled with great pieces of art and varied exhibits. If you stop inside, visit the Winter Garden on the ninth floor, a luminous space below the peaked glass ceiling.

Walk east on Van Buren (just north of the library). As you approach Wabash Avenue, look southeast. See how that shiny blue skyscraper with the undulating form—Roosevelt University's 469-foot-tall Wabash Building—towers high above the classic gray building just south of it? When that shorter structure, the Auditorium, opened in 1889, it was one of Chicago's tallest buildings. (It's now 238 feet tall, but it originally had a turret jutting up to 270 feet.) But it looks squat next to its neighbor, which rose up in 2011.

South of Van Buren, a mural with red, gray, and yellow shapes covers 8,100 square feet on the wall of the Buckingham student housing high-rise mural. Titled *Almost Full,* it was painted in 2015 by Italian street artist Never 2501 (also known as Jacopo Ceccarelli). It's the northernmost picture in the Wabash Arts Corridor, a "living urban canvas" sponsored by Columbia College Chicago. At the northeast corner of Van Buren and Wabash, that 601-foot-high metal-and-glass box (formerly known as the CNA Center) is Chicago's only red skyscraper. Built in 1972, it was painted red to match the corporate color of its original owner, CNA Financial.

Continue east on Van Buren, where the Chicago Club is on the south side of the street. This elite private club moved here in 1893, taking over a former Art Institute facility. But that building fell down during remodeling, so this eight-story red-granite clubhouse replaced it in 1929. The architects reused the triple-arched entrance from the earlier, collapsed building.

When you reach Michigan Avenue, you'll see Grant Park across the street. Staying on Michigan's west side, turn south toward the ❷ **Fine Arts Building.** Architect Solon S. Beman's elegant structure was a factory and showroom for horse-drawn Studebaker buggies when it opened in 1885, but when the buggies moved out in the mid-1890s, it was transformed into an arts center. Creative Chicagoans—everyone from Frank Lloyd Wright to L. Frank Baum—hung out in these hallways. Suffragists met here, and it was Harriet Monroe's base for editing *Poetry Magazine*. From 1912 to 1917, the innovative and influential Chicago Little Theatre performed on the fourth floor, and the Fine Arts movie theater operated here from 1982 to 2000. The Fine Arts Building—where the elevators are still operated manually—opens its doors to the public on the second Friday evening of each month, giving visitors a chance to visit artist studios. The building's 740-seat Studebaker Theater reopened for live performances in 2016.

The next building to the south is immense: the ❸ **Auditorium Theatre** was said to be the largest structure in the United States when it opened in 1889. Remarkably, its 110,000 tons of granite, limestone, and marble sit on top of Chicago's mushy land. Architect-engineer Dankmar Adler used a floating foundation of crisscrossed timbers and railroad beams encased in concrete. Each pier sank gradually into the soil as the structure's weight was added. It worked—but the building has settled as much as 29 inches in some places. The Auditorium hosted performances by John Philip Sousa and Sarah Bernhardt, as well as speeches by Booker T. Washington and President Theodore Roosevelt.

Roosevelt University has owned the building since 1946. After sitting dormant for two decades, it reopened in 1967, hosting concerts by Jimi Hendrix, the Who, Pink Floyd, the Doors, David Bowie, the Grateful Dead, and Bruce Springsteen. The golden-hued theater is an awe-inspiring space, with 3,500 carbon-filament bulbs illuminating its arches and lush details—fashioned by Adler's partner, Louis Sullivan, along with a young draftsman named Frank Lloyd Wright.

At the next corner, turn west on Ida B. Wells Drive, which was called Congress Parkway until it was renamed in 2019 for the legendary civil rights crusader. Walk west in the covered promenade. This sidewalk was inserted into the building when the street was widened in 1952. Peer through the Auditorium's glass doors for a glimpse of the stained glass. And if you get a chance, take one of the Auditorium's informative guided tours.

Continue west, past the Harold Washington Library Center, then turn south on Dearborn Street, heading into ❹ **Printers Row.** As you look south, you can see Dearborn Station's tower two blocks in the distance. After that depot opened in 1885, this area became the Midwest's printing center. Rand McNally, R. R. Donnelley & Sons, and M. A. Donohue & Company made books, maps, magazines, railroad timetables, and catalogs here. The neighborhood's last printing business, Palmer, moved out in 2018. On one weekend every year—typically in early June—booksellers take over this street for the Printers Row Lit Fest.

As you walk south on Dearborn, the Hotel Blake lies on the street's west side and comprises three buildings: the Duplicator Building from 1886, the Morton Building from 1896, and a newer hotel from 1987. Immediately south of this triumvirate is the 14-story Pontiac Building. The oldest skyscraper by architects Holabird & Roche still standing, it was built in 1891. Note the building's elegant use of oriels—bay windows that protrude from the main wall but don't extend all the way down to the ground.

Cross Harrison Street, continuing south. The 22-story Transportation Building takes up half a block along Dearborn's west side. South of that, there's a gap in the buildings with a fountain. Federal Street, once called Custom House Place, is over on the park's east side. This was a notorious red-light district from the 1870s until 1903.

❺ **Sandmeyer's Bookstore,** a mom-and-pop shop in business since 1982, is just south of the park. South of that is one of the neighborhood's gems, the Second Franklin Building. Architect George C. Nimmons applied the Prairie School's design principles to this printing plant, which opened in 1912. On the wall facing Dearborn, tile artworks by Oskar Gross outline the history of printing.

On Dearborn's east side, this block includes Grace Place, a church in a renovated printing plant from 1915. South of that is the Donohue Building from 1883, the neighborhood's first major printing plant. And at 701 S. Dearborn, Kasey's Tavern has been operating for 33 years, in a space occupied by various bars and restaurants since 1883.

At the end of the block, Dearborn Station's clock tower rises up 138 feet. By the 1920s, 146 trains arrived here each day, carrying 17,000 passengers. The station served seven railroads, including the Atchison, Topeka & Santa Fe, which explains why people sometimes came here hoping to glimpse celebrities hopping on trains bound for Los Angeles. The station closed in 1971, as Amtrak consolidated rail service at Union Station. Other old depots were demolished, but Dearborn Station was converted to retail and office space in the 1980s. On the depot's east side, along Plymouth Court, you'll find ❻ **Jazz Showcase,** a 170-seat concert venue where Joe Segal greeted fans at the door for seven decades, after opening the club in 1947.

Walk east on Polk, cross State Street, and then turn north. Looking across to the northwest corner, you'll see Jones College Prep, a high-rise high school completed in 2013. Designed by Perkins+Will to meet environmental standards, it has opaque glass panels, calibrated to regulate the sun's heat and light.

Turn east on Balbo Drive. At this corner, you're next to the South Loop Club, an old-time bar in the ground floor of an Art Deco building from 1930. The sign on the building's corner says 7TH ST. HOTEL, a remnant of the early 1930s, when Balbo was called Seventh Street. Mayor Edward Kelly renamed Seventh Street after Italo Balbo, the head of Italy's air force, who had led a squad of seaplanes across the Atlantic Ocean and landed on Lake Michigan in 1933 during the world's fair. In recent years, many Chicagoans have urged the city to change the street's name, pointing out that Balbo was a brutal paramilitary leader who served the fascist Benito Mussolini.

As you reach the end of the hotel, look back at the wall that faces east. It's covered with the comic book–style mural *Make Your Own Luck,* depicting motorcycle riders, by Brooklyn duo ASVP. Farther east on Balbo, a 165-foot-tall mural titled *Beacon* by Jeff Zimmerman covers the west-facing wall of the 30 East high-rise. ❼ **Buddy Guy's Legends,** the music venue owned by the famous Chicago blues guitarist, is on Balbo's south side. Guy, who moved his club here in 2010, performs a string of 16 sell-out shows every January.

When you reach Wabash Avenue, look farther east to see the ❽ **Merle Reskin Theatre.** When it opened in 1910, it was the Blackstone Theatre. This is where Lorraine Hansberry's *A Raisin in the Sun* made its Chicago premiere in 1959 before moving to Broadway. Since 1989, DePaul University has owned the 1,325-seat venue.

At the northeast corner of Balbo and Wabash, Heidi Unkefer's mural *Slime Mountain* oozes from the wall next to the parking lot. Walk south on Wabash. Over the next four blocks, you'll see several murals in the Wabash Arts Corridor. Also keep an eye on the views toward the east, where the rear sides of Michigan Avenue's hotels and other buildings are visible, along with some glimpses of Grant Park.

The walk ends at Wabash and Roosevelt. Several CTA train lines and bus routes stop at Roosevelt just west of Wabash.

The Loop, Part 3

Points of Interest

① **Harold Washington Library Center** 400 S. State St., 312-747-4300, chipublib.org/locations/34

② **Fine Arts Building** 410 S. Michigan Ave., 312-566-9800, fineartsbuilding.com

③ **Auditorium Theatre** 50 E. Ida B. Wells Dr., 312-341-2310, auditoriumtheatre.org

④ **Printers Row** Dearborn St. and adjacent streets between Ida B. Wells Dr. and Polk St.

⑤ **Sandmeyer's Bookstore** 714 S. Dearborn St., 312-922-2104, sandmeyersbookstore.com

⑥ **Jazz Showcase** 806 S. Plymouth Ct., 312-360-0234, jazzshowcase.com

⑦ **Buddy Guy's Legends** 700 S. Wabash Ave., 312-427-1190, buddyguy.com

⑧ **Merle Reskin Theatre** 60 E. Balbo Dr., 312-922-1999, theatre.depaul.edu

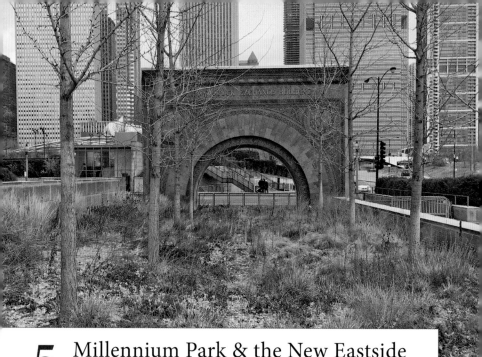

5 Millennium Park & the New Eastside
Chicago's Garden of Delight

Above: The arch of the Chicago Stock Exchange Building stands outside the Art Institute.

BOUNDARIES: Randolph St., Michigan Ave., Adams St., Lake Shore Dr.
DISTANCE: 2 miles
DIFFICULTY: Easy
PARKING: Millennium Park's underground garage
PUBLIC TRANSIT: Take any CTA train downtown and exit near State and Lake; take a Metra train
   downtown; any of the CTA buses running on Michigan Avenue

Millennium Park is a work of art—but one with which you can play. The park's most famous public artworks aren't just statues that you study with your arms folded. The Bean is more like a giant funhouse mirror. Ever since it opened in 2004, Millennium Park has been a magnet for visitors. On this walk, you'll explore this marvelous public space, along with the adjacent Maggie Daley Park, an inventively designed collection of playground spaces; the Art Institute's Modern Wing; and the New Eastside, a neighborhood filled with modern skyscrapers. Millennium Park is open daily,

6 a.m.–11 p.m. Before visiting, check to see if a concert or festival is underway; most such events are free. Like any walk in Chicago's downtown area, this one is worth taking at night as well as during the day; after dusk, the city lights transform the scenery.

Walk Description

Begin at the southeast corner of Michigan Avenue and Randolph Street, walking a short distance south on Michigan and then turning east toward Millennium Monument. Evoking ancient Greece or Rome, this semicircular row of 40-foot-high Doric-style limestone columns stands next to a circular pool with water spraying up at its center. The columns are a replica of a peristyle that stood here from 1917 to 1953, though the old one was 15% larger.

Walk south through Wrigley Square, a lawn lined with benches. Turn east on the tree-lined promenade that points toward the curvy metal structure of the Jay Pritzker Pavilion. This is where the city installs a huge Christmas tree each year. South of the sidewalk, ❶ **Park Grill** serves food on a plaza May–October. Mid-November–mid-March, the same space becomes the McCormick Tribune Ice Rink.

Continue east, taking the stairs up to the ❷ **Jay Pritzker Pavilion,** then walk south along the venue's west side. Huge pieces of gleaming stainless steel sprout above the stage, like a blooming metallic flower, reaching 120 feet high. Designed by Frank Gehry, who gained fame with his Guggenheim Museum in Bilbao, Spain, the pavilion opened in 2004. Speakers hang from a trellis over the 4,000-seat bowl and 95,000-square-foot lawn. This is one of the best places to see live music in Chicago, and almost all of the concerts here are free, including rock concerts every summer, plus festivals of blues, jazz, gospel, house, and world music. The Grant Park Orchestra and Chorus also perform here. Around midday on some summer weekdays, you can watch the orchestra rehearsing. And the pavilion also hosts free movie screenings.

Take the sidewalk leading east from the pavilion toward the massive shiny metal sculpture titled ❸ *Cloud Gate,* which quickly became Chicago's most recognizable work of public art after its 2006 unveiling. Everyone calls it the Bean because it's shaped like a kidney bean—one that's 66 feet long and 42 feet high, weighing 110 tons. Welded together with no visible seams, 168 stainless steel plates cover the surface. It's spectacular to see warped reflections of Chicago's skyline (and the sky itself) bending across the Bean's metal. "Chicago is a very vertical city, and I wanted to make a horizontal sculpture that would draw in the clouds as well as the buildings," *Cloud Gate*'s creator, London-based Mumbai native Sir Anish Kapoor, told the *Sun-Times.* The lower part of the structure is wiped down by hand twice a day with a cleaning solution, while the entire Bean gets cleaned

How Chicago Made Its Lakefront

How did downtown Chicago end up with so much open land along its lakefront? The history goes back to a US government map from 1839, when federal authorities were selling Chicago land. In the spot where Millennium Park and Grant Park are now, the map declared: "public ground forever to remain vacant of buildings."

In Chicago's early years, the land was called Lake Park, but it was just a narrow strip. Back then, the lakeshore was just east of today's Michigan Avenue. In the 1850s, the Illinois Central Railroad constructed tracks parallel to Michigan Avenue. Today, the rails run underneath a portion of the Art Institute building, but they were originally on trestles above the lake's water. After the Great Chicago Fire of 1871, debris was dumped between Michigan Avenue and the trestles, turning it into solid land. Later, park officials extended the land farther east. In 1899 the park was renamed in honor of President Ulysses S. Grant.

Aaron Montgomery Ward, whose mail-order retail company had a building across the street from the park, began a series of legal battles in 1890 to ensure that the land remained open space, just as that map had promised. Ward and his allies won court rulings, putting up high legal hurdles against anyone who wanted to construct buildings east of Michigan Avenue.

The Illinois Central Railroad lowered its tracks below ground level after the City Council passed an ordinance in 1919 to beautify the lakefront, but the rails remained an eyesore. Parking lots just southeast of Michigan Avenue and Randolph Street weren't attractive either. In the 1990s, Mayor Richard M. Daley reportedly said, "Let's cover it with a park." Millennium Park was built on top of those tracks. When it finally opened in 2004, its price tag had ballooned to $475 million (including $225 million covered by private donations). The 24.5-acre park quickly became one of Chicago's most beloved places. A 2017 study used pings from cellphones to estimate how many people were visiting Millennium Park—concluding that the park had nearly 13 million visits in one 6-month period. That would make it Chicago's most visited place.

twice a year with 40 gallons of detergent. Walk into the space under the Bean, a concave chamber known as an omphalos, where the reflections are darker and more intimate.

While you're near the Bean, look at the "street wall" of buildings facing Michigan Avenue. Look northwest toward the corner of Michigan and Randolph, where you'll see the Chicago Cultural Center. Turning south, you'll see the Michigan Boulevard Building; the Illinois State Medical Society; the former Montgomery Ward & Co. Tower Building; Willoughby Tower; and the Chicago Athletic Association, an 1893 building with a Venetian Gothic facade. Designed by Henry Ives Cobb, it reopened as a hotel in 2015, including Cindy's rooftop bar and restaurant. South of the hotel, you'll see a high-rise with a facade designed by Louis Sullivan. It's one of a trio of structures called the Gage Group Buildings, designed by Holabird & Roche for three millinery firms. South of them stands another Holabird & Roche design, the University Club of Chicago.

Walk south from the Bean, then take the next sidewalk west. Just before you get back to Michigan Avenue, take a sidewalk south toward a pair of 50-foot black rectangular structures encased in glass blocks. This is ❹ **Crown Fountain,** designed by Barcelona-born artist Jaume Plensa and built in 2004. On the facing walls, LED video screens show the faces of 1,000 everyday Chicagoans. Water sprays out—looking like it's coming from their rounded mouths. Children love splashing in the 232-by-48-foot reflecting pool in between the faces, where the water is one-eighth of an inch deep.

Walk north from the fountain, then go back east. As you approach the Pritzker Pavilion trellis, look for the ramp leading south onto the Nicholas Bridgeway, a pedestrian bridge. Architect Renzo Piano's bridge, which opened in 2009, is supposed to look like a ship's hull. Walk south on the 620-foot bridge, which reaches a height of 60 feet as it passes over Monroe Street toward the ❺ **Art Institute of Chicago's Bluhm Family Terrace,** which features sculptures, alongside the Terzo Piano restaurant. (No admission fee is required for this area of the museum. But note that the bridge closes when the Art Institute is closed; if necessary, you can use the crosswalk over Monroe Street.) Look down at the railways coming from the south, running underneath a portion of the Art Institute building, and disappearing under Monroe; Millennium Park was built above those tracks. Take the escalator or elevator down to the ground floor. You're inside the Modern Wing, an Art Institute expansion that opened in 2009. Like the Nichols Bridgeway, it was designed by Piano.

Coming out of the escalator or elevator, turn left and then left again, going north through the glass doors. Turn east on Monroe Street's sidewalk. As you approach the next corner, a large arch lies to your south. Go south on the walk just west of the arch, walking a few feet and turning to look at this architectural fragment from the Chicago Stock Exchange Building, an 1893 masterpiece by Louis Sullivan and Dankmar Adler that stood at Washington and La Salle Streets until it was demolished in 1972. Photographer Richard Nickel, who was fighting to preserve it, died when a staircase collapsed on him inside the building. You can see another remnant of the Chicago Stock Exchange Building inside the Art Institute: a reconstruction of the Trading Room.

Walk south and east around the landscaped area at the arch's base. Walk north to the intersection, crossing Monroe and reentering Millennium Park. Walk northwest into the ❻ **Lurie Garden,** where the wide range of plants offers a four-season experience. In early spring, see bulbs and perennials emerging. In summer and fall, butterflies and birds flock to this spot. And in winter, snow and ice form graceful shapes on the seed heads and grasses. The garden includes a 15-foot-high shoulder hedge, as well as a footbridge over shallow water.

Exit the garden's northeast corner, where you'll be back on the edge of the Pritzker Pavilion's lawn. Take the ramp onto the BP Pedestrian Bridge, which ascends at a gentle 5% incline, with a hardwood walking surface and a brushed stainless-steel exterior. Designed by Gehry, this 925-foot-long bridge takes a serpentine route over Columbus Drive. As you reach the bridge's end, you'll be in the middle of ❼ **Maggie Daley Park,** named after former mayor Richard M. Daley's wife, who died in 2011. Open since late 2014, the 16-acre park offers more recreation than Millennium Park: a skating ribbon for in-line skates and scooters; a climbing wall; tennis courts; a play garden; picnic groves; and a miniature golf course, where you can putt underneath a miniature Willis Tower or a replica of the Picasso sculpture. At evening, the park is illuminated with lights atop tripods that resemble the poles of tepees. Walk northeast through the park toward a serene space called the Cancer Survivors' Garden. Go north through the garden, emerging onto Randolph Street.

Take the crosswalk north over Randolph, then continue north one block on Field Boulevard, entering the New Eastside neighborhood's Lakeshore East development, where more than a dozen skyscrapers have gone up since 2002. Continue north into ❽ **Lakeshore East Park,** a rectangle of green space. At the park's northeast corner, you'll see Vista Tower, a shiny glass skyscraper with three undulating towers, designed by Jeanne Gang and completed in 2020. At 1,198 feet, it's Chicago's third-tallest building—and the world's tallest structure designed by a woman. Look over to the park's northwest corner to see another marvelous work of artistic architecture by Gang: Aqua at Lakeshore East, a 2009 skyscraper covered with curvy white concrete balconies that resemble waves of water.

Exit the park's southwest corner, going up the stairs, and then walk east, crossing Columbus Drive. Turn south, walking along the Aon Center, a 1,100-foot-tall white rectangle known as the Amoco Building when it was completed in 1973. It was Chicago's third-tallest building until Vista Tower was built. At Aon's southeast corner, you'll find artist Harry Bertoia's *Sounding Sculpture,* a group of flexible metal rods that sway in the wind, making a sound like tinkling bells. Walk west along Randolph Street toward another part of the sculpture. Looking south across Randolph, you'll see the ❾ **Harris Theater,** a venue for dance and classical music, as well as the back side of the structure holding up Pritzker Pavilion's metal curves.

Continue west to Randolph and Michigan, where the walk ends.

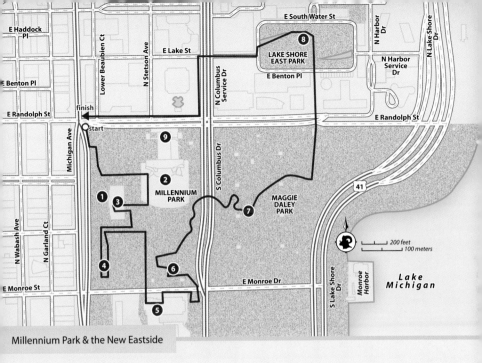

Points of Interest

1 **Park Grill** 11 N. Michigan Ave., 312-521-7275, parkgrillchicago.com; McCormick Tribune Ice Rink: 1 N. Michigan Ave., 312-742-1168, millenniumpark.org

2 **Jay Pritzker Pavilion** Southwest of Randolph St. and Columbus Dr., 312-742-1168, millenniumpark.org

3 *Cloud Gate* **(the Bean)** East of Michigan Ave. between Washington St. and Madison St.

4 **Crown Fountain** Northeast of Michigan Ave. and Monroe St.

5 **Art Institute of Chicago's Bluhm Family Terrace and Modern Wing** entrance on Monroe St. between Michigan Ave. and Columbus Dr., 312-443-3600, artic.edu

6 **Lurie Garden** Northwest of Monroe St. and Columbus Dr.

7 **Maggie Daley Park** Northeast of Monroe St. and Columbus Dr., 312-552-3000, maggiedaleypark.com

9 **Lakeshore East Park** 450 E. Benton Pl., 312-742-3918, chicagoparkdistrict.com/parks-facilities/lakeshore-east-park

9 **Harris Theater** 205 E. Randolph St., 312-334-7777, harristheaterchicago.org

6 Grant Park
Chicago's Front Lawn

Above: Clarence F. Buckingham Memorial Fountain

BOUNDARIES: Monroe St., Michigan Ave., Roosevelt Rd., Lake Shore Dr.
DISTANCE: 1.8 miles
DIFFICULTY: Easy
PARKING: Grant Park or Millennium Park's underground garage
PUBLIC TRANSIT: Take any CTA train downtown and exit near Monroe; take a Metra train downtown;
    any CTA bus running on Michigan Avenue

The older areas of Grant Park don't get as much hype these days as Millennium Park, but they still deserve their reputation as Chicago's front lawn. This walk begins with a stroll alongside the Art Institute, followed by a wandering route through the park. It's also an architectural tour de force, with lovely views of the city's skyscrapers, especially the historic buildings facing Michigan Avenue. And you'll get glimpses of Lake Michigan too.

Grant Park is open daily, 6 a.m.–11 p.m. Before visiting, check to see if a festival or special event is happening. Taste of Chicago takes place during a stretch of several days each July, with restaurants selling food out of tents set up on streets within Grant Park. The event also includes concerts. You'll need a ticket if you try to enter the Lollapalooza rock-and-pop festival, which takes over a large portion of Grant Park for a few days around early August.

Walk Description

Start at the southeast corner of Monroe Street and Michigan Avenue, walking south. On your east is the ❶ **Art Institute's Stanley McCormick Memorial Court,** with flowers and prairie grass amid sculptures, including Henry Moore's bronze abstracted human figure *Large Interior Form* and Alexander Calder's *Flying Dragon*. Continuing south on Michigan, you'll be greeted by the Art Institute's iconic lions. They're bronze versions of plaster statues that stood outside the Fine Arts Palace of the 1893 World's Columbian Exposition. When the lions were installed here in 1894, their sculptor, Edward Kemeys, said they're "guarding the building." The south lion is "attracted by something in the distance which he is closely watching," while the north lion "has his back up, and is ready for a roar and a spring," he said. The lions flank the front steps of the oldest portion of the Art Institute, which has been expanded nine times since 1901, making it the country's second-largest art museum. The museum was designed by Shepley, Rutan, and Coolidge with a triangular pediment, statues of goddesses, and friezes copied from the Parthenon.

Look across Michigan Avenue at the Chicago Symphony Orchestra's home base, ❷ **Orchestra Hall,** an early-1900s landmark by Daniel Burnham. Just south of that is another Burnham design, the Railway Exchange Building, 17 stories high with a white-glazed terra-cotta skin, now adorned with a Motorola sign on the roof. Continue south. To your east is the South Garden, where honey locusts, cockspur hawthorns, and flowering shrubs are arranged around a rectangular pool with low jets of water. The edges of the raised plant beds offer nice spots to sit. Sculptor Lorado Taft's *Fountain of the Great Lakes* stands against the wall on the east side. Unveiled in 1913, it has five bronze nymphs, each representing one of the Great Lakes.

Continue south, crossing Jackson Boulevard. Walk southeast into Grant Park's Sir Georg Solti Garden, decorated with British artist Dame Elisabeth Frink's bust of Solti—the Hungarian-born conductor and pianist who led the Chicago Symphony Orchestra (CSO) from 1969 to 1991. Continue south, heading toward the Paris Metro Entryway near Michigan Avenue. Installed in 2003—a gift from the Union League Club of Chicago and the transit authority in Paris—this is a replica of the subway entrances that Hector Guimard designed for Paris in 1900.

Follow the sidewalk as it bends southeast along Congress Plaza Drive. Two giant bronze statues of American Indian men riding horses are across the roadway here. ❸ *The Bowman* and *The Spearman* were sculpted in Zagreb by Croatian artist Ivan Mestrovic and installed here in 1928. Each is 17 feet high, standing on an 18-foot granite pedestal. Mestrovic chose to omit their bow and spear, leaving them up to our imagination.

Follow the sidewalk, heading east on the north edge of Ida B. Wells Drive. After you've passed over the railroad tracks, Art on the Farm lies to your north. The nonprofit Urban Growers Collective and the Chicago Park District instruct teens on how to grow vegetables and herbs here. Walk north to *Abraham Lincoln, Head of State,* a statue often called ❹ **Seated Lincoln.** It was sculpted by Irish-born Augustus Saint-Gaudens a year before his death in 1907—but it wasn't installed in the park until 1926, taking its place on a 150-foot-wide marble setting designed by architect Stanford White. Plans for a nearby statue of George Washington never came to fruition, leaving Lincoln as the lone figure in this area called the Court of Presidents.

Walk southeast toward the corner of Ida B. Wells and Columbus Drives. Look back west—from here, you can see some of the Loop's most massive structures looming behind the Michigan Avenue street wall. Take the crosswalk east over Columbus, and up ahead you'll see the ❺ **Clarence F. Buckingham Memorial Fountain.** One of the world's largest fountains, it operates May–mid-October, with a "major water display" at the top of every hour. As many as 15,000 gallons of water spray through 134 jets during each 20-minute display, which includes a central column shooting up 150 feet. With four basins clad in elaborately carved granite and pink Georgia marble, the fountain can hold 1.5 million gallons. It opened in 1927 and was designed by Edward Bennett (who cowrote the *Plan of Chicago* with Daniel Burnham). French artist Marcel Loyau made the sculptures, including four Art Deco–style seahorses. Art collector Kate Sturges Buckingham funded the fountain, naming it after her brother. According to the Chicago Park District, she "worked night after night with technicians, trying out various colors of glass and adjusting the control of electric current" to produce "blends … that pleased her—and indeed, there is a mystical aura around the lighted fountain suggesting moonlight—in fairyland." Today, the water displays after-dusk feature illumination and colors shining from 820 lights, concluding each night with a display at 10:35 p.m. The original pumps and motors are still in operation underneath the fountain.

Walk south through the South Rose Garden, which features sculptor Leonard Crunelle's *Fountain Figures.* The two on this side of Buckingham Fountain are *Turtle Boy* and *Dove Girl.* When you reach Balbo Drive, look south for a view of Hutchinson Field—a long stretch of grass that serves as one of the main concert spaces during Lollapalooza. It's where Barack Obama spoke to an enormous audience on November 4, 2008, the night he was elected president. Huge crowds

John Alexander Logan Monument in Grant Park

also gathered here in 2013 to celebrate the Chicago Blackhawks' Stanley Cup win and in 2016 to rejoice at the Chicago Cubs' World Series victory.

Walk west along Balbo's north side. As you near Michigan, turn north into the **6** **Spirit of Music Garden.** A 14-foot-tall bronze sculpture of a woman stands here. She holds a lyre in her left hand, with her right hand aloft. Czech immigrant Albin Polasek sculpted *Spirit of Music* in 1923, paying tribute to Theodore Thomas, the German immigrant who was the CSO's first conductor, from 1891 to 1905. The space just north of the monument includes Chicago SummerDance's open-air floor, where people dance to live bands and DJs on many summer evenings.

Walk west onto the sidewalk next to Michigan Avenue, then go south across Balbo Drive. Over the next two blocks, walk through the Formal Gardens east of the sidewalk. You'll reach a mound topped by the **7** **John Alexander Logan Monument,** which was dedicated in 1897. Born in Illinois, Logan was a Union Army general in the Civil War. As a leader in the Grand Army of the Republic veterans' organization, he led efforts to establish Memorial Day (originally Decoration Day) as a holiday. This spot—with a bronze figure of Logan, sculpted by Saint-Gaudens, riding a horse sculpted by Alexander Phimister Proctor—was intended to be Logan's resting place. But he was buried in Washington, DC, and this tomb has always been empty. During the 1968 Democratic National Convention, protesters covered this hill, some climbing on top of Logan and his horse.

Walk south two blocks, staying parallel with Michigan Avenue. As you reach 11th Street, a set of east–west sidewalks crosses your path. A bust of the department store magnate Aaron Montgomery Ward, sculpted in 1972 by Milton Horn, was moved here in 2005. In 1890 Ward began a 20-year legal battle to keep Grant Park "open, free, and clear."

A block farther south, the Rosenberg Fountain, sculpted in 1893 by Franz Machtl, stands near Michigan Avenue. As a newsboy in Chicago, Joseph Rosenberg had trouble persuading merchants to spare him any water. When he died in 1891, he left a $10,000 bequest to erect an ornamental drinking fountain. This 11-foot-tall bronze figure of Hebe, a cupbearer to the gods in Greek mythology, stands near Rosenberg's childhood home—but it no longer provides drinking water.

Walk south through ❽ *Agora,* a crowd of 106 headless, armless bodies sculpted in iron. The Polish artist Magdalena Abakanowicz created this installation in 2006, calling it the Greek word for "meeting place." Some of the rusty 9-foot-tall figures look like they're frozen in midstride. Some are clustered together; others stand alone. "I think about the experience of crowds as brainless organisms acting on command, worshipping on command and hating on command," Abakanowicz, who died in 2017, told the *Tribune* in 2005. "I speak about the time of Hitler, which was my childhood, and the time of Stalin, and other influences of leaders. . . . Every sculpture can be turned into decoration. But if you have 100, you are confronted by them and must think and imagine and question yourself. This is what I want." Walk northeast to ❾ **Grant Skate Park,** often filled with youngsters attempting stunts on their skates, skateboards, and bikes.

Walk to the grassy area south of the skate park. Two pieces of Milford granite with ornamental designs sit in the grass. This is nearly all that remains of Central Station, a depot that stood just across the street from here—south of what's now Roosevelt Road—from 1893 until 1974. Historian Tim Samuelson has said it was a "virtual Ellis Island of the rails for hundreds of thousands of African American Southerners who escaped the boot of Jim Crow between World War I and 1960." During the depot's demolition, a railroad employee saved these fragments. Three decades later, they were placed in the park.

Walk south to Roosevelt Road, where this walk ends. You can head a couple of blocks west to depart via various CTA train and bus lines at the Roosevelt station just west of Wabash. Or go east to start Walk 7, touring the Museum Campus. Or go south to begin Walk 11, visiting the Near South Side.

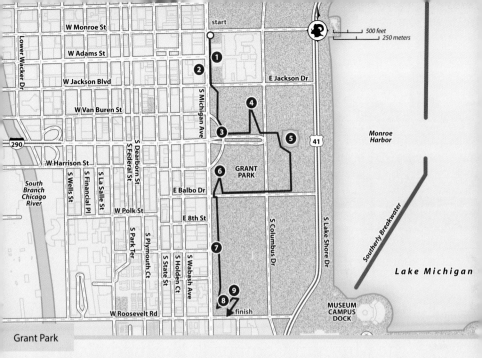

Points of Interest

1 **Art Institute of Chicago** 111 S. Michigan Ave., 312-443-3600, artic.edu

2 **Orchestra Hall, Chicago Symphony Center** 220 S. Michigan Ave., 312-294-3000, cso.org

3 *The Bowman* and *The Spearman* Michigan Ave. and Congress Plaza Dr.

4 **Seated Lincoln** Northwest of Ida B. Wells Dr. and Columbus Dr.

5 **Clarence F. Buckingham Memorial Fountain** 301 S. Columbus Dr., 312-742-3918, chicagoparkdistrict.com/parks-facilities/clarence-f-buckingham-memorial-fountain

6 **The Spirit of Music Garden** Northeast of Michigan Ave. and Balbo Dr., chicagoparkdistrict.com/parks-facilities/spirit-music-gardens

7 **John Alexander Logan Monument** 337 E. Randolph St., chicagoparkdistrict.com/parks-facilities/john-alexander-logan-monument

8 *Agora* Northeast of Michigan Ave. and Roosevelt Rd.

9 **Grant Skate Park** Northeast of Michigan Ave. and Roosevelt Rd., 312-742-3918, chicagoparkdistrict.com/parks-facilities/grant-skate-park

7 The Museum Campus & Northerly Island
Outside the Exhibit Halls

Above: The walkway along Lake Michigan near the Adler Planetarium

BOUNDARIES: Roosevelt Rd., Lake Shore Dr., Lake Michigan, Cermak Rd.
DISTANCE: 4.8 miles
DIFFICULTY: Easy
PARKING: Paid parking at the Field Museum
PUBLIC TRANSIT: CTA 130 Museum Campus bus, exiting at the stop south of the Field Museum; or
   walk about 0.5 mile east from the CTA's Roosevelt station

The Field Museum, Shedd Aquarium, and Adler Planetarium—along with Soldier Field, which hosts Chicago Bears games as well as blockbuster concerts and other big events—are clustered south of Grant Park. Even if you don't go inside the museums, the campus itself is a delightful place for a stroll. (If you *do* plan to go inside the museums—and if you live in Illinois—check their websites for the days when state residents get in for free.)

The 57-acre park became the Museum Campus in 1998, after Lake Shore Drive's northbound lanes, which used to run on Soldier Field's east side, were moved to the stadium's west side, opening up space. This area—stretching farther south into Burnham Park and Northerly Island— is where Chicago held its second world's fair, A Century of Progress International Exposition, in 1933 and 1934. The expo's streamlined buildings were brightly colored, creating a Rainbow City that contrasted with the White City of the 1893 fair.

Northerly Island is actually a peninsula. In the 1909 *Plan of Chicago*, Daniel Burnham and Edward Bennett envisioned a chain of man-made islands extending from Grant Park south to 51st Street. Only one was created—the northernmost one in the plan, hence the name for this chunk of landfill. After the location hosted the world's fair, it became an airport in 1948 and was soon named after *Chicago Herald and Examiner* publisher Merrill C. Meigs. Small planes took off and landed here until one night in 2003, when Mayor Richard M. Daley ordered bulldozers to carve giant Xs in the runway, abruptly demolishing all debate about the airport's future. Northerly Island was transformed into a 40-acre nature preserve in 2015, a delightful spot for watching birds and gazing toward the skyline. It also includes the Huntington Bank Pavilion, and the park may close early on the afternoons of concert days, so check the schedule.

Walk Description

Begin in the area north of ❶ **Soldier Field.** The acropolis-style columns of the original stadium, built in 1924, are still standing, but a new stadium was squeezed between them during a controversial overhaul in 2003. Walk north to the ❷ **Field Museum,** going up the steps and looking at the details, including sculptor Henry Hering's winged female figures representing fields of science. Walk west on the terrace, then turn the corner, heading north. A life-size replica of a Brachiosaurus, 75 feet long and 40 feet high, stands at the northwest corner. Partially based on bones that the Field Museum's first paleontologist, Elmer Riggs, found in 1900 in Colorado, it's made of plastic and metal, designed to withstand Chicago's weather.

Take the steps down and walk across the museum's north side through the Rice Native Gardens. Filled with species like nodding wild onion, swamp milkweed, and big bluestem, these gardens offer glimpses of what Chicago's original prairie landscape was like. The Field Museum, at this location since 1921, has nearly 40 million artifacts and specimens. The 55-foot-tall *Big Beaver Totem Pole,* carved in 1982 by Norman Tait, a member of the Nisga'a Band, Tsimshian Tribe of British Columbia, stands north of the front steps. *Olmec Head Number 8* sits at the museum's northeast corner. Carved by Ignacio Perez Solano, this 7-foot-tall, 7-ton rock is a replica of a sculpture discovered in 1939. The original was created by the Olmec people, who lived 3,000 years ago in what's now the Mexican state of Veracruz. This replica, installed in 2000, was a gift from the Veracruz state government.

Walk east toward ❸ **Shedd Aquarium,** where *Man With Fish* lies just south of the entrance. Created in 2001 by Germany's Stephan Balkenhol, this 16-foot-tall painted bronze depicts an expressionless man embracing a fish that's as big as he is. Water sprays from the fish's mouth. The Shedd is home to 32,000 animals—1,500 different species—making it one of the world's largest indoor collections of aquatic creatures. With a Beaux Arts design by Ernest Graham, this octagonal building opened in 1930, doubling in size with later expansions. Neptune's trident points up from the 4,500-square-foot octagonal skylight's peak. And the front entrance's 500-pound cast-bronze doors are ornamented with images of sea life.

Walk northwest along the front of the aquarium, taking a sidewalk down the slope toward the lake. Then turn right onto the Lakefront Trail, taking it east as it runs along the water's edge north of the Shedd. This stretch of walkway offers expansive views of the skyline and Lake Michigan. Waves lap against the trail's edge, and there's no railing, so proceed with caution. Watch out for water splashing up onto the trail and making the surface slippery. (These areas are sometimes closed to the public when waves are high.) Follow the trail as it bends south around the aquarium and then heads east toward the ❹ **Adler Planetarium,** along a set of stairs that are ideal for sitting.

As you approach the Adler's dome, walk up the steps and head toward the building. The Nicolaus Copernicus Monument—a replica of an 1823 sculpture in Warsaw, Poland, honoring the father of modern astronomy—is west of the Adler. Built in 1930 and designed by Ernest A. Grunsfeld Jr., the original planetarium building is a dodecagon—a 12-sided polygon—covered with a darkly speckled rock known as gneiss, or rainbow granite, and topped by a copper dome. Italian immigrant Alfonso Iannelli designed the gold-surfaced bronze plaques on the 12 sides, each depicting a zodiac sign. Wrapping around the Lake Michigan side, architect Dirk Lohan's glass-enclosed Sky Pavilion was added in 1999, including Galileo's Café.

A 13-foot bronze sundial sits in the northwest part of the plaza, near the water. Called *Man Enters the Cosmos,* it was sculpted by British artist Henry Moore—and you can actually use it to tell the time. A rod called a gnomon casts a shadow down onto the sundial's circular base. Check the spot where the shadow falls to see the time (but add an hour if daylight saving time is in effect). Return to the trail along the water on the Adler's north side, walking east and then south as it curves around the building. On the Adler's east side, a small, round structure stands next to the water. This is the Doane Observatory, which has the largest aperture telescope available to the public in the Chicago area. Visitors can sky-gaze here during the Adler's Doane at Dusk

A view of the Chicago skyline from Northerly Island

programs, which are free and open to the public. Continue south. Sixty stones are arranged like a galaxy on the grass west of the path. Installed in 1999, this is *Americas' Courtyard* by Brazilian wife-and-husband artists Denise Milan and Ary Perez. The four avenues running through the stones are positioned to mark the points on the horizon where the sun rises and sets each year on summer and winter solstices.

Continuing south, the path leads to the ❺ **12th Street Beach,** a stretch of sand hidden away from the city. Del Campo Tacos is open here during warm weather. West of the beach you'll see Northerly Island's 30,000-capacity concert amphitheater, ❻ **Huntington Bank Pavilion.** Follow the path that leads south from the beach into Northerly Island's nature areas. As the path bends west across the scrubby landscape, follow it past a white tent that's used for weddings and events. Continue to the ❼ **Northerly Island Fieldhouse,** on the peninsula's west shore facing Burnham Harbor. This building was the terminal for Meigs Field. Built in 1961 out of glass, steel, and precast masonry, it still looks like a midcentury airport structure. The same architects, Consoer & Morgan, designed the 1952 air traffic control tower south of here. The terminal now serves as a fieldhouse, where park employees answer visitors' questions.

Head for the fieldhouse's east side and walk south on the paved trail just west of the tent. This curving path will take you down the peninsula between man-made hills and a lagoon. The land you're traversing used to be a runway for small airplanes. It's quiet because the sloping land shields you from Lake Shore Drive's noise. If you look northwest, the city's skyline will disappear behind the hills at various points, peeking above them elsewhere.

This is one of the best places for bird-watching in Chicago, with more than 230 species listed. Look for *Ammodramus* sparrows, including Nelson's sparrow and the shy and uncommon Le Conte's sparrow. Rarities like the sage thrasher and Brewer's sparrow have made cameos here. During one visit, I spied a great blue heron, cleaning its feathers as it sat on some stumps of wood in the lagoon. Northerly Island also had the first documented sighting of a black meadowhawk dragonfly in Illinois.

When you reach the south end of the trail, turn back north. Back at the trail's north end, walk west toward the fieldhouse. Then turn right, walking north on Linn White Drive. As you continue north, with Burnham Harbor to your west, take the sidewalk along the water's edge. Go north for a mile, emerging onto Solidarity Drive. Walk west, turning south when you reach Museum Campus Drive.

At the corner with McFetridge Drive, walk east into the ❽ **Gold Star Families Memorial and Park,** a 5-acre area that pays tribute to Chicago police officers who have died in the line of duty. Walk south through the memorial, visiting the "sacrifice space," where the names of more than 450 officers are inscribed on black granite. Just east of that circular concrete wall, you may (or may not) want to visit the controversial Balbo Monument, a column from ancient Rome. Because it was a gift from Italy's Benito Mussolini, many Chicagoans have called for its removal. Continue south through the police memorial, then walk up Burnham Park's sledding hill. At the top, you can see the McCormick Place convention center to the south. Go down the winding path on the hill's south side.

Follow Museum Campus Drive north. Just before you reach McFetridge Drive, walk west into the Soldier Field Children's Garden, where spheres representing Earth can be climbed on or walked through. There's also a jungle gym resembling a spiderweb. Walk west and north through the garden, emerging back on the roadways between the Field Museum and Soldier Field, where the walk ends.

The Museum Campus & Northerly Island

Points of Interest

1 Soldier Field   1410 S. Museum Campus Dr., 312-235-7000, soldierfield.net

2 Field Museum   1400 S. Lake Shore Dr., 312-922-9410, fieldmuseum.org

3 Shedd Aquarium   1200 S. Lake Shore Dr., 312-939-2438, sheddaquarium.org

4 Adler Planetarium   1300 S. Lake Shore Dr., 312-922-7827, adlerplanetarium.org

5 12th Street Beach   On the lakeshore south of the Adler Planetarium, 312-742-3224, chicagoparkdistrict.com/parks-facilities/12th-street-beach

6 Huntington Bank Pavilion   1300 S. Linn White Dr., 312-540-2668, pavilionnortherlyisland.com

7 Northerly Island Fieldhouse   1521 S. Linn White Dr., 312-745-2910, chicagoparkdistrict.com/parks-facilities/northerly-island-park

8 Gold Star Families Memorial and Park   Southeast of McFetridge Dr. and Museum Campus Dr.

8 Chicago Riverwalk
The City's Backyard Patio

Above: Looking across the Chicago River at night toward the Wrigley Building

BOUNDARIES: Ontario St., Lake Michigan, Lake St., Canal St.
DISTANCE: 2.2 miles
DIFFICULTY: Easy
PARKING: Paid garages and lots
PUBLIC TRANSIT: CTA's Brown or Purple Line to Merchandise Mart

For much of Chicago's history, the river that shares the city's name was nothing to brag about. It was a dirty, smelly channel functioning as a sewer. Today, it's cleaner and more attractive— although human contact with the water is still considered dangerous because of the bacteria levels. Don't even try swimming in the Chicago River, but *do* enjoy looking at it. And there's no better place to experience it than the Chicago Riverwalk.

The south bank of the Chicago River's Main Stem—the section just west of Lake Michigan— used to be covered with wholesale produce markets. Those were demolished in the 1920s to make way for Wacker Drive, a double-decker roadway. A section of the south bank was transformed into a pedestrian area in 2005. Extended in 2015 and 2016—with even more attractive landscaping—the Chicago Riverwalk (chicagoriverwalk.us) now stretches from Lake Street east to Lake Shore Drive. It's open daily, 6 a.m.–11 p.m., and it's worth seeing at night, when the city's lights are reflected in the water. In addition to the Riverwalk itself, this walk will take you around the junction of waterways known as Wolf Point.

Walk Description

Begin outside the ❶ **Merchandise Mart,** near the Brown Line stop on Wells Street. The Mart was the world's largest building when it opened in 1930, with 4.2 million square feet of floor space. It's no longer even in the top 40 biggest buildings, but it still has an impressively huge presence, with its steel-framed structure clad in limestone, terra-cotta, and bronze. Designed by Alfred Shaw as a "city within a city," the Art Deco behemoth was originally a wholesale center for Marshall Field & Company. It was owned for five decades by the Kennedy family, after Joseph P. Kennedy, John F. Kennedy's father, purchased it in 1945. It hosts trade shows and expos such as the Chicago Antiques + Art + Design Show. The hundreds of tenants include furniture and clothing showrooms; Motorola Mobility and other corporate offices; Illinois Institute of Art classrooms; and 1871, a hub for digital startups.

Walk south on Wells, then go west on Merchandise Mart Plaza. Eight bronze busts of American merchants stand in this corridor. Halfway along the Mart's front side, enter the main doors to see the south lobby. Seventeen murals, depicting "a panorama of the world's commerce and industry," by Jules Guerin are high up on the walls.

Exit and continue west. As you approach the Franklin–Orleans Street Bridge, take in the views. The area just ahead of you is called Wolf Point. This is where the Chicago River's branches come together. Look toward the river's south side, just west of the Franklin–Orleans Street Bridge. The 487-foot-tall skyscraper at 333 Wacker Drive faces the water with a curving green glass facade. Completed in 1983, it was designed by Kohn Pederson Fox Associates.

Turning your eyes west, look for the 150 North Riverside skyscraper southwest of the Lake Street Bridge. Some people call it The Tuning Fork or The Guillotine. At ground level, the core wall facing north is only 39 feet wide. Amazingly, the building gets wider as it rises up to its eighth floor, where it's 120 feet wide. From there, the walls go straight up, reaching a height of 724 feet. How does this 2017 skyscraper (designed by Goettsch Partners and Magnusson Klemencic Associates) pull off this feat? It has a massive central concrete spine, with caissons reaching 110 feet underground. Now, look north of that bridge: River Point, a 732-foot-tall office tower that opened in 2016, has a curved-glass wall facing the river. Two parabolic arches—one at ground level and another at the top—look like they've been sliced out of the surface.

Turn north on Orleans. After about a block, look for stairs leading down from either side. Go down and turn west on Kinzie Street, taking the bridge across the river. This was where one of the city's oddest calamities began on April 13, 1992: the Great Chicago Flood. Crews who were replacing pilings caused a leak in an old freight tunnel below the river, and 250 million gallons of water gushed into the tunnel system, flooding basements all over the Loop. Looking south, you'll see a bridge that's almost always raised. The Chicago and North Western Railway's Kinzie Street railroad bridge was the world's longest and heaviest bascule bridge when it opened in 1908. Trains used it to deliver goods to the Merchandise Mart, Tribune Tower, the Curtiss candy factory, and other companies. No one has used it since 2000, when the *Sun-Times* moved its printing operations. To keep the bridge in active status, Union Pacific lowers it once a year and runs a Hy-Rail truck over it.

Continue across the river and turn south on Canal Street. Go east into the driveway just north of the Residences at River Bend. Take the walkway that runs south along the water. When the walkway ends, take the stairs up and go east across the Lake Street Bridge. When you reach the other side, look east across Wacker Drive. This is where Mark Beaubien opened Chicago's earliest lodging house, the Sauganash Hotel, in 1831. When Chicago became a town in 1833, the hotel hosted the first elections and town meetings. Seven years later, it served as Chicago's first theater. Nine years after the hotel burned down in 1851, the Wigwam was constructed at the site and hosted the 1860 Republican National Convention, where Abraham Lincoln was nominated for president.

At the northwest corner of Lake and Wacker, take the stairs down to the Chicago Riverwalk and head north, following the corridor as it bends east, where you'll pass underneath the Franklin–Orleans Street Bridge. Wherever the Riverwalk runs below a bridge, a metal awning juts out over the walkway, with a shiny surface that captures reflections from the water and nearby buildings.

The space between Franklin and La Salle Streets has seven piers for fishing and sightseeing, with floating trays of plants anchored in between. Next to the Franklin–Orleans Street Bridge, a control center runs 34 projectors. This is where colored pixels shine across the river, transforming 2 acres of the Merchandise Mart's walls into a video canvas. ❷ **Art on the Mart,** the world's largest permanent digital art projection, made its debut in 2018. The hour-long display begins after dark every night April–October.

Continuing east: The area from La Salle to Wells Street is filled with a zero-depth fountain. The next block, from La Salle to Clark Street, has stairs facing the river, like the seats of an outdoor

Reversing the River

The Chicago River isn't really just one river. It's a system of rivers, tributaries, and canals, with a total 156 miles. The Main Stem runs west from Lake Michigan, north of the Loop. It originally followed a serpentine path, but early Chicagoans straightened it out. At Wolf Point, it splits into the North Branch and the South Branch.

In September 1673, Louise Jolliet and Jacques Marquette arrived at a spot they'd heard about from the Miami Indians—a portage where boats could be carried across land. After seeing it, Jolliet remarked, "It would only be necessary to make a canal, by cutting through but half a league of prairie." That idea of connecting the Great Lakes with the Mississippi River's watershed helped motivate people to create a city where Chicago is today. Inspired by Jolliet's vision, the 97-mile Illinois & Michigan Canal opened in 1848.

Chicago was dumping its sewage, including animal waste from the Union Stock Yards, into the river. "The water is so thick with filth that it can scarcely ripple," the *Tribune* reported in 1893. "It is positively black in color, covered with a thick greasy slime, and dotted with gas bubbles. . . . A sort of miasma at once disgusting and unhealthy hung over the foul stream, which had no perceptible current one way or the other. Refuse of various sorts was floating on the surface." City officials ran pipes miles out into Lake Michigan, hoping they could find clean water farther from the shore. It didn't always work. Thousands died of typhoid fever, and the city feared a cholera outbreak.

In 1892 a newly formed unit of government—known today as the Metropolitan Water Reclamation Sanitary District—began digging the 28-mile Chicago Sanitary and Ship Canal. It was the biggest excavation project in world history up until that time, with steam shovels, conveyor belts, horse-drawn plows, donkey carts, men pushing wheelbarrows, and dynamite blasts moving 43 million cubic yards of earth. After the canal opened in January 1900, a *New York Times* headline declared, WATER IN CHICAGO RIVER . . . NOW RESEMBLES LIQUID. The article reported, "The impossible has happened! The Chicago River is becoming clear!"

The water now flows from the North Branch and the Main Stem into the South Branch, flowing down toward the canal. From there, it runs into the Des Plaines River, then the Illinois River, then the Mississippi River, and finally into the Gulf of Mexico.

The Chicago River remained putrid for the next century. Unlike every other metropolitan area in the United States, Chicago was allowed to ignore federal laws requiring the disinfection of human and industrial waste before it's dumped into waterways. Finally, in 2011, the Obama administration ordered local authorities to clean up their act. With the addition of new germ-killing equipment, the Chicago River is getting cleaner. More people are boating and fishing in the river, but bacteria levels are still too high for swimming.

Reversing the river caused one unforeseen problem: By connecting the Gulf of Mexico with the Great Lakes, the canal created a pathway for invasive species. Government agencies and environmental groups are now trying to prevent species such as Asian carp from swimming upstream and entering Lake Michigan.

theater. This block also has a spot where you can catch a Chicago Water Taxi. Looking across to the north bank, you'll see Encyclopaedia Britannica's headquarters inside a seven-story redbrick building with an elegant clock tower, constructed in 1914. In 1915 it served as a makeshift hospital and morgue for the Eastland Disaster. That was the deadliest single catastrophe in Chicago history. On July 24, 1915, the SS *Eastland* was docked near Clark Street, preparing to take Western Electric workers on an excursion. As the top-heavy boat filled up with people, it rolled over and 844 people, including 22 entire families, died.

Continue east. Small boats can dock between Clark and Dearborn Streets alongside a patio. This is also where ❸ **Tiny Tapp & Cafe** serves craft cocktails, craft beer, sandwiches, and coffee. Walk east under the Dearborn Street Bridge, entering a plaza with ❹ **City Winery**'s patio, as well as high-backed benches and steps that go right down to the water's edge. Look north to see Marina City's twin cylindrical towers.

The block east of State Street includes the ❺ **Vietnam Veterans Memorial Plaza,** where the names of more than 2,900 Illinois servicemen killed or missing in action are inscribed. Next to a fountain, steps lead up to street level. Looking across to the river's north side, you can't miss Trump International Hotel & Tower—a shiny, silver-blue skyscraper completed in 2009 with a huge sign spelling out the name of its famous developer. Designed by Skidmore, Owings & Merrill, it's 1,389 feet tall, including its spire.

Continue east. The ❻ **McCormick Bridgehouse & Chicago River Museum** is just west of Michigan Avenue's DuSable Bridge. Open May–October, the museum spirals up five stories from river level into a historical bridge house. Inside, you'll see the gears that lift and lower the bridge. Look over at the river's north side to see skyscrapers from the 1920s: the Wrigley Building, Tribune Tower, and the InterContinental hotel. Continue east under Michigan Avenue, gazing over at the glass walls of the Apple Store on the north bank. This is the Riverwalk's oldest stretch, spruced up in 2019 with new landscaping, seating, plazas, and access points. Here, you can buy tickets for ❼ **Chicago's First Lady Cruises,** or dine and drink at the ❽ **Northman Beer & Cider Garden.**

After going east under Columbus Drive, gaze up at the wavy shape of Vista Tower, Chicago's third-tallest building. Designed by Jeanne Gang, it's the world's tallest structure designed by a woman, as of 2020. Continue east into the Riverwalk Gateway tunnel under Lake Shore Drive, decorated with 28 ceramic panels by Ellen Lanyon, a series of pictures showing how important the river has been to the city's history. Exiting the tunnel, you'll be at the spot where the river connects with Lake Michigan. Notice the pier that extends out into the lake here, leading to the Chicago Marine Safety Station, a hub for police and fireboats. The pink stone structure here is part of the system controlling the flow of water from Lake Michigan into the river.

Walk out onto the pier, taking in views of **9** **DuSable Harbor** to your south and Navy Pier to your north. Head back to land and walk south. Concrete objects resembling giant toy jacks sit in the grass here. The U.S. Army Corps of Engineers uses these Core-loc Armoring Devices to protect shorelines.

To end the walk, you have two options: Head toward Millennium Park and the Loop by walking south on the Lakefront Trail, then going west on Randolph Street. Or head toward **10** **Navy Pier,** going up the ramp to the Lake Shore Drive Bridge and walking north.

Another Nearby Walk: Navy Pier

Originally named Municipal Pier when it was built in 1916, **10** **Navy Pier** became a shopping mall and lakefront plaza in 1995, later getting a refreshed look with renovations that began in 2012. Attractions include the Centennial Wheel, a 196-foot-tall Ferris wheel with 42 climate-controlled gondolas; the Chicago Children's Museum; an AMC IMAX movie theater; the Chicago Shakespeare Theater; Chicago Public Radio's studios; Festival Hall, which hosts events like Expo Chicago, a massive marketplace of art held each fall; and Offshore, a 36,000-square-foot rooftop bar.

Walk through the building's interior, following the winding passageway amid the shops and stores. But also make sure to walk on the wide outdoor plaza along the southern edge, which is lined with excursion boats. Out at the pier's windswept eastern tip, you can look out across Lake Michigan or gaze back at the Chicago skyline.

Spend some time wandering around Polk Bros Park, west and south of Navy Pier's entrance. Just to the northwest, you'll find Milton Lee Olive Park and Jane Addams Memorial Park. A roundtrip along Navy Pier's length and through the parks adds up to about 2 miles.

(For a map of Navy Pier and the surrounding area, see navypier.org/visit/navy-pier-map.)

Points of Interest

1 **Merchandise Mart** 222 W. Merchandise Mart Plaza, 800-677-6278, themart.com

2 **Art on the Mart** Chicago Riverwalk east of Orleans/Franklin St., artonthemart.com

3 **Tiny Tapp & Cafe** 55 W. Riverwalk South, instagram.com/tinytappchicagoriverwalk

4 **City Winery at the Chicago Riverwalk** 11 W. Riverwalk South, 312-229-5593, citywinery.com/chicago/riverwalk

(continued on next page)

Chicago Riverwalk

(continued from previous page)

⑤ Vietnam Veterans Memorial Plaza Chicago Riverwalk between State St. and Wabash St.

⑥ McCormick Bridgehouse & Chicago River Museum 99 Chicago Riverwalk, just west of Michigan Ave., 312-977-0227, bridgehousemuseum.org

⑦ Chicago's First Lady Cruises 112 E. Wacker Dr. (Chicago Riverwalk east of Michigan Ave.), 847-358-1330, cruisechicago.com

⑧ The Northman Beer & Cider Garden Riverwalk between Michigan Ave. and Columbus Dr., 312-228-1911, thenorthman.com

⑨ DuSable Harbor South of the mouth of the Chicago River, 312-742-3577, chicagoharbors.info/harbors/dusable

⑩ Navy Pier 600 E. Grand Ave., 312-595-7437, navypier.org (also see "Another Nearby Walk: Navy Pier," on the previous page)

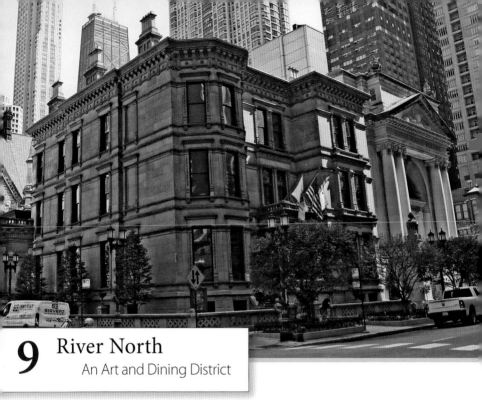

9 River North
An Art and Dining District

Above: Northeast of Wabash Avenue and Erie Street are the Richard H. Driehaus Museum and Murphy Auditorium.

BOUNDARIES: Franklin St., Chicago River, Lake Michigan, Division St.
DISTANCE: 2.9 miles
DIFFICULTY: Easy
PARKING: Metered street parking, paid lots and garages
PUBLIC TRANSIT: CTA Brown or Purple Line to Chicago Ave.

River North is one of Chicago's hottest areas for restaurants, bars, hotels, and galleries, along with the offices of tech companies. It takes some imagination to picture what it looked like in earlier eras. In the late 1800s and early 1900s, it was an industrial area with so much pollution that people called it Smokey Hollow. It included a bohemian enclave of artists known as Tower Town. Later, as the Magnificent Mile became a prestigious retail corridor, River North evolved, with industrial spaces converted into galleries. Strolling here today, you see Chicagoans and tourists popping in and out of restaurants, amid a mix of old buildings juxtaposed with sleek high-rises.

River North 53

Walk Description

As you exit the CTA's Chicago Avenue station, you're in the ❶ **River North Art District.** Walk half a block south on Franklin Street, then head east on Superior Street, amid art galleries. When you reach Wells Street, you may want to visit the galleries north and south of Superior. Many galleries hold their exhibit openings on the first Friday evening in odd-numbered months, and *Chicago Gallery News* offers free guided tours at 11 a.m. Saturdays, departing from 714 N. Wells.

The tavern at the northeast corner of Superior and Wells was the site of a famous undercover sting. The *Sun-Times* bought it in 1977, calling it the Mirage—and staffing it with journalists who posed as bartenders. Their investigation caught inspectors taking bribes to ignore health and safety violations. Today, the building is the Brehon Pub.

Continue east on Superior. At 154 W. Superior, a two-story Italianate row house built in 1888 looks as though it's being crushed between modern high-rises. Turn north on Clark. A rare large-scale example of French Renaissance Revival architecture stands at the northwest corner of Clark and Chicago Avenue. Designed by J. E. O. Pridmore, it opened in 1901 as the Bush Temple of Music, serving as the Bush and Gerts Piano Company's headquarters. It was rehabbed into an apartment building in 2016.

Continue north. After you cross Delaware Place, enter Washington Square Park on Clark's east side. The ❷ **Newberry,** an independent research library, is at the park's north end. This tranquil spot with a fountain was nicknamed Bughouse Square in the early 20th century, when anarchists, socialists, poets, preachers, and hobos used it as their platform for speeches. The tradition faded, but the Newberry holds annual Bughouse Square Debates here. Washington Square Park is also where gay activists gathered on June 27, 1970, before marching in the earliest version of what became the annual Chicago Pride Parade. Built in 1893 and designed by Henry Ives Cobb, the Newberry is a treasure trove with more than 1.6 million books, 5 million pages of historical manuscripts, and 600,000 maps. As long as you're 14 or older, you can sign up for a reader's card and examine this rare stuff at a table inside.

Go to the park's northeast corner and cross to the east side of Dearborn Street. The church standing here, which has been a Harvest Bible Chapel since 2012, opened as Unity Church in 1867. The Great Chicago Fire destroyed its wooden portions, but the Gothic-style Joliet limestone walls survived; Edward Burling and Dankmar Adler designed the rebuilt church in 1873.

Walk south on Dearborn, where row houses from the late 19th century stand along the east side. Dr. Robert Newton Tooker, author of *Tooker's Diseases of Children,* lived at 863, where he died of apoplexy in 1902. Walk into the alley south of his house, Tooker Place, far enough to see the parking garage behind the house. It occupies the spot where the Dill Pickle Club hosted masquerade balls and candid talk about taboo topics for two decades starting around 1914.

Continue south on Dearborn. Look for two sculpted faces on the wall in front of 827–831, fragments from Louis Sullivan and Adler's Schiller Theater, which was demolished in 1960. Continue south across Chicago Avenue. Along Dearborn's east side, construction began in 2019 on One Chicago Square, two glass skyscrapers with planned heights of 971 and 574 feet. When you reach Superior Street, go to the southwest corner, where the ❸ **Poetry Foundation**'s building is encased inside what looks like a corrugated metal box. A section of the wall is actually a screen you can peek through to see a courtyard. Architect John Ronan's 2011 building hosts free poetry and arts events.

Walk east on Superior. At the northeast corner with State Street, ❹ **Holy Name Cathedral,** the seat of the Roman Catholic Archdiocese of Chicago, opened in 1875. This Gothic Revival limestone building with a 210-foot spire has been renovated several times. Continue east on Superior, then go south on Wabash Avenue. ❺ **St. James Cathedral** is at the southeast corner of Wabash Avenue and Huron Street. Abraham Lincoln worshipped inside this church after he was elected president in 1860. Eleven years later, the Episcopal church's bells rang out, warning the neighborhood about the Great Chicago Fire. The flames destroyed much of the 1857 building, but the stone walls and bell tower endured. The foyer contains something else that survived the fire: a memorial to parishioners who died in the Civil War.

Just south of the church is a mansion from the Gilded Age—originally the home of Samuel M. Nickerson, who made a fortune in liquor and explosives before founding the First National Bank of Chicago. Built in 1883, it was designed by Burling (the same architect responsible for St. James Church) and Francis M. Whitehouse, using 17 types of marble. After investment manager Richard H. Driehaus spent five years restoring the building, it opened in 2008 as the ❻ **Richard H. Driehaus Museum,** hosting exhibits on Gilded Age art, architecture, and design.

Another castle of that era stands at the southwest corner of Erie and Wabash. With a peach-pink facade, this 1886 mansion (designed by Henry Ives Cobb and Charles Sumner Frost) was the home of Ransom R. Cable, president of the Chicago, Rock Island and Pacific Railway. The next occupant was John Carroll, who drove the horse-drawn hearse carrying Lincoln's body. Today, it's the offices of Driehaus Capital Management LLC. Return to Wabash and continue south.

Cross Ontario Street, where Medinah Temple lies on Wabash's west side. The Shriners constructed this building in 1912 in the Moorish Revival style. Though built by Christians, it looks like an Islamic structure, with copper onion domes, textured brickwork, stained glass windows, and Arabic script that reads "There is no god but Allah." A Bloomingdale's store occupied the building from 2003 until 2020.

Look at ❼ **Pizzeria Due** on Wabash's east side, inside a Second Empire–style house, which lumber merchant Nathan Mears built in the 1870s. Now walk south toward Ohio Street. ❽ **Pizzeria Uno** is at the southwest corner, inside another mansion built by the Mears family. This is where deep-dish pizza was invented in the 1940s, though there's debate about exactly who invented it: owner Richard Novaretti, also known as Ric Riccardo; his partner, Ike Sewell; or bartender Adolpho "Rudy" Malnati Sr., whose son Luciano later launched Lou Malnati's Pizzeria. At the southeast corner, ❾ **Eataly** is a mall filled with Italian restaurants, cafés, lunch counters, and food shops.

Walk west on Ohio. Tree Studios and its annexes stand west of Medinah Temple. Judge Lambert Tree and his wife, Anne, built this complex in 1894, requiring that only artists could live in it. Turn north on State Street, walking along the Tree Studios complex, where the tenants include Pops for Champagne, which features live jazz as well as bubbly wine, and Alliance Patisserie.

Turn west on Ontario, then north on Dearborn, where ❿ **Tao** restaurant occupies a granite fortress on the west side. Designed by Henry Ives Cobb, it opened in 1892 as the Chicago Historical Society. It later served as a lodge for the Loyal Order of Moose, a design school, and recording studios. From 1985 to 2014, it was a series of nightclubs: the Limelight, Excalibur, Vision, and Castle Chicago. The opulent Asian restaurant Tao opened here in 2018.

Walk north, then go west on Erie and south on Clark. The two-story Portillo's restaurant at Clark and Ontario is chock-full of Chicago memorabilia. A strikingly contemporary McDonald's restaurant—a glass box under a white pavilion with 1,062 rooftop solar panels—fills the block southwest of Clark and Ontario. Designed by Chicago architect Carol Ross Barney, who also worked on the Chicago Riverwalk, it opened in 2018.

Turn west on Ohio Street. At the northwest corner of Ohio Street and La Salle Drive, ⓫ **Ohio House Motel** opened in 1960, offering cheap lodging in a two-story structure designed by Arthur Salk. Continue west on Ohio, then go south on Wells, past bars and restaurants including GT Fish & Oyster and Lou Malnati's Pizzeria. Turn east at Hubbard Street. Half a block east of Clark, in the alley running north from Hubbard, a door leads down to Three Dots and a Dash, a renowned tiki bar.

East of the alley, a six-story office building called Courthouse Place was the Cook County Criminal Court Building 1893–1929. This block of Hubbard is Honorary Clarence S. Darrow Way, named for the Chicago lawyer who argued many cases here. In 1924 he pleaded that Nathan Leopold and Richard Loeb should not get the death penalty for killing 14-year-old Bobby Franks in "the crime of the century." A judge spared their lives, sending them to prison. The same year, juries found Beulah Annan and Belva Gaertner not guilty of killing their lovers, prompting a *Tribune* reporter who'd covered their trials, Maurine Dallas Watkins, to write the play *Chicago,* which became a Broadway musical and an Oscar-winning 2002 movie.

Walk east on Hubbard, then north on Dearborn, going as far as the alley. The Chicago Fire Department's 1st District Headquarters is north of the alley today, but from 1872 to 1929 that land was the site of Cook County Jail, connected to the courthouse by a bridge. On November 11, 1887, four anarchists convicted in the Haymarket case went to the scaffold here. In 1921 convicted cop killer "Terrible Tommy" O'Connor busted out of the jail and disappeared—never to be found—inspiring Ben Hecht and Charles MacArthur's 1928 play *The Front Page.*

Turn back south, crossing Hubbard. ⑫ **Harry Caray's Italian Steakhouse**—started in 1987 by the popular sportscaster, who died in 1998—is at the southeast corner with Kinzie Street. The building is Chicago's only remaining example of Dutch Renaissance architecture, built in 1895 for the Chicago Varnish Company and designed by Cobb. Al Capone's chief enforcer and successor, Frank Nitti, lived on the fourth floor.

Continue south on Dearborn, where Marina City looms on the east side. Its two towers are often described as corncobs, but architect Bertrand Goldberg compared their exteriors to sunflower petals. Completed in 1967, the complex was designed to be a "city within a city." Halfway down the block, walk east between Hotel Chicago and the ⑬ **House of Blues,** a concert venue crammed with colorful art that opened in 1996. Turn north on State Street. ⑭ **The Museum of Broadcast Communications** is to your west. Open at this location since 2012, it features memorabilia from TV and radio history. Go north across Kinzie to Rossi's, a dive that's been serving cheap beer for half a century. Continue north and turn east on Hubbard, where you'll find ⑮ **Andy's Jazz Club & Restaurant** and ⑯ **Shaw's Crab House.**

On the north side of Hubbard, take the stairs up to Wabash and walk south. Cross to the east side and look for a path along Trump International Hotel & Tower's north side. Take that path east into a park with views of the Chicago River. Continue east into the plaza between the Wrigley Building's two structures.

This walk ends as you reach Michigan Avenue. You can depart via CTA bus lines on Michigan Avenue or go a few blocks northwest to the Red Line's Grand station.

Points of Interest

❶ **River North Art District** Vicinity of Superior St. and Franklin St., rivernorthartgalleries.com

❷ **The Newberry** 60 W. Walton St., 312-943-9090, newberry.org

❸ **Poetry Foundation** 61 W. Superior St., 312-787-7070, poetryfoundation.org

(continued on next page)

River North

(continued from previous page)

④ **Holy Name Cathedral** 730 N. Wabash Ave., 312-787-8040, holynamecathedral.org

⑤ **St. James Cathedral** 65 E. Huron St., 312-787-7360, saintjamescathedral.org

⑥ **Richard H. Driehaus Museum** 40 E. Erie St., 312-482-8933, driehausmuseum.org

⑦ **Pizzeria Due** 619 N. Wabash Ave., 312-943-2400, pizzeriaunodue.com

⑧ **Pizzeria Uno** 29 E. Ohio St., 312-321-1000, pizzeriaunodue.com

⑨ **Eataly** 43 E. Ohio St., 312-521-8700, eataly.com/us_en/stores/chicago

⑩ **Tao** 632 N. Dearborn St., 224-888-0388, taochicago.com

⑪ **Ohio House Motel** 600 N. La Salle Dr., 312-943-6000, ohiohousemotel.com

⑫ **Harry Caray's Italian Steakhouse** 33 W. Kinzie St., 312-828-0966, harrycarays.com

⑬ **House of Blues** 329 N. Dearborn St., 312-923-2000, houseofblues.com/chicago

⑭ **Museum of Broadcast Communications** 360 N. State St., 312-245-8200, museum.tv

⑮ **Andy's Jazz Club & Restaurant** 11 E. Hubbard St., 312-642-6805, andysjazzclub.com

⑯ **Shaw's Crab House** 21 E. Hubbard St., 312-527-2722, shawscrabhouse.com/chicago

10 The Magnificent Mile
Chicago's Top Shopping

Above: The Water Tower, 875 N. Michigan (formerly the John Hancock Center), and Water Tower Place

BOUNDARIES: Chicago River, Rush St., Cedar St., Lake Michigan
DISTANCE: 1.6 miles
DIFFICULTY: Easy
PARKING: Paid garages
PUBLIC TRANSIT: Any of the CTA bus routes that stop on Michigan Ave. near Tribune Tower; or walk
    east from the Red Line's Grand station

The Magnificent Mile is nearly always bustling. The stores and restaurants are the main attractions on this 13-block stretch of North Michigan Avenue, but it's also a prime spot for people-watching and architectural sightseeing.

Its origins go back to the opening of Michigan Avenue's bridge in 1920, which spurred construction north of the river. But then the Depression hit, stalling development. After Arthur

Rubloff and William Zeckendorf bought much of the property along North Michigan Avenue, Rubloff unveiled his plan to create what he called the Magnificent Mile in 1947. That kicked off a retail boom.

The wealthy Streeterville neighborhood lies east of Michigan Avenue and includes Northwestern Memorial Hospital, Ann & Robert H. Lurie Children's Hospital, and Northwestern University's downtown campus. The River North neighborhood (Walk 9) is to the west.

Walk Description

Begin at Michigan Avenue and Illinois Street. The skyscraper at the northeast corner embodies the stylish architecture of the 1920s. It's now the ❶ **InterContinental Chicago Magnificent Mile,** but the Chicago Shriners Club built the 42-story south tower in 1929 as the Medinah Athletic Club. Within four years, the Depression drove the club into bankruptcy. Architect Walter W. Ahlschlager borrowed elements from Egyptian, Greek, Celtic, Mesopotamian, medieval European, Gothic, and Art Deco styles. The hotel has a junior Olympic swimming pool on the 14th floor, where *Tarzan* film star and Olympian Johnny Weissmuller trained. Over on Michigan Avenue's west side, the ❷ **Purple Pig** serves pig's tails and pig's ears, along with more typical porcine dishes like pork chops, ham, and bacon.

Walk north, and you'll see an opening in the buildings where Michigan Avenue passes over Grand Avenue—a reminder that the Magnificent Mile is one story above ground level here. A building at 520 includes the ❸ **Gwen Hotel**—named after noted artist Gwen Lux, who sculpted mythological figures including Helios, Atlas, and Diana on the limestone panels above the entrance in collaboration with her then-husband Eugene Lux. This wall was salvaged from the McGraw-Hill Building, built in 1929 and demolished in 1998. ❹ **The Shops at North Bridge,** a four-level mall anchored by Nordstrom, fills a stretch north of the Gwen.

Farther north, one of the street's boldest buildings is the Burberry store (completed in 2012), which looks like it's encased inside a shiny black package featuring the clothing brand's signature check pattern. A bit farther north and across the street, the ❺ **Starbucks Reserve Roastery** was the world's largest Starbucks when it opened in 2019, with four floors plus a roof deck, featuring a cocktail bar, an Italian bakery, and demonstrations on "the art, science and theater of coffee." It's not unusual to see a line of people on the sidewalk waiting to get in.

Farther north, the ❻ **Allerton Hotel** is a rare Chicago example of North Italian Renaissance architecture. Completed in 1924, it was a residential "club hotel" catering to single young men with white-collar jobs. Near the top, a sign advertises the Tip Top Tap, a 23rd-floor lounge where

Frank Sinatra and Bob Hope reportedly performed in the 1940s and 1950s. The Tip Top Tap hasn't actually been open since the 1960s.

When you reach Chicago Avenue, go to the northwest corner—and the ❼ **Water Tower,** one of very few buildings around here that survived the Great Chicago Fire of 1871, when "the whole neighborhood, for blocks around, became a 'sea of fire,' " according to a city report. Ever since, it has been a symbol of Chicago's rebirth. Built in 1869 and designed by William W. Boyington—who also designed the pumping station across the street—the 182.5-foot-tall yellow-limestone tower was a fancy disguise for an unglamorous piece of infrastructure: a standpipe that regulated water flowing from a crib 2 miles out into Lake Michigan. When Oscar Wilde visited Chicago in 1882, he called it a "castellated monstrosity." The city now runs a gallery inside the Water Tower. The surrounding park, named Jane M. Byrne Plaza, is usually busy with pedestrians passing through and people relaxing in chairs. The ❽ **Loyola University Museum of Art** is west of the plaza's north end, inside Lewis Towers, a 1926 building that originally served as the Illinois Women's Athletic Club.

Walk northeast through the plaza. At Pearson Street, go east across Michigan Avenue. ❾ **Water Tower Place,** a mall and 74-story high-rise, is on the northeast corner. Inside, eight stories of retail spaces encircle an atrium. Water Tower Place was a big deal when it opened in 1975, with as much retail space as the rest of North Michigan Avenue combined. And it remains popular today, with a Macy's, the region's only American Girl store, and more than 100 other shops, a dozen restaurants, and the Broadway Playhouse.

The Chicago Avenue Pumping Station lies on the southeast corner of Pearson and Michigan. Walk through the first entrance on the building's north side, entering a space where you can look through glass walls at the pipes and machinery. Turn left, walking east to the next room. The acclaimed ❿ **Lookingglass Theatre Company** has occupied the space to your right since 2003. Turn left, heading into a foyer with an information center for tourists, along with a library branch. Exit onto Pearson. Walk back west, then go south on Michigan.

Turn east on Chicago Avenue. On the street's north side, a two-story limestone fire station with glossy red front doors houses the Chicago Fire Department's Engine Company 98 and Ambulance 11. Built in 1902, it's among the city's oldest active fire stations, with a design by Charles Hermann that complements the Water Tower. As you continue east, the street's north side features Seneca Park, including Deborah Butterfield's 1990 sculpture *Ben,* a horse that looks like it's assembled out of tree branches but is actually bronze.

At the next corner, turn north on Mies van der Rohe Way, entering the plaza in front of the ⓫ **Museum of Contemporary Art Chicago** (MCA). Located here since 1996, the museum showcases post-1945 art in its large galleries. German architect Josef Paul Kleihues's building has an aluminum facade and a limestone base, with a set of 32 wide steps leading up to the entrance. Large sculptures are sometimes displayed in the plaza. At the southeast corner, there's a ground-level entrance to the gift shop, a trove of quirky oddities. At the northeast corner, doors lead into the MCA's theater.

Go to the MCA's north end, then turn east on Pearson, walking along Lake Shore Park. Turn north on Lake Shore Drive. After you pass Chestnut Street, look at the pair of box-shaped glass-and-steel residential high-rises at 860 and 880 N. Lake Shore. Completed in 1951 and known as the Glass House apartments, they were the first residential skyscrapers designed by Ludwig Mies van der Rohe, the influential German-born Chicago architect.

Turn west on Delaware Place. As you approach Michigan Avenue, the building originally known as the John Hancock Center—now called ⓬ 875 North Michigan—dominates Delaware's south side. When this 100-story skyscraper was completed in 1969, it was the world's second-tallest building. Just east of the Hancock, there's a small building called the Casino Club. This private club, which has been here since 1928, refused to sell its property in the 1960s, forcing Skidmore, Owings & Merrill's architect Bruce Graham and engineer Fazlur Khan to rethink the original plan for building two skyscrapers on this block. Khan figured out a new way to construct a single tower tall enough to serve the project's needs. Unlike all previous skyscrapers, 875 is a giant tapered rectangular tube, supported by trusses on each side. The exterior structure is what holds up the 1,128-foot building, allowing for wide-open spaces inside. Those huge X-shaped braces on the exterior enable "Big John" to resist the wind. The 360 Chicago observatory offers 360-degree views from the 94th floor. For an extra fee, visitors can enter the Tilt, a box on the building's edge with floor-to-ceiling windows that slowly tilts to 30 degrees. The Signature Room restaurant occupies the 95th floor, with a bar called the Signature Lounge one story up.

West of the skyscraper, Fourth Presbyterian Church is the oldest structure on North Michigan Avenue other than the Water Tower. Completed in 1914, it was designed by a leading architect of the Gothic Revival style, Ralph Adams Cram, while Howard Van Doren Shaw designed the Tudor-style parish buildings around its courtyard.

Walk north on Michigan. The ⓭ 900 North Michigan Shops mall is anchored by Bloomingdale's. The Palmolive Building, a 1929 Art Deco skyscraper designed by Holabird & Root, stands at the southeast corner of Michigan and Walton Place. This was the Playboy Building from 1965 to 1989, housing the magazine's editorial and business offices—with 9-foot-high illuminated letters at the top, spelling out PLAYBOY. Installed in 1930, an aerial beacon named for aviator Charles Lindbergh was atop the building, with an arc light rotating 360 degrees and projecting a beam into the night sky, reportedly visible from as far away as Cleveland. The light was shut off in 1981 when neighbors complained. In 2007 the light began shining again, every night, 8 p.m.–midnight, but with a modification—now its beam is directed in an arc over Lake Michigan. The building's Palmolive name was restored after new owners converted it into condos.

Farther north, the ⓮ **Drake** hotel dates back to 1920. Architects Benjamin Marshall and Charles Fox designed the Italian Renaissance–style building. The hotel's Coq d'Or bar has been serving liquor since a day after Prohibition was lifted in 1933. The Palm Court is famous for its afternoon tea, a ritual that Diana, Princess of Wales, participated in during her stay in 1996. In the Cape Cod room, you can see the spot on the wooden bar where Joe DiMaggio and Marilyn Monroe carved their initials.

Across the street, ⓯ **Spiaggia** has been acclaimed by many critics as Chicago's best Italian restaurant for more than three decades. For a less pricey meal, try the adjacent Café Spiaggia. Continue north on Michigan, crossing Oak Street. As you approach the pedestrian tunnel under Lake Shore Drive, pause to look back at the Drake's northern face, with the Palmolive Building and its beacon towering up behind it—and farther back, the Hancock overshadowing both. Go through the tunnel under Lake Shore Drive—emerging on the sands of ⓰ **Oak Street Beach,** a great spot for looking at Lake Michigan and vistas of Chicago.

To depart, use one of the many bus routes that stop at Michigan Avenue and Delaware Place.

Points of Interest

❶ **InterContinental Chicago Magnificent Mile** 505 N. Michigan Ave., 312-944-4100, icchicagohotel.com

❷ **The Purple Pig** 444 N. Michigan Ave., 312-464-1744, thepurplepigchicago.com

❸ **The Gwen Hotel** 521 N. Rush St., 312-645-1500, thegwenchicago.com

❹ **Shops at North Bridge** 520 N. Michigan Ave., 312-327-2300, theshopsatnorthbridge.com

❺ **Starbucks Reserve Roastery** 646 N. Michigan Ave., 312-283-7100, starbucksreserve.com

❻ **Allerton Hotel** 701 N. Michigan Ave., 312-440-1500, warwickhotels.com/allerton-hotel-chicago

❼ **Chicago Water Tower** 806 N. Michigan Ave.

❽ **Loyola University Museum of Art** 820 N. Michigan Ave., 312-915-7600, luc.edu/luma

❾ **Water Tower Place** 835 N. Michigan Ave., 312-440-3580, shopwatertower.com

❿ **Lookingglass Theatre** 821 N. Michigan Ave., 312-337-0665, lookingglasstheatre.org

(continued on next page)

(continued from previous page)

11 **Museum of Contemporary Art Chicago** 220 E. Chicago Ave., 312-280-2660, mcachicago.org

12 **875 North Michigan (John Hancock Center)** 875 N. Michigan Ave., 875northmichiganavenue.com; 360 Chicago Observation Deck Chicago, 888-875-8439, 360chicago.com

13 **900 North Michigan Shops** 900 N. Michigan Ave., 312-915-3916, shop900.com

14 **The Drake, a Hilton Hotel** 140 E. Walton Pl., 312-787-2200, thedrakehotel.com

15 **Spiaggia** 980 N. Michigan Ave., 312-280-2750, spiaggiarestaurant.com

16 **Oak Street Beach** 1000 N. Lake Shore Dr., 312-742-3224, chicagoparkdistrict.com/parks-facilities/oak-street-beach

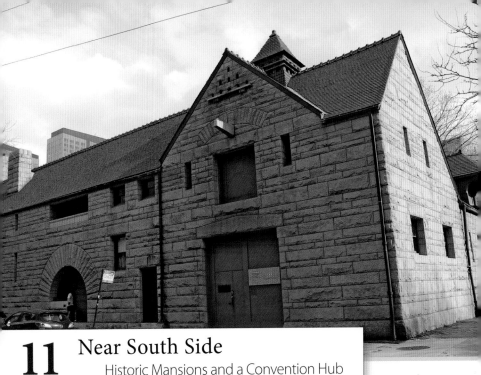

11 Near South Side
Historic Mansions and a Convention Hub

Above: The Glessner House Museum

BOUNDARIES: 18th St., Lake Shore Dr., 24th St., Wentworth Ave.
DISTANCE: 2.1 miles
DIFFICULTY: Easy
PARKING: Free and metered street parking
PUBLIC TRANSIT: CTA 1, 3, or 4 bus to Michigan and Cullerton; or walk from the Green Line's
    Cermak-McCormick Place station

At the turn of the 20th century, the Near South Side included Chicago's most notorious red-light district, as well as Millionaires' Row. After weathering many changes, the area is vibrant and varied today, with a bounty of architectural gems and historically significant places.

Residential construction has boomed since 1980, with high-rises popping up in a landscape once dominated by rails. One of the area's biggest attractions is the McCormick Place convention center, but it was surrounded for decades by boring streets. Officials tried to remedy that by backing the construction of a new megahotel and an arena in 2017.

Walk Description

Begin at Michigan Avenue and Cullerton Street. Towering above the northwest corner, ❶ **Second Presbyterian** is one of only two churches in the Chicago area designated as a National Historic Landmark. Built in the 1870s (after the Great Chicago Fire destroyed the congregation's previous home) and designed by James Renwick, it has nine Tiffany stained glass windows and 13 murals by Frederic Clay Bartlett. The sanctuary, redesigned by Howard Van Doren Shaw after another fire gutted it in 1900, is one of the country's largest intact interiors in the Arts and Crafts style.

At the southwest corner, the word *Locomobile* is visible at the top of a three-story building from 1909. Northeast of the intersection, a building with a green mansard roof was the B. F. Goodrich Company Showroom when it opened in 1924. Both buildings are remnants of the days when this stretch of Michigan was Motor Row.

Walk east on Cullerton and then north on Indiana Avenue. On the street's east side, the ❷ **Clarke House Museum** is Chicago's oldest surviving house. Built in 1836 for Henry B. Clarke in the Greek Revival architectural style, it has been moved twice, ending up here in 1977, surrounded by the Chicago Women's Park and Gardens. The city maintains it as a free museum, offering guided tours at 1 and 2:30 p.m. on Wednesdays, Fridays, and Saturdays. Walk into the lovingly landscaped park. Installed north of the house in 2011, Louise Bourgeois's sculpture *Helping Hands* honors social reformer Jane Addams. Looking east, you'll see a line of historical mansions on the opposite side of Prairie Avenue. Head north from the middle of the park, exiting into a courtyard. ❸ **The Spoke & Bird,** a bistro and coffee house with a patio for alfresco dining or sipping, is to your west.

The fortresslike ❹ **Glessner House Museum** is on your east. Walk east on 18th Street, alongside this National Historic Landmark designed by H. H. Richardson and completed in 1887. Note the odd shape of the service entrance on the north side: a circular arch with an off-center set of stairs leading into a dark nook. With its rusticated granite walls, the Glessner House looks forbidding, but its interior living spaces are cozy. Walk around to the main entrance on the east side. Guided tours (at 11:30 a.m., 1 p.m., and 2:30 p.m., Wednesday–Sunday) cost $15 for adults.

Another remarkable work of architecture is across the street, on the southeast corner of Prairie and 18th. Designed by Solon S. Beman in the Châteauesque style and completed in 1892 at an astronomical cost of $1 million, it was the mansion of piano manufacturer William W. Kimball.

Walk one block east on 18th, entering the Battle of Fort Dearborn Park. Dedicated in 2009, this 0.5-acre marks the place—or at least, one possible place—where the Battle of Fort Dearborn happened on August 15, 1812, when Potawatomi warriors ambushed US soldiers and white civilians marching south from the fort, killing more than 50 people. Some historians say the clash actually happened several blocks north of here.

Return west on 18th, then turn south on Prairie. From the 1870s through the early 1900s, this was Millionaires' Row. The wealthy occupants included Marshall Field, Philip Armour, and railroad car manufacturer George Pullman. But as they died, their descendants moved away. Field's former mansion at 1905 S. Prairie was demolished in 1955, but his son Marshall Field Jr.'s Queen Anne–style mansion, designed by Beman, still stands at 1919. The department store heir died here of a gunshot wound in 1905. An inquest ruled he'd accidentally shot himself while cleaning his gun, but some witnesses said he'd been shot at the Everleigh Club brothel that evening, while other people suggested it was a suicide.

After crossing Cullerton and continuing south, look at the three-story Harriet F. Rees House at 2017 S. Prairie. Built in 1888, it stood for 126 years a block south of here, but then the landmark was moved in 2014 to make way for Wintrust Arena. Weighing 762 tons, it's one of the heaviest buildings ever moved in the United States.

When you reach 21st Street, you'll see ❺ **Wintrust Arena,** a big metallic box on the southwest corner that hosts DePaul University basketball games, concerts, and other events. The 1,205-room Marriott Marquis Chicago Hotel, which opened as part of the same $700 million project in 2017, is on the southeast corner, where ❻ **Showroom Food Hall** offers a variety of foods.

Walk east on 21st. The building just east of Prairie District Park's playground was the final home of Chess Records in the late 1960s; today it's the Chess Lofts condominiums. Turn north on Calumet Avenue, walking half a block—far enough to see a mansion with a tall third-story mansard roof, built in 1870 for banker Calvin T. Wheeler. The ❼ **Wheeler Mansion** is now a boutique hotel. Return south on Calumet, crossing 21st. The building at the southeast corner opened in 1912 as the R. R. Donnelley & Sons Co. Calumet Plant. The printing company asked architect Shaw "to make the building . . . something that will be beautiful not only today, but one hundred years from now." Today, it's a 1.1 million-square-foot data hub called the Lakeside Technology Center—the nerve center for Chicago's commodity markets and one of the world's largest data centers.

Walk south on Calumet, continuing south as the street runs into King Drive. After about a block, you'll reach a square with a fountain and five tall rectangular columns. This is the main entrance to ❽ **McCormick Place,** North America's largest convention center. Originally constructed in 1960, then rebuilt after a 1967 fire, McCormick Place has expanded over the years. Crowds flock here for industry events like the Chicago Auto Show every February (open to anyone who buys a ticket) and the Sweets & Snacks Expo (sorry, not open to the public), as well as volleyball and chess tournaments; pop culture confabs (like 2019's Star Wars Celebration); and meetings of groups ranging from the North American Spine Society to the National Funeral Directors Association. The complex also includes the Arie Crown Theater, a food court, and giant corridors.

Return north on King Drive as it curves west and turns into Cermak Road. When you reach Michigan Avenue, you'll see a glass-covered building at the northeast corner, including South Loop Market. This is the former site of the Lexington Hotel, Al Capone's primary residence from 1928 until he was arrested in 1931. The building was demolished in 1995.

Cross to the west side of Michigan and walk half a block north to see the **❾ Willie Dixon's Blues Heaven Foundation,** a small museum in the former office and studio of Chess Records at 2120 S. Michigan Ave.—an address that's also the title of an instrumental track by the Rolling Stones, who recorded five songs here in 1964. Founded in 1950 by brothers Leonard and Phil Chess, the label recorded some of the earliest rock songs—by Chuck Berry and others—and many influential blues musicians, including Bo Diddley, Willie Dixon, Howlin' Wolf, Muddy Waters, Buddy Guy, and Etta James. The company moved several times during its history, operating here 1957–1965, recording in one tiny, unventilated room. The museum is open Tuesday–Saturday, noon–4 p.m., with tours at the top of each hour.

Return south to Cermak, then walk west. At Cermak and Wabash Avenue, a White Castle restaurant is on the northwest corner. Compare it with the former White Castle #16 on the southeast corner, now occupied by **❿ Chef Luciano Kitchen & Chicken.** The city designated this 1930 structure as a landmark, calling it "the best-surviving example in Chicago of the buildings built by the White Castle System of Eating Houses, Inc." Designed by Lewis E. Russell, it's an early example of programmatic architecture, in which a building functions as a kind of advertisement.

Continue west, passing under the steel-and-glass tube of the Cermak–McCormick Place Green Line station, which opened in 2015. After you cross State Street, the Hilliard Towers Apartments will be on Cermak's north side—two cylindrical towers next to two half-circle buildings. It's no coincidence that the round high-rises resemble downtown's Marina City: both projects were designed in the 1960s by Bertrand Goldberg. These were originally the Raymond Hilliard Homes, a public housing project. It's now mixed-income housing. They stand on land that was part of the Levee red-light district in the early 1900s, including Chicago's most famous brothel, the luxurious Everleigh Club.

Walk west across Clark to the Red Line's Cermak-Chinatown station, where this walk ends. Or you can continue west and explore Chinatown on Walk 12.

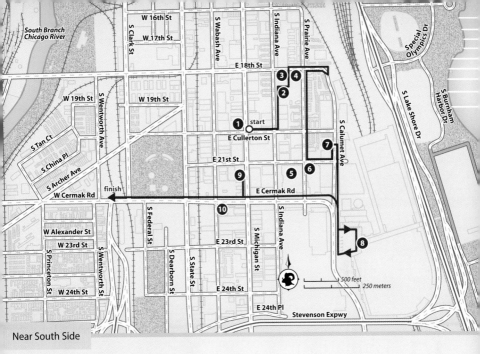

Near South Side

Points of Interest

1. **Second Presbyterian Church** 1936 S. Michigan, 312-225-4951, 2ndpresbyterian.org
2. **Clarke House Museum** 1827 S. Indiana Ave., 312-744-3316, clarkehousemuseum.org
3. **The Spoke & Bird** 205 E. 18th St., 929-263-2473, spokeandbird.com
4. **Glessner House Museum** 1800 S. Prairie Ave., 312-326-1480, glessnerhouse.org
5. **Wintrust Arena** 200 E. Cermak Road, 312-791-6900, wintrustarena.com
6. **Showroom Food Hall** 21st St. and Prairie Ave., 312-824-0500, marriottmarquischicago.com
7. **Wheeler Mansion** 2020 S. Calumet Ave., 312-945-2020, wheelermansion.com
8. **McCormick Place** 2301 S. King Dr., 312-791-7000, mccormickplace.com
9. **Willie Dixon's Blues Heaven Foundation** 2120 S. Michigan Ave., 312-808-1286, bluesheaven.com
10. **Chef Luciano Kitchen & Chicken** 49 E. Cermak Rd., 312-326-0062, chefluciano.com

12   Chinatown
A Thriving Asian Enclave

Above: Looking north up Wentworth Avenue on a stormy afternoon

BOUNDARIES: Clark St., Stevenson Expressway, Canal St., 16th St.
DISTANCE: 3 miles
DIFFICULTY: Easy
PARKING: Paid parking lots northeast of Cermak Rd. and Wentworth Ave., free and metered
   street parking
PUBLIC TRANSIT: Red Line to Cermak/Chinatown

Even as the Chinese areas of some US cities shrink or fade away amid gentrification, Chicago's Chinatown is thriving—with 24% population growth between 2000 and 2010, including a new influx of Asian immigrants. Chinatown is a colorful place to walk, where some buildings imitate traditional Asian architecture. Sculptures of guardian lions stand next to some entrances, and there's Chinese writing everywhere. Some restaurants have one menu in English, plus another menu in Chinese, featuring dishes less familiar to most Americans. There are even a few eateries serving Korean, Thai, or Japanese food, alongside many Chinese bakeries, candy shops, and groceries. The neighborhood celebrates the Lunar New Year with a parade every February, but it's a festive and fascinating place to visit any time.

Walk Description

Starting at the Red Line station, walk west on Cermak Road's north side, where the ornate Nine Dragon Wall stands. Around 25 feet long, it's a smaller reproduction of a wall in Beijing that depicts nine regal dragons. Completed in 2003, it's an example of the spirit screens that the Chinese used centuries ago, believing they blocked evil spirits.

Cross to the west side of Wentworth Avenue, then go south, crossing Cermak. The next several blocks of Wentworth are the heart of old Chinatown. Walk under the red Friendship Gate, built in 1975. Above the words WELCOME TO CHINATOWN, the gate says TIAN XIA WEI GONG, meaning "The world belongs to the people" or "What is under heaven is for all." This ancient Confucian phrase describes humanity as family. It was a favorite saying of Sun Yat-sen, the Republic of China's provisional first president after the overthrow of the last emperor in 1911. That revolution helped inspire Chinese immigrants, who were facing harassment and high rents in the South Loop, to move en masse to this neighborhood around 1912, with the On Leong Merchants Association leading the way.

On Leong's old headquarters are on the west side of Wentworth near the arch, with pagoda-style towers. Completed in 1928, it was designed by Norwegian American architects Christian Michaelsen and Sigurd Rognstad, who relied on photos of Chinese buildings in a German book. The terra-cotta ornaments, including symbols of the six Confucian virtues, are mostly glazed red (the color of joy) or jade green (symbolizing affluence). The animal figures face outward or toward another animal, because it's considered bad luck to show them with their backs turned on one another. The building came to be known as Chinatown's unofficial city hall—but federal agents discovered it was also operating as a gambling parlor, where people wagered on games of fan-tan and pai gow. The Justice Department seized the building in 1988. The Chinese Christian Union Church later bought this city-designated landmark and reopened it as the ❶ Pui Tak Center, providing education and services for Chinese immigrants.

Walk south on Wentworth's west side. Michaelsen and Rognstad also designed the ornate building with dragon-encircled terra-cotta columns at 2238 S. Wentworth, now occupied by ❷ Emperor's Choice, one of Chinatown's most popular restaurants. Looking across the street and a bit south, you'll see another Chinese design by these Scandinavian Americans: the large brick structure with recessed balconies between two rectangular towers decorated with herons and parrots. That was the legendary Won Kow Restaurant for 90 years, until the owners retired in 2018.

At the next corner, take Alexander Street half a block west to see St. Therese Chinese Catholic Church, which served an Italian congregation before it began celebrating Mass in Chinese in 1960. Along with some distinctively Asian touches, like lion statues, the church still contains elements of its Italian history, including the shrine of Santa Maria Incoronata. Return east to Wentworth and continue south.

At 23rd Street, you can walk half a block west to visit the ❸ **Chinese American Museum of Chicago,** where the exhibits explore the history of Chinese immigrants in America. St. Therese School is across the street from the museum, and this block also includes the popular restaurant Go 4 Food. Return east to Wentworth, and continue south. Another restaurant that's a favorite in Chinatown, Little Sheep Mongolian Hot Pot, is along this stretch.

When you reach 24th Place, walk west for a block to ❹ **Sun Yat-Sen Park,** a spot next to the Stevenson Expressway with chess tables near a bust of the park's namesake. Return east to Wentworth, then head north up the street's east side. Recommended restaurants along here include Chiu Quon Bakery & Dim Sum (at 2253) and Slurp Slurp Noodles (2247). After passing under the arch, turn west on Cermak. The fire station at 212 W. Cermak was in the 1991 movie *Backdraft*.

The black granite Chinese American Veterans Memorial sits at the southwest corner of the intersection with Archer and Princeton Avenues. Cross over to the intersection's north side, where ❺ **Chinatown Square** covers 45 acres along Archer. Walk northeast through the central corridor of this two-story outdoor mall, which was built in 1993 on a rail yard. One of the largest Chinese shopping centers in the United States between San Francisco and New York City, it has several of Chinatown's most-praised restaurants: BBQ King House, Cai, Chi Cafe, Hing Kee Restaurant, Joy Yee's Noodle Shop, MCCB Chicago, MingHin Cuisine, Qing Xiang Yuan Dumplings, and Saint Anna Bakery & Café. Amid gift shops, bookstores, medical offices, bakeries, and candy stores, several cafés serve bubble tea. Near the mall's center, walk out into the open square on its south edge, a gathering place featuring statues of 12 animals, one for each year in the Chinese zodiac cycle, sculpted at Xiamen University in China. Nearby, artists Yan Dong and Zhou Ping's *Chinese in America* mural is made from 100,000 mosaic tiles. Continue northeast through the mall. As you exit, the ❻ **Richland Center Chinatown Food Court** (including the acclaimed Mala Spicy Spirit Temptation) and Pop KTV, a popular karaoke spot, are just northeast of the mall.

Walk north on Wentworth, then west on Cullerton Street, entering the newer residential section of Chinatown, where the streets are filled with neat redbrick town houses. At the next corner, turn north on Wells Street. When the street ends, turn west, entering ❼ **Ping Tom Memorial Park**—a former rail yard that the Chicago Park District transformed in 1998, creating a lovely spot for strolling along the Chicago River's South Branch. Named after a neighborhood leader whose company built Chinatown Square, the park features a pagoda-like pavilion, a playground, and pretty views at sunset. When you look south, the Canal Street railroad bridge and its two 185-foot towers dominate the vista. A houselike structure sits on top of the bridge's 1,500-ton span, which can be raised 111 feet in about 45 seconds. Built in 1914, it's the only vertical-lift bridge on the Chicago River.

Head north, going under the 18th Street bridge—past *All as One,* a lovely blue, white, and gold floral mural by Andy Bellomo, Chester Chow, and Anna Murphy that *Chicago* magazine called the city's best place for a selfie—and entering the park's newer north area, where paths run along the river. Kayaks can be rented at the park's boathouse, and there's a public dock for boats without motors. When you look north, the scenery includes another railway span across the water—the St. Charles Air Line Bridge, which was the world's longest and heaviest single-leaf bridge when it was built in 1919—as well as downtown's skyline. This vista is changing, with the construction of a development called the 78—a whole new neighborhood on 62 acres of previously vacant land north of Chinatown.

Turn back south, exiting the park where you came in. Continue east on 19th Street, then go south on Wentworth. Cross Archer and continue south, walking alongside the ❽ **Chinatown**

The Friendship Gate over Wentworth Avenue

Chinatown

Branch of the Chicago Public Library, where vertical metal fins line the curved two-story structure's glass curtain wall. Designed by Skidmore, Owings & Merrill and Wight and Company, the distinctive building opened in 2015, quickly becoming a new nexus of Chinatown's community. Continue south. The walk ends at Wentworth and Cermak, where you can leave via the Red Line.

Points of Interest

1. **Pui Tak Center** 2216 S. Wentworth Ave., 312-328-1188, puitak.org
2. **Emperor's Choice** 2238 S. Wentworth Ave., 312-225-8800, chicagoemperorschoice.com
3. **Chinese American Museum of Chicago** 238 W. 23rd St., 312-949-1000, ccamuseum.org
4. **Sun Yat-Sen Park** 251 W. 24th Pl., chicagoparkdistrict.com/parks-facilities/sun-yat-sen-park
5. **Chinatown Square** Archer Ave. between Princeton Ave. and Wentworth Ave.
6. **Richland Center Chinatown Food Court** 2002 S. Wentworth Ave.
7. **Ping Tom Memorial Park** 19th St. and Wells St., 312-225-3121, chicagoparkdistrict.com/parks-facilities/tom-ping-memorial-park
8. **Chinatown Branch, Chicago Public Library** 2100 S. Wentworth Ave., 312-747-8013, chipublib.org/locations/20

13 Bronzeville
Chicago's Black Metropolis

Above: The Illinois Institute of Technology's McCormick Tribune Campus Center

---

BOUNDARIES: Dan Ryan Expwy., 31st St., Martin Luther King Dr., 47th St.
DISTANCE: 3.5 miles
DIFFICULTY: Easy
PARKING: Free and metered street parking
PUBLIC TRANSIT: Red Line to Sox/35th

When African Americans began their Great Migration from the South circa 1916, many flocked to Chicago. One of the few places where they had the opportunity to settle in this segregated city was a section of the South Side called the Black Belt. Around 1930, James J. Gentry, a theater editor for a black newspaper called the *Chicago Bee,* coined a new name for the neighborhood: Bronzeville. In the mid-20th century, Bronzeville rivaled New York City's Harlem as black America's most prominent cultural hub and business center. In later decades, Bronzeville was plagued by poverty and crime, but its fortunes have been on the rise in recent times, even if it hasn't gentrified as quickly as some boosters had anticipated.

Walk Description

Walk east on 35th Street from the Dan Ryan Expressway. When you reach Dearborn Street, turn north on the sidewalks through the Illinois Institute of Technology campus. The college traces its roots back to 1893, when the Armour Institute opened as a school for engineering, chemistry, architecture, and library science. It became Illinois Tech in 1940 when it merged with Lewis Institute. Later, Hungarian immigrant artist László Moholy-Nagy's Institute of Design and the Chicago-Kent College of Law became parts of Illinois Tech. While serving as the architecture department's director from 1938 to 1958, Ludwig Mies van der Rohe left his modernist imprint on the campus, designing 20 buildings in his minimalist style: steel and concrete frames with curtain walls of brick and glass.

After you've gone about a block north, ❶ **S. R. Crown Hall** will be to your east, with a wall of rectangular windows. Designed by Mies and constructed in 1955, it's a National Historic Landmark. To create an interior space without obstructing columns, Mies suspended the roof from four steel girders supported by eight external columns spaced 60 feet apart. The building sits on the spot where the Mecca Flats apartment complex—a vibrant African American community—was demolished in 1952 despite a decade-long fight by tenants to save it.

When you reach 33rd Street, walk a block west, where you can see two of the oldest campus buildings flanking 33rd: the Main Building, from 1893, and Machinery Hall, from 1901. Walk back east on 33rd, then go north on the pedestrian corridor you were following earlier. Look for *Man on a Bench,* George Segal's white-resin-covered bronze sculpture of a man, who appears to be African American. This popular spot for student selfies sits on a 6-by-9-foot piece of land called Park 474, the Chicago Park District's smallest park. A bit farther north, take the path that runs east, and then go south on State Street. Across the street, Dutch architect Rem Koolhaas's sleek ❷ **McCormick Tribune Campus Center** opened in 2003. Overhead, the Green Line L tracks are sheathed inside a 530-foot-long concrete and stainless steel tube.

Turn east on 33rd Street. At the southeast corner of 33rd and State, State Street Village is a trio of five-story dorms designed by Helmut Jahn, with exterior glass walls to muffle the noise from passing L trains. This corner is also where 3-year-old Sam Cooke (the King of Soul) lived when his family moved from Mississippi in 1933.

At Indiana Avenue, the limestone walls of ❸ **Pilgrim Baptist Church** are at the southeast corner. Designed by Dankmar Adler and Louis Sullivan and completed in 1891, it was the Kehilath

Anshe Ma'arav synagogue until 1922, when a Baptist congregation took over the building, which had a pyramid-shaped roof. This is where Thomas A. Dorsey, who was Pilgrim Baptist's music director for decades, began creating a new genre of music called gospel in the 1930s. Albertina Walker, Mahalia Jackson, Aretha Franklin, and the Staples Singers sang here. A fire gutted the church in 2006, leaving just the walls, which have been propped up by a steel support skeleton ever since. There are plans to construct the National Museum of Gospel Music within the old church's shell.

Walk north on Indiana. Unity Hall, a decrepit building at 3140 S. Indiana, was built in 1887 as a Jewish social club. It later housed the Peoples Movement Club, a black political organization led by alderman Oscar Stanton De Priest. Go west on 31st Street, along the south edge of Dunbar Park. Just across from Prairie Avenue, you'll see Debra Hand's sculpture of ❹ **Paul Laurence Dunbar,** the first prominent African American poet, who lived in Chicago for a time and spoke at the 1893 world's fair. Erected in 2014, this 6-foot-tall bronze is reportedly the first full-figure statue of a famous African American in a Chicago park.

Continue east on 31st, then turn south on Calumet Avenue, which is lined with beautiful homes dating back to the 1880s and 1890s. The Joseph Deimel House at 3141, constructed in 1887, is the last survivor of more than 20 houses that Adler and Sullivan designed for Jewish clients in this neighborhood. The Robert Roloson Houses, with four high-pitched gables at the addresses from 3213 to 3219, comprise the only row house development ever designed by Frank Lloyd Wright, who remodeled them in 1894.

When you reach 35th Street, cross to the south side and walk a short distance west to see the building at 315. Now a cosmetics store called ❺ **Urban Beautique,** it was built as an automobile garage in 1909. After it was remodeled in 1921, it became one of Chicago's most famous jazz clubs, the Sunset Café, where Louis Armstrong, Cab Calloway, and Earl Hines played in front of mixed-race audiences. After 1937, it was renamed the Grand Terrace Cafe, becoming a hot spot for bebop in the 1940s.

Go one block east on 35th, arriving at the wide intersection with Martin Luther King Jr. Drive. Chicago was the first city to name a street after King, bestowing the honor on this thoroughfare—which had been called South Park Way and, before that, Grand Boulevard—on July 31, 1968. That was less than four months after the civil rights leader's assassination. Mayor Richard J. Daley (who often opposed King) presided over a ceremony at the ❻ **Victory Monument** on the island in the middle of King Drive south of 35th. Cross to the island for a closer look. Created by French immigrant Leonard Crunelle, it was dedicated in 1928, with bronze panels honoring the Illinois National Guard's Eighth Regiment, an African American unit that served during World

War I. A sculpture of a soldier was added on top in 1936. Look to the east side of King Drive to see a landmark building from 1921: formerly the headquarters of the Supreme Life Insurance Company—the largest African American–owned business in the northern United States—it now includes the Senegalese restaurant **❼ Yassa.**

Walk west, crossing King Drive's southbound lanes and going all the way to the sidewalk along the west frontage street. Head south. This stretch is lined with the distinctive Chicago homes called greystones, including many that were rehabbed in recent years. Highlights include the Martin Roche–John Tait House (at 3614), designed in 1888 by noted architect Martin Roche, who lived there in a third-floor suite above his sister and her husband; the **❽ Ida B. Wells-Barnett House** (3624), where the legendary anti-lynching crusader lived from 1919 to 1929; and the opulent D. Harry Hammer House (3656), designed by William Clay in 1885, a rare example of the big houses that once stood on corners along boulevards.

If you're hungry for one of the South Side's most popular traditional dishes, cross King Drive to **❾ Chicago's Home of Chicken and Waffles** (3947). As you continue south, you may want to take short side trips to see nearby historical sites: Author **❿ Richard Wright's former home** is at 3743 S. Indiana, a block west on 38th; Wendell Phillips High School lies west on Pershing Road; and **⓫ Nat "King" Cole's former home** is at 4023 S. Vincennes, east on 41st Street.

A historical marker at 41st and King honors Bessie Coleman, who became the first black woman licensed to fly airplanes in 1920. The Metropolitan Apostolic Community Church is an imposing presence at the same intersection. Built in 1890, the Romanesque church with reddish-brown stones is where A. Philip Randolph organized the Pullman Porters Union. Activists saved the church after learning of demolition plans in 2001. At the northeast corner of 43rd and King, the Belmonte Flats were constructed in 1893; poet Gwendolyn Brooks lived in a kitchenette in the building in the 1930s, upstairs from the storefront where Bronzeville Boutique is today.

Walk west on 43rd. At the northwest corner of 43rd and Calumet, the Forum was built in 1897, with a second-floor ballroom that hosted concerts by Muddy Waters, B. B. King, and Nat "King" Cole. It's been vacant for decades, but the owners have plans to revive it. Go south on Calumet, and when the street ends, continue south on the path through **⓬ Hadiya Pendleton Park,** which was renamed in 2015 as a tribute to a 15-year-old girl murdered in 2013, a week after she'd performed as a drum majorette at President Barack Obama's second inauguration. Pendleton was shot to death in a different park by gang members who mistook her for a rival. This park named in her honor features sculptures of musical instruments and school books—poignant reminders of Chicago's tragic violence.

Exit the park, walking south on Calumet, then go east on 44th Street. Cross King Drive to see the former home of ⑬ **Louis Armstrong** at 421 E. 44th, then backtrack west and turn south on King. This stretch includes the Parkway Ballroom (4455), a social hub for decades; the former home of ⑭ **Groucho, Chico, Harpo, Zeppo, and Gummo Marx** (4512), where they lived while starting on the vaudeville circuit in the 1910s; and the former home of Oscar Stanton De Priest (4536), Chicago's first black alderman and the first black congressman elected from a northern state.

At King Drive and 47th Street, sculptures by Ed Dwight—depicting a guitar player, saxophonist, trumpeter, and singer—stand on 27-foot-high cylinders at each corner. This is the focal point of the Chicago Blues District. ⑮ **Peach's,** a restaurant famed for its comfort food, is at the northwest corner. Walk west on 47th. At the northeast corner of 47th and Calumet, study the disturbing 1975 mural *Wall of Daydreaming and Man's Inhumanity to Man* by William Walker, Mitchell Caton, and Santi Isrowuthalkul, which vividly visualizes the social ills of urban life. A block farther west, the *Blues Mural* at Prairie Avenue had a cameo in *The Blues Brothers,* serving as the exterior wall of a fictional music store run by Ray Charles.

The walk ends at 47th and Prairie, where you can depart by taking a CTA Green Line train.

Points of Interest

① **S. R. Crown Hall** 3360 S. State St., arch.iit.edu/about/sr-crown-hall

② **McCormick Tribune Campus Center** 3201 S. State St., web.iit.edu/event-services/meeting-spaces/mccormick-tribune-campus-center

③ **Pilgrim Baptist Church** 3301 S. Indiana Ave., 312-842-4417, nationalmuseumofgospelmusic.org

④ **Paul Laurence Dunbar Monument** 300 E. 31st St., chicagoparkdistrict.com/parks-facilities/paul-laurence-dunbar-monument

⑤ **Urban Beautique (former Sunset Cafe)** 315 E. 35th St., 312-877-5717

⑥ **Victory Monument** King Dr. south of 35th St.

⑦ **Yassa African Restaurant** 3511 S. King Dr., 773-488-5599, yassarestaurant.com

⑧ **Ida B. Wells-Barnett House** 3624 S. King Dr.

⑨ **Chicago's Home of Chicken and Waffles** 3947 S. King Dr., 773-536-3300, chicagoschickenandwaffles.com

⑩ **Richard Wright's home** 3743 S. Indiana Ave.

(continued on next page)

(continued from previous page)

11 Nat "King" Cole's home 4023 S. Vincennes Ave.

12 Hadiya Pendleton Park 4345 S. Calumet Ave., 312-747-6707, chicagoparkdistrict.com/parks-facilities/pendleton-hadiya-park

13 Louis Armstrong's home 421 E. 44th St.

14 Marx Brothers' home 4512 S. King Dr.

15 Peach's 4652 S. King Dr., 773-966-5801, peachson47th.com

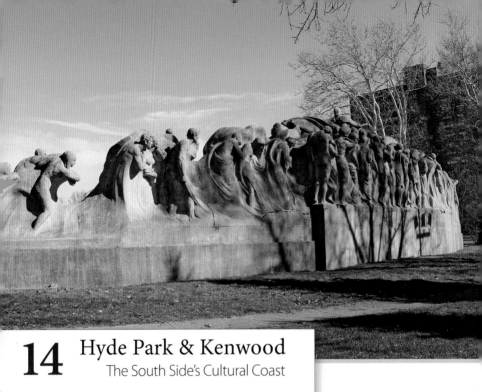

14 Hyde Park & Kenwood
The South Side's Cultural Coast

Above: Lorado Taft's Fountain of Time *sculpture*

BOUNDARIES: Payne Dr., 60th St., Lake Park Ave., 48th St.
DISTANCE: 5 miles
DIFFICULTY: Easy
PARKING: Free street parking on the Midway Plaisance
PUBLIC TRANSIT: CTA 2 Hyde Park Express bus to Midway Plaisance and Cottage Grove; Red Line to 63rd St.; 53 bus to 63rd Street and St. Lawrence; Green Line to King Drive

Hyde Park is a politically liberal and racially diverse hub for culture and arts, anchored by the elite University of Chicago and its array of Gothic buildings. Three years after Hyde Park was annexed by Chicago, it was the site for the World's Columbian Exposition of 1893, attracting 27 million visitors. But the fairground's temporary buildings didn't last long, so it will take imagination to picture that White City. There's no shortage of beautiful architecture, however. (To see more sights connected with the 1893 fair, visit Jackson Park in Walk 15.) The university opened in 1892, initially funded by oil magnate John D. Rockefeller on land donated by Marshall Field. At latest count, it's had nearly a hundred Nobel Prize laureates.

Just north of Hyde Park, Kenwood was one of Chicago's most affluent neighborhoods at the turn of the 20th century, but some areas fell into poverty after World War II. Kenwood has been on the rebound in recent decades, and marvelous houses line the streets at the neighborhood's south end.

Walk Description

Begin your walk near Cottage Grove Avenue and the Midway Plaisance. West of the intersection, walk over to sculptor Lorado Taft's 1922 masterpiece ❶ *Fountain of Time.* Taft spent more than a decade creating it, inspired by Henry Austin Dobson's poem *The Paradox of Time*: "Time goes, you say? Ah no, Alas, time stays, we go." Father Time, a hooded figure with a scythe, stands on one side of a reflecting pool. On the other side, a hundred or so humans march through the cycle of life, forming one mountainous mass more than 100 feet long. Taft molded the hollow, steel-reinforced sculpture from 250 tons of concrete mixed with pebbles. Time took its toll on the artwork, but a restoration was completed in 2007.

Fountain of Time lies at the northeast corner of Washington Park. The Midway Plaisance, a 660-foot-wide boulevard-style park, extends east from here toward Jackson Park. All of this green space was originally South Park, a 1,055-acre landscape designed in 1871 by Frederick Law Olmsted and Calvert Vaux. Olmsted's vision for a canal running through the Midway never came to fruition. Neither did Taft's idea to populate it with sculptures. In 1893 the Midway was the entertainment zone for the World's Columbian Exposition, with foreign villages, ethnological displays, and amusements.

Walk south to 60th Street, and then go east along the Midway's south edge. Looking north, you'll see the University of Chicago's (U of C's) castles of learning. After you cross Drexel Avenue, the ❷ **Reva and David Logan Center for the Arts** is on the south side of 60th, dominated by an 11-story tower. Open since 2011, the complex hosts performances, art exhibits, and lectures. Farther east, Taft's house and Midway Studios, a converted barn where he sculpted in the early 1900s, are at the southwest corner of 60th and Ingleside.

At Ellis Avenue, walk north across the Midway. Ellis and the other four streets crossing the Midway are illuminated at night by 40-foot-tall light masts. Installed in 2011, they look like giant fluorescent light bulbs planted vertically in the ground. As you reach the Midway's midpoint, look east to see a skating rink. That's where the world's first Ferris wheel operated during the 1893 fair, standing 264 feet high.

After you've crossed both of the Midway's roadways, go east through the Readers Garden and the North Winter Garden. A sculpture of naturalist Carl Linnaeus stands amid these gardens, replicating a monument in Stockholm. Make your way to the gardens' northeast corner, passing through the spot that was the Street of Cairo, where scantily clad belly dancers did the hootchy-kootchy during the 1893 fair.

At Woodlawn Avenue, go north across 59th Street. Ida Noyes Hall, constructed in 1916 as a gymnasium and social center for U of C's women, is at the northeast corner. Inside, it looks like an English Tudor manor house, decorated with carved wood and gessoed ceilings. On the ground floor, the former gym is now the Max Palevsky Cinema, where ❸ **Doc Films** shows an eclectic selection of movies.

On the northwest corner of Woodlawn and 59th, the ❹ **Rockefeller Memorial Chapel** is the tallest building on campus, a 32,000-ton church constructed in 1928 almost entirely out of limestone—with no structural steel except for supports in the 207-foot-high tower's carillon and roof. That carillon is the world's second heaviest, with 72 bronze bells weighing a total of 100 tons. Outside, the walls are populated with more than 100 stone sculptures, depicting Biblical figures along with Zoroaster, Plato, Dante, John Milton, Woodrow Wilson, Theodore Roosevelt, and even some U of C students from the early 20th century. The chapel hosts carillon, organ, and choral concerts, as well as occasional rock and jazz shows.

Walk north on Woodlawn. At the northeast corner of Woodlawn and 58th, the ❺ **Frederick C. Robie House** is one of Frank Lloyd Wright's masterpieces. There may be no finer example of the architect's Prairie style, with strong horizontal lines echoing the Midwestern landscape. Robie, a bicycle and car company owner, lived in the house for less than two years after it was completed in 1910. It later served as a Chicago Theological Seminary dormitory and escaped demolition plans in 1957. The Frank Lloyd Wright Trust, which completed an $11 million restoration in 2019, offers guided tours. The building just north of the Robie House includes ❻ **Seminary Co-op,** an academic bookshop in business since 1961 (at this location since 2012), with an eclectic mix of 100,000 books on its shelves. Where Woodlawn meets 59th, walk west, following a corridor toward the ❼ **Oriental Institute Museum,** which displays ancient artifacts from the Middle East, most excavated by U of C archaeologists.

Continue west across University Avenue, entering the Main Quadrangle. This is the heart of the campus that Henry Ives Cobb designed in 1892, a pastoral space where students sit with books, socialize, or play Frisbee. From the quad's center, walk south toward the William Rainey

Harper Memorial Library, constructed in 1912. No longer filled with books, it's a popular spot for studying. Cut west between Swift Hall and Haskell Hall, where you can see Bond Chapel's steeple. This stone cloister was constructed in 1926, connected with the U of C's Divinity School. Walk south around the chapel, entering a cozy courtyard. Head north, along the chapel's west side.

After you return to the Main Quad, take the sidewalk leading north under the metal arch for Hull Court. Walk north through Cobb Gate, designed in 1897 by its namesake. Passing under the limestone archway—decorated with winged dragons that supposedly represent U of C admissions officers—is a ritual for freshmen. According to legend, the sculptured creatures ascending the arch symbolize students in their first, second, and third years, while the fellow at the peak is ready for his diploma.

Cross 57th Street, walking toward the **8** **University of Chicago Library's Joseph Regenstein Library,** a concrete structure with grooved limestone slabs forming grid patterns on the outer walls. An example of the Brutalist style from 1970, it was designed by Walter Netsch. Walk west to the Joe and Rika Mansueto Library's 240-foot-long elliptical glass dome, which has 691 panels curving up to a height of 35 feet. Designed by Helmut Jahn and completed in 2011, the dome sits on top of a tightly packed storage facility that can hold 3.5 million volumes.

At the corner, walk north on Ellis. That 14-foot-tall bronze blob north of the dome is British artist Henry Moore's 1967 sculpture *Nuclear Energy,* looking like a melting human skull or a mushroom cloud. It's at the spot where a team of scientists led by Enrico Fermi created the first human-made self-sustaining nuclear chain reaction at 3:25 p.m. on December 2, 1942, as part of the Manhattan Project that developed the first atomic bomb. They used a pile of 40,000 graphite blocks enclosing 19,000 pieces of uranium metal and uranium oxide fuel in an abandoned rackets court under the stands of Stagg Field, which was later demolished.

Walk north, crossing 56th Street. Go east through the lot south of **9** **Court Theatre,** then continue through the sculpture garden of the **10** **Smart Museum of Art** (where the admission is free). Exit east, then walk northeast through a plaza between the high-rises of the Campus North Residential Commons, which includes restaurants and a café.

When you reach 55th Street and University Avenue, head south on University, a street with historical buildings. Walk east on 57th, strolling past the Quadrangle Club, University Church, First Unitarian Church of Chicago, the University of Chicago Institute of Politics, and 57th Street Books. Go north through Bikler Park, continuing north on Kenwood Avenue. When the street bends east at 54th, go straight north through Nichols Park. At the north end of that park, turn east on 53rd, Hyde Park's main street for shops and restaurants.

At the northeast corner of 53rd and Dorchester, a plaque marks the place where Barack Obama kissed his future wife, Michelle, for the first time. Another three blocks east, the ⑪ **Valois** diner has been in business since 1921. Obama was a regular here during his days as a U of C professor. Across the street, the Hyde Park Bank, a gem from 1929, was designed by K. M. Vitzthum & Company with Art Deco flourishes. The ⑫ **Promontory** nightclub and concert venue is down the alley just east of the bank. But we're going to head north on the restaurant-lined Harper Court, following it as it curves west.

Walk north on Harper Avenue until you reach Hyde Park Boulevard, then go west. Turn north on Dorchester Avenue, entering Kenwood. After one block, look at the one-story brick buildings at the northwest corner of Dorchester and Madison Park. Designed in 1961 by Y. C. Wong, the Atrium Houses look like windowless bunkers, but they actually have glass-walled atriums inside. Former White Sox owner Bill Veeck lived in the unit at 1380 E. Madison Park. Walk west on Madison Park, an enclave constructed in the late 1800s with a park in between the street's lanes.

Exiting Madison Park, turn north on Woodlawn Avenue, which is lined with elegant houses. Muhammad Ali lived at 4944. Nation of Islam founder Elijah Muhammad lived in the complex at the northeast corner with 49th Street, where the stained glass windows include Muslim motifs. An Italianate country villa at 4812 is one of the area's oldest homes, built in 1873.

Turn west on 48th Street. When you reach Greenwood Avenue, you're a bit south of the property where murderer Nathan Leopold lived, but his family's mansion at 4754 was demolished in the 1960s. Walk south on Greenwood. As you approach Hyde Park Boulevard, you'll see signs warning: SIDEWALK CLOSED and RESIDENTIAL TRAFFIC ONLY. Barack Obama and his family lived in the house at 5046 before he was elected president. They rarely visit now, but Secret Service agents still guard the premises. You can take the sidewalk on the south side of the street, where ⑬ **KAM Isaiah Israel Congregation** is at the northeast corner of Greenwood and Hyde Park. The Byzantine-inspired synagogue was designed by Alfred S. Alschuler and built in 1924.

Walk west on Hyde Park Boulevard to Drexel Boulevard. An 1881 sculpture of real estate speculator Francis M. Drexel stands west of the intersection on a pedestal with sculpted images, including Neptune riding a dolphin. This fountain is the oldest existing public sculpture in any Chicago park.

The walk ends here, but you can walk west to explore Washington Park. Or head south on Cottage Grove Avenue to the ⑭ **DuSable Museum of African American History.** To depart, take a 15 Jeffrey local bus west to the Red Line.

Hyde Park & Kenwood

Points of Interest

1. *Fountain of Time* Cottage Grove Ave. and Midway Plaisance, chicagoparkdistrict.com /parks-facilities/washington-fountain-time
2. Reva and David Logan Center for the Arts 915 E. 60th St., 773-702-2787, arts.uchicago.edu
3. Doc Films Ida Noyes Hall, 1212 E. 59th St., 773-702-8574, docfilms.uchicago.edu
4. Rockefeller Memorial Chapel 5850 S. Woodlawn Ave., 773-702-2667, rockefeller.uchicago.edu
5. Frederick C. Robie House 5757 S. Woodlawn Ave., 312-994-4000, flwright.org/visit/robiehouse
6. Seminary Co-op Bookstore 5751 S. Woodlawn Ave., 773-752-4381, semcoop.com
7. Oriental Institute Museum 1155 E. 58th St., 773-702-9514, oi.uchicago.edu
8. University of Chicago Library 1100 E. 57th St., 773-702-8740, lib.uchicago.edu
9. Court Theatre 5535 S. Ellis Ave., 773-753-4472, courttheatre.org
10. Smart Museum of Art 5550 S. Greenwood Ave., 773-702-0200, smartmuseum.uchicago.edu
11. Valois 1518 E. 53rd St., 773-667-0647, valoisrestaurant.com
12. The Promontory 5311 S. Lake Park Ave. W, 312-801-2100, promontorychicago.com
13. KAM Isaiah Israel Congregation 1100 E. Hyde Park Blvd., 773-924-1234, kamii.org
14. DuSable Museum of African American History 740 E. 56th Pl., 773-947-0600, dusablemuseum.org

15 Jackson Park & South Shore
From the World's Fair to Obama

Above: These women appear to be holding up the Museum of Science and Industry. Pillars sculpted as women are called caryatids.

BOUNDARIES: 71st St., 56th St., Stony Island Ave., Lake Michigan
DISTANCE: 4.2 miles
DIFFICULTY: Easy
PARKING: Free street parking on 71st St. west of South Shore Dr.; paid parking lots in Jackson Park
PUBLIC TRANSIT: CTA 6, 26, and 71 bus routes to South Shore Dr. and 71st St.; Metra Electric District
 train to South Shore

With its 170 acres of woodlands, prairie, savanna, lagoons, and dunes, Jackson Park is one of Chicago's most beautiful places, masterfully designed by Frederick Law Olmsted and Calvert Vaux. It served as the fairgrounds for the 1893 World's Columbian Exposition, but only a few traces of that famous event remain. As this book was being written, the Obama Presidential Center—a complex honoring and exploring former President Barack Obama's legacy—was being planned on the park's west edge. This walk starts at the landmark South Shore Cultural Center before heading north into Jackson Park.

Walk Description

Begin at South Shore Drive and 71st Street, where the ❶ **South Shore Cultural Center** is at the northeast corner. Walk through the gates, past the stables where 32 geldings in the Chicago Police Department's Mounted Patrol Unit live. Head up the drive toward the Mediterranean Revival–style clubhouse, designed by architects Marshall and Fox in 1916, back when this was the South Shore Country Club. The club went out of business in the 1970s after refusing to lift its ban on African American members. The Chicago Park District now runs the nine-hole golf course. The building includes the Parrot Cage Restaurant, a teaching program of the Washburne Culinary Institute. Barack and Michelle Obama held their wedding reception here in 1992, and the front colonnade can be seen in *The Blues Brothers*—serving as the Palace Hotel Ballroom, where Jake and Elwood perform. A beach lies just north of the building. And off in the park's northeast corner, a boardwalk leads across 6 acres of dunes, prairie, wetlands, and a meadow.

Return to the park's entrance, then walk north along South Shore Drive, with the golf course on your east and the South Shore neighborhood's residential high-rises to your west. This is the southern end of the Lakefront Trail. Follow the trail as it bends northwest, entering Jackson Park. The La Rabida Children's Hospital is on the street's north side. Constructed in 1932, it stands on the site of the 1893 world's fair's Spanish Pavilion.

Continue west along the yacht-filled harbor. Follow the trail as it turns north, running along Lake Shore Drive. At the harbor's north end, turn east toward ❷ **63rd Street Beach.** Walk on the L-shaped pier extending 1,800 feet out into the lake, where you can see downtown to the north, Indiana's industrial shoreline to the south, and water stretching toward the eastern horizon. Take the pier back to land, then head west. Just before you reach Lake Shore Drive, veer north and take the tunnel underneath the road. Head south toward Hayes Drive, then walk west along that street.

Look for the ❸ **Statue of the Republic,** a gilded bronze sculpture in the traffic island where Hayes Drive meets Richards Drive; cross the roadways to the island for a closer look. (This configuration of roads may change as the Obama Presidential Center is built, but the sculpture will remain.) This 24-foot-tall female figure may seem giant, but it's smaller than artist Daniel Chester French's original—a 65-foot gilded plaster monument that presided over the Court of Honor during the 1893 world's fair, east of here. It became a symbol of the fair but was destroyed in an 1896 fire. Like the original, this replica from 1918 depicts a mythic woman with her arms raised, holding a scepter labeled Liberty and an orb where an eagle perches.

Cross to the north side of the intersection and walk west along Hayes. (The planned site of the ④ **Obama Presidential Center,** including a museum, a public meeting space, and a library, is just northwest of here.) From Hayes, veer north on the path to the Wooded Island. Cross the pedestrian bridge to the island and head north, using any of the paths through the woods. Along the way, stop on the island's eastern edge and look north across the lagoon at the Museum of Science and Industry. Originally constructed as the Palace of Fine Arts, it's the only surviving structure from the 1893 fairgrounds.

As you approach the island's north end, you'll reach the ⑤ **Japanese Garden.** Yoko Ono's *Sky Landing* sculpture, with curvy 12-foot-tall shapes representing lotus petals, was installed west of the garden entrance in 2016. She described it as the "place where the sky and earth meet and create a seed to learn about the past and come together to create a future of peace and harmony, with nature and each other." This is where the Japanese government constructed Ho-o-Den (Phoenix Pavilion) in 1893, modeling it after a classical temple. It was later destroyed by fire, but the site still feels like a piece of Japan dropped into the Midwest: a peaceful garden where water falls over rocks into the lagoon. In 2013, 160 cherry trees were planted nearby; they bloom 6–10 days each year, in late April or early May.

Looking north across Columbia Basin at the Museum of Science and Industry

Walk to the island's north tip and take the bridge. The Clarence Darrow Memorial Bridge crosses the channel to your east, and the Columbia Basin is north of that. Darrow, the legendary lawyer, lived a few blocks west of here, and he could see this bridge from his home. Before he died in 1938, he predicted that his spirit would make its presence known at this bridge. Ever since, Darrow's admirers have tossed flowers in the water here on the anniversary of his death, at 10:10 a.m., March 13. As of 2020, officials were planning a new bridge to replace the old one, which was closed to pedestrians in 2015.

Walk north toward the **❻ Museum of Science and Industry.** This Beaux Arts building was sturdier than others constructed for the 1893 fair. It housed the Field Museum until that institution moved downtown in 1920. With a new limestone exterior, it reopened as the Museum of Science and Industry in the 1930s. As you reach the museum, turn east, walking along the south wall, where you can see caryatids—pillars sculpted as women. This plaza on the museum's south side goes right up to the water's edge, allowing you to dip your fingers or toes in the Columbia Basin, where gondolas carried fairgoers in 1893.

After you reach the museum's east end, walk north. If you'd like to go inside the museum, enter through the north side. The walk ends here, but you can head through the tunnel under Lake Shore Drive to visit the 57th Street Beach. To depart, walk to 56th Street and Hyde Park Boulevard—just north of the museum—and take a CTA 6 Jackson Express bus.

Another Nearby Walk: South Lakefront Trail

Starting at the 57th Street Beach, walk north on the Lakefront Trail, which runs through Burnham Park, a strip of green space and beaches between Lake Shore Drive and Lake Michigan. Just north of 57th Street Beach, visit **❼ Promontory Point.** At 47th Street, take the bridge over Lake Shore Drive, then walk north to visit the **❽ Burnham Nature Sanctuary** before heading back over the bridge to continue north. At 35th Street, take the bridge over Lake Shore Drive to see the **❾ Stephen A. Douglas Tomb and Memorial,** the resting place of the "Little Giant" famous for his debates with Abraham Lincoln. You can end the walk there—at the 4-mile mark—by catching a CTA 35 bus west to the Red Line. Or return over the bridge and continue north another 2.5 miles to McCormick Place. (See Walk 11.)

(See tinyurl.com/southlakefronttrail for a map.)

Jackson Park & South Shore

Points of Interest

1 **South Shore Cultural Center** 7059 S. South Shore Dr., 773-256-0149, chicagoparkdistrict.com/parks-facilities/south-shore-cultural-center-park

2 **63rd Street Beach** 6301 S. Lake Shore Dr., 312-742-7529, chicagoparkdistrict.com /parks-facilities/63rd-street-beach

3 **Statue of the Republic** Hayes Dr. and Richards Dr., chicagoparkdistrict.com/parks-facilities /statue-republic

4 **Obama Presidential Center (planned)** Southeast of Stony Island Dr. and Midway Plaisance, obama.org

5 **Japanese Garden** Wooded Island in Jackson Park, 773-256-0903, chicagoparkdistrict.com /parks-facilities/japanese-garden

6 **Museum of Science and Industry** 5700 S. Lake Shore Dr., 773-684-1414, msichicago.org

Another Nearby Walk: South Lakefront Trail

7 **Promontory Point** 5491 S. Lake Shore Dr., chicagoparkdistrict.com/parks-facilities /promontory-point

8 **Burnham Nature Sanctuary** 4700 S. Lake Shore Dr., chicagoparkdistrict.com/parks-facilities /burnham-wildlife-corridor

9 **Stephen A. Douglas Tomb and Memorial** 636 E. 35th St., 312-225-2620, www2.illinois.gov/dnrhistoric/experience/sites/northeast/pages/douglas-tomb.aspx

16 Wolf Lake
Wildlife on the Industrial East Side

Above: A man fishes in Wolf Lake near a hunter's blind.

BOUNDARIES: 112th St., Ave. O, 131st St., Illinois–Indiana state line
DISTANCE: 5.2 miles
DIFFICULTY: Moderate
PARKING: Free parking in Eggers Grove lots south of 112th St. near Ave. E
PUBLIC TRANSIT: Red Line to 69th Street, then a CTA 30 South Chicago bus to Ewing and 112th
   Street; walk five blocks east

Industry and wildlife exist side by side in the East Side, the corner of Chicago that's along the Indiana state line. That boundary runs through the middle of Wolf Lake, an 800-acre body of water surrounded by wetlands, woods, prairies, oak savannas, factories, and a superhighway. In spite of all of the changes imposed by mankind, it remains a haven for fish, fowl, fauna, and flora—including some endangered and threatened species.

Dikes were erected in Wolf Lake in the 1950s, as the lake was being dredged—providing soil to construct the Chicago Skyway. That left Wolf Lake's Illinois side divided into five pools. *Chicago*

Wilderness magazine said that these barriers "effectively cordoned the lake off from some of its urban surroundings and their pollutants." Human development also blocked Wolf Lake's connection to Lake Michigan, and the water now flows south toward the Calumet River.

To reach Wolf Lake, you'll walk through Eggers Grove, a Cook County Forest Preserve with a cattail marsh beloved by birds—and bird-watchers. Be prepared for the possibility that you'll walk through some wet areas.

Walk Description

Start at 112th Street and Avenue E, walking south on the entrance road for cars into ❶ **Eggers Grove**. At a T-intersection, you'll see the Eggers Grove Comfort Station to the east, a 1930s structure with public restrooms. Go the other direction, following the road as it curves south. The road ends in a loop. Look for a dirt trail next to a placard that says ANCIENT SAND DUNES. Take this footpath 0.75 mile south amid the oak, elm, basswood, and cherry trees. At times, you'll be able to see Eggers Marsh off to the east. During one walk in early spring, I heard what sounded like hundreds of chorus frogs in the wetlands west of the path.

At the south end of the woods, you'll emerge into a clearing where a tall set of power lines runs east–west. This is where I encountered a garter snake slithering into a mound of brush. We'll continue taking the trail south across the clearing, but there's also a spur running east here along the marsh. That's worth exploring—you might see grebes, geese, ducks, marsh wrens, and yellow-headed blackbirds, and this marsh is one of the few remaining local wetlands where Virginia rails nest. If you go exploring that way, return to this spot when you're ready to continue.

Follow the trail south beneath the buzzing electrical lines, walking into the woods on the clearing's other side. You're now entering the ❷ **William W. Powers State Recreation Area**—the only state park within Chicago city limits. After a short distance, you'll enter a second clearing. Walk east, looking for patches of concrete and rusty metal plates on the ground. Constructed in the 1950s, this was Nike Ajax Site C-44, one of 22 missile sites that the US military operated around Chicago during the Cold War. If the Soviet bomber planes had ever approached, guided missiles with nuclear-tipped warheads would have launched out of these 80-by-80-foot reinforced concrete bunkers. The Nike bases were demolished in the 1970s.

Walk straight east from the concrete and look for a sunken trail that leads into the woods. After following that for just a short distance, you'll reach a set of railroad tracks. Follow them south, where you'll hit the road at Wolf Lake's north end.

Walk east on the roadway, then turn south on State Line Road, which runs south through the middle of the lake on a long, straight embankment. Illinois is to your west, while the Indiana portion of Wolf Lake is to the east, where the horizon is lined with factories, clouds of white smoke, power lines, and the Chicago Skyway. You'll probably see fishermen with lines and nets along this roadway. Largemouth bass, northern pike, and bluegill are common in the lake. These waters are also home to the lake sturgeon, which is endangered in Illinois and Indiana, and the banded killifish, a species considered threatened in Illinois. You may also notice wooden structures camouflaged with grass or cattails. These are the blinds where hunters wait for a shot at geese and ducks during waterfowl hunting season, usually September–January. Wolf Lake is one of just a few places where hunting is legal in Chicago, and only shotguns are allowed. Hunters are required to use one of the park's 20 or so blinds, assigned by lottery each summer.

Swans—including tundra swans, which migrate to the Arctic during the summer—are common on the lake. Trumpeter swans live here year-round, competing with invasive Eurasian mute swans. During one of my walks, I saw eight swans splashing in the water on the Indiana side. Amid birdcalls and gently lapping waves, I heard the distant roar of semitrucks on the Skyway, freight trains blasting their horns, and something that sounded like an air-raid siren coming from the factory zone. Be on the lookout for uncommon bird species like the little blue heron, yellow-crowned night heron, and black-crowned night heron. The lake is also home to various species of newts, salamanders, and mudpuppies.

After you've gone about 0.3 mile south on State Line Road—getting about halfway across the lake—turn back the way you came. When you reach the lake's north shore, walk west on the road about 400 feet. At the railroad crossing, look south: the Indiana Harbor Belt Railroad's freight trains cross the lake here on an embankment. Walk south on the gravel path through the shrubbery just west of the tracks, taking in more sights of the lake all around you. After 0.3 mile, you'll reach a causeway on your right that leads west, away from the railroad tracks. Walk west on this strip of land to Wolf Lake's western shore.

This section of the William W. Powers State Recreation Area includes a picnic grove, as well as a disarmed Nike missile, displayed as a monument dedicated to service members who worked nearby. Some of the open ground here was originally cleared by beavers. The animals still live around Wolf Lake, taking down trees to construct dams—and presenting a challenge for the state's foresters.

Walk north, taking the road that runs into the woods. Follow that road until you reach a curve, where the road bends east. Look for a sign pointing west toward a bike trail, and take that spur. You will emerge in a long clearing where the paved Burnham Greenway runs north–south, alongside more power lines. Walk north on the path, which follows the former route of some railroad tracks that are no longer used.

An infamous place is along this stretch—probably around where the power lines turn east, running above the path. The landscape has changed, but this is where Nathan Leopold and Richard Loeb left the body of Bobby Franks after killing him on May 21, 1924, putting the corpse in a culvert underneath the rails. Leopold, who had led bird-watching tours in this area, dropped his fake tortoiseshell spectacles. Those eyeglasses helped police solve the "crime of the century."

After a mile or so, the distinctively checkered steeple of St. Simeon Serbian Orthodox Church is visible in the neighborhood to the west. You will end up back at 112th Street, the conclusion of this walk. If you'd like to continue, follow the path a mile north into the East Side neighborhood. That stretch is called the John "Beans" Beniac Greenway Park—named after a local resident who devoted many hours to cleaning up the tires and trash that had turned this corridor into an eyesore in the 1970s.

The north shore of Wolf Lake

Points of Interest

1 **Eggers Grove** South of 112th St. at Ave. E, 800-870-3666, fpdcc.com/eggers-grove

2 **William W. Powers State Recreation Area** 12949 Ave. O, 773-646-3270, www.dnr.illinois.gov/parks/pages/williamwpowers.aspx

17 West Loop
Once a Food Market, Now a Foodie Haven

Above: Restaurants along Lake Street

BOUNDARIES: I-290, Jefferson St., Grand Ave., Damen Ave.
DISTANCE: 4.1 miles
DIFFICULTY: Easy
PARKING: Free and metered street parking near Halsted St. and Van Buren St.
PUBLIC TRANSIT: Blue Line to UIC-Halsted; walk east out of the station toward Halsted St.

For more than a century, the area along Randolph Street west of the Loop was Chicago's main food marketplace. Starting in 1850, truck farmers sold produce in the street. Later, the district evolved into a distribution hub for meatpackers and other food companies, and the streets were filled with forklifts, refrigerated trucks, and workers in bloody aprons. Most of that industry has vanished, replaced by trendy restaurants and hotels, pricey apartments, and offices for modern businesses like Google.

This walk goes through the heart of the West Loop's foodie zone, but it also explores surrounding sections of the Near West Side, including Greektown, Union Park, and the site of the Haymarket Square tragedy.

Walk Description

Walk north on Halsted Street from the Eisenhower Expressway, and enter Greektown. Until the 1960s, many Greek immigrants lived south of here, but their neighborhood was demolished to make way for the expressway and the University of Illinois. After that, many Greek restaurants opened on this stretch. At the northeast corner of Halsted and Van Buren Streets, the ❶ **National Hellenic Museum** celebrates Greek culture. As you continue north, the next two blocks contain a cluster of Greek restaurants, including Nine Muses, Artopolis, Meli, Athena, Greek Islands, and Santorini. At the southeast corner of Halsted and Jackson Streets, the Athenian Candle Company has been in business for nearly a century.

At Adams Street, go east over the Kennedy Expressway. As you approach Desplaines Street, you will notice ❷ **Old St. Patrick's Catholic Church** at the northwest corner. Dedicated in 1856 for an Irish parish, it is Chicago's oldest public building. When fire swept across the city in 1871, St. Pat's was just two blocks west of the destruction. Thomas A. O'Shaughnessy, inspired by the entwined Celtic lines of Ireland's Book of Kells, created the church's renowned stained glass windows between 1912 and 1922. Walk north on Desplaines, then east on Madison Street, where Claes Oldenburg's 1977 sculpture *Batcolumn*—a 101-foot-tall steel lattice shaped like a baseball bat—towers in front of the Harold Washington Social Security Administration Building. Turn north on Jefferson Street, then west on Randolph Street.

Stop at Desplaines Street, observing how Randolph widens as it continues west. Hay was sold here 1860–1875, and thus it became known as Haymarket Square. That name is connected with one of Chicago history's most significant events: the Haymarket Square tragedy of May 4, 1886. It happened during a strike calling for workdays to be limited to 8 hours. Around 175 officers marched north here toward a labor rally. Walk north on Desplaines, where you'll see sculptor Mary Brogger's ❸ **Haymarket Memorial,** dedicated in 2003. That's where protesters were speaking on top of a wagon, denouncing earlier police attacks against laborers. As the police approached and ordered the crowd to disperse, a bomb came flying from the alley south of that wagon, exploding amid the officers. Gunfire erupted, and by the end of the melee, seven policemen and at least four people in the crowd were dead or fatally wounded. No one was charged with throwing the bomb, but eight men were arrested for conspiracy, including four who were hanged; three were later pardoned.

Continue north to Kinzie Street, where **❹ Blommer Chocolate** sits at the northeast corner. This factory is the source of a delicious aroma that often wafts through Chicago's air. Continue north on Desplaines, then northwest on Milwaukee Avenue. The area around the intersection of Milwaukee, Grand Avenue, and Halsted Street has several restaurants and taverns, including **❺ Richard's Bar,** an old-school joint open since Prohibition. Head south on Halsted. As you reach Hubbard Street, note the murals stretching in either direction on the railroad embankment.

Continue south, then go west on Fulton Market, a street described in 1892 as "the great emporium for meat of all kinds." Many of the buildings had large loading bays at street level, making it easy to load and unload trucks. Today, most of those garage-door-style openings have been transformed into windows. The block west of Green Street has two large brick buildings with terracotta letters declaring the name of the meatpacking collective that constructed them in 1887: Fulton Street Wholesale Market Co. Today, these historical buildings contain some of the city's most acclaimed food establishments, including the **❻ Publican,** a high-ceilinged space resembling a European beer hall, where chef Paul Kahan has been serving pork, beer, and oysters since 2008. (There's also a café, bakery, and whole-animal butcher shop across the street called Publican Quality Meats.) Another block west, you'll reach **❼ Next** restaurant, where culinary wizard Grant Achatz totally overhauls the cuisine every few months, conjuring up a new theme—but you'll need to buy a ticket in advance to get a table. The same goes for Next's sister cocktail bars, the Aviary and the Office. The trendy **❽ Ace Hotel Chicago** is on Morgan Street just north of Fulton Market.

Walk south on Morgan, then east on Lake under the shadow of the L tracks, alongside walls painted with murals. Just north of Lake on Green Street, the 12-story **❾ Hoxton** hotel opened in 2019, featuring hip restaurants, an underground cocktail lounge, and communal spaces that are open to walk-in visitors, including even the rooftop pool.

Turn south on Halsted and then west on Randolph. As Randolph's vegetable marketplace expanded in the early 20th century, more blocks were widened, stretching farther west. Today, it's the main artery through the city's preeminent dining scene. People wait in line for hours at **❿ Au Cheval** for the cheeseburgers. Across the street, **⓫ Girl & the Goat** is the main culinary outpost for Stephanie Izard, the first woman to win Bravo's *Top Chef.* Just south of Randolph on Green, **⓬ Soho House Chicago** is a hotel and a private club for people working in creative fields.

Southwest of Randolph and Green, **⓭ Nellcôte** serves cocktails and European small plates in a seven-story building from 1912—an example of the structures that grocery commission merchants used for storing nonperishable canned goods, coffee, and spices. It was designed by the district's leading architects, Frommann and Jebsen, who are also known for creating Chicago's Schlitz-tied houses (saloons that originally served nothing but Schlitz beer).

Farther west, McDonald's nine-story global headquarters are at the southwest corner of Randolph and Carpenter Streets, where the company moved 2,000 employees in 2018, taking over the former location of Oprah Winfrey's Harpo Studios. The fast-food complex includes Hamburger University, a training facility for restaurant managers, and ⓮ **McDonald's Global Menu Restaurant,** where the menu includes items from the company's overseas locations.

Continue west on Randolph. When Randolph intersects with Ogden Avenue and bends northwest, go west across Ogden, continuing into ⓯ **Union Park.** Since 2006, the historical park has hosted the Pitchfork Music Festival for three days each summer. Cross south over Washington Boulevard to see the bronze sculpture honoring Mayor Carter H. Harrison Sr., who lived nearby on Ashland Avenue. The Democrat was assassinated at the end of the 1893 world's fair; his son, also named Carter H. Harrison, later served as mayor too. Looking west, you'll see the First Baptist Congregational Church across Ashland Avenue, which was called the Union Park Congregational Church and Carpenter Chapel when it was completed in 1871.

Walk north on Ashland, crossing under the L, and then go west on Fulton Street, entering an industrial area where the ⓰ **Goose Island Beer Company**'s production brewery features a taproom and tours. Founded in 1988 and brewing in this facility since 1995, Goose Island helped launch the craft beer movement. The ⓱ **Intelligentsia Coffee Chicago Roasting Works** lies just west of the brewery, supplying coffee to some of the city's best cafés and offering public tours and classes.

To finish the walk, you can either head west to Damen Avenue and catch a CTA 50 Damen bus or go north on Wolcott Avenue to Grand Avenue, where you can take a 65 Grand bus.

Points of Interest

❶ National Hellenic Museum 333 S. Halsted St., 312-655-1234, nationalhellenicmuseum.org

❷ Old St. Patrick's Catholic Church 700 W. Adams St., 312-648-1021, oldstpats.org

❸ Haymarket Memorial 175 N. Desplaines St., chicago.gov/city/en/depts/dca/supp_info /chicago_s_publicartthehaymarketmemorial.html

❹ Blommer Chocolate 600 W. Kinzie St., 312-226-7700, blommer.com

❺ Richard's Bar 491 N. Milwaukee Ave., 312-733-2251

West Loop

6 The Publican 837 W. Fulton Market, 312-733-9555, thepublicanrestaurant.com

7 Next 953 W. Fulton Market, nextrestaurant.com

8 Ace Hotel Chicago 311 N. Morgan St., 312-764-1919, acehotel.com/chicago

9 The Hoxton 200 N. Green St., 312-761-1700, thehoxton.com/illinois/chicago/hotels

10 Au Cheval 800 W. Randolph St., 312-929-4580, auchevaldiner.com/chicago

11 Girl & the Goat 809 W. Randolph St., 312-492-6262, girlandthegoat.com, girlandthegoatceries.com/

12 Soho House Chicago 113-125 N. Green St., 312-521-8000, sohohousechicago.com

13 Nellcôte 833 W. Randolph St., 312-432-0500, nellcoterestaurant.com

14 McDonald's Global Menu Restaurant 1035 W. Randolph St., 312-291-9224, mcdonalds.com

15 Union Park 1501 W. Randolph St., 312-746-5494, chicagoparkdistrict.com/parks-facilities/union-park

16 Goose Island Beer Company 1800 W. Fulton St., 800-466-7363, gooseisland.com/fulton-brewery

17 Intelligentsia Coffee Chicago Roasting Works 1850 W. Fulton St., 312-563-0023, intelligentsiacoffee.com/chicago-roasting-works

18 Little Italy & Vicinity
An Old-World Enclave

Above: The Christopher Columbus Monument in Arrigo Park

BOUNDARIES: I-290, Damen Ave., Maxwell St., Clinton St.
DISTANCE: 3.9 miles
DIFFICULTY: Easy
PARKING: Metered street parking
PUBLIC TRANSIT: Blue Line to Illinois Medical District

Little Italy is one of the West Side's most charming neighborhoods, retaining its identity after many decades of upheaval. It's centered on Taylor Street, a quaint main street renowned for its restaurants. This walk begins in the Illinois Medical District, a 560-acre cluster of hospitals west of Little Italy. Later on the route, we'll see the University of Chicago at Illinois campus—a controversial construction project that destroyed a large chunk of Italian and Greek residential areas in the

1960s—as well as the legendary social reformer Jane Addams's headquarters, the former site of the Maxwell Street Market, and the spot where the Great Chicago Fire of 1871 started.

Walk Description

Begin at the CTA Blue Line's Illinois Medical District stop, in the middle of the Eisenhower Expressway at Ogden Avenue. Walk south on Ogden, then cross to the south side of Congress Parkway. Walk east, veering southeast through a park where the 28-foot-high Art Deco ❶ **Louis Pasteur Monument,** sculpted in 1928 by Léon Hermant, honors the French scientist who pioneered vaccines and the germ theory of disease. South of the park, a block is filled by the old Cook County Hospital, Paul Gerhardt's Beaux Arts building from 1914, decorated with terra-cotta lions and cherubs amid three-story fluted Ionic columns. After the hospital closed in 2002, a $1 billion project to restore the facade and gut the interior began in 2018, transforming it into a hotel, retail, and office complex.

At the park's southeast corner, cross Harrison Street and go south on Wood Street. The street is lined with medical facilities, including John H. Stroger Jr. Hospital (which replaced the old Cook County Hospital) and the University of Illinois College of Medicine. Half a block south of Polk Street, look for a marker on the west side of Wood, which explains that this was the location of ❷ **West Side Park,** where the Chicago Cubs played 1893–1915.

Next, turn east on Taylor Street. Continue east across Ashland Avenue, entering Little Italy, where Taylor Street is lined with century-old buildings. Restaurants fill many of these storefronts, including Italian eateries along with many others. ❸ **Pompei Bakery** is one of Chicago's oldest restaurants. Luigi Davino opened the original location in 1909, selling only bread and cheese pizza. Farther east, Rosebud has been open since 1975. Nearby, Patio is one of the city's oldest hot dog stands, in business since 1948. That's the same year when the Conte Di Savoia delicatessen—another block east—opened for business. Farther east, Scafuri Bakery was founded in 1904 by immigrant Luigi Scafuri. It closed in 2007, but a new generation of the family revived it in 2013.

At the northwest corner of Taylor and Ada Streets, the Chicago Public Library's ❹ **Little Italy Branch** opened in 2019. At the northeast corner, that brick building with red boards filling the windows is the last surviving structure from the Jane Addams Homes. Completed in 1938 with federal money, they became part of a sprawling public housing complex known as the ABLA Homes, with a population of 17,000. By the 1980s, they were notorious as a gang battleground. Most of the buildings were demolished after being vacated in 2002.

Walk north on Ada. When the street turns east, continue north into Arrigo Park. Veer north-west toward the ❺ **Christopher Columbus Monument.** Moses Jacob Ezekiel, a prominent Jewish artist from Virginia, sculpted this 9-foot-tall bronze for the Italian Pavilion at the 1893 world's fair. For the next 66 years, it stood above the entrance to the Loop's Columbus Memorial Building. After that building was demolished, the statue spent seven years in storage before being installed here in 1966.

Walk north on Loomis Street. A poplar known as Dead Man's Tree once stood at 725 S. Loomis. In 1921 the names of men were either tacked onto the tree or carved into its trunk, stating that they would be the next victims during a murderous political feud. In 2019 a sapling was growing at the same spot.

Walk east on Flournoy Street, where ❻ **Notre Dame de Chicago** is on the north side. The most prominent landmark associated with Chicago's 19th-century community of French immigrants, the Roman Catholic church was completed in 1892. Walk south on Ada, then go east on Lexington Street, where Italianate row houses made with blocks of yellow Joliet limestone are clustered on the north side. They were built in the 1870s, when this was an Irish enclave. Farther east, the Shrine of Our Lady of Pompeii is Chicago's oldest Italian American church, constructed in 1923. At the end of the park, go south on Lytle Street, then a block east on Cabrini Street. Just before you reach Racine Avenue, look for a marker on the building on the street's north side. It honors Frances Xavier Cabrini, an Italian immigrant who founded the Missionary Sisters of the Sacred Heart of Jesus. Before her death in 1917, she founded a hospital in this building, providing assistance to people in the neighborhood. Canonized in 1946 by Pope Pius XI, she was the first US citizen to become a saint.

Walk south on Racine, then east on Taylor. A few blocks farther east, ❼ **Al's No. 1 Italian Beef** is one of the best-known purveyors of Italian beef. It's named after Albert Ferreri, who reportedly invented the sandwich. Starting in 1938, he sold the sandwiches out of a shop in this neighborhood. After a split in the family business in the 1960s, his brother-in-law, Christopher Pacelli, opened this restaurant, roasting beef in house with a secret mix of spices. Across the street from Al's, Mario's Italian Lemonade serves Italian ice during warm months. The DiPaolo family has owned Mario's since the stand opened in 1954.

When you reach Morgan Street, take the sidewalk that runs at a northeast angle into the ❽ **University of Illinois at Chicago** (UIC) campus. Continue along a diagonal route as you thread your way amid architect Walter Netsch's Brutalist-style concrete, brick, and stone buildings. You're following the former pathway of Blue Island Avenue, which was demolished in the early 1960s to make way for the university, along with 105 acres of the surrounding neighborhood. Residents led by Florence Scala protested Mayor Richard J. Daley's plans but to no avail. When the campus opened in 1965, it included a more extensive network of elevated walkways, but many of those features were removed in the 1990s.

Continue northeast to the corner of Harrison and Halsted Streets. Walk a block south on Halsted, where the **9** **Jane Addams Hull-House Museum** is on the west side. Addams, the first American woman to receive the Nobel Peace Prize, moved here in 1889, when this was a neighborhood of poor immigrants from various corners of Europe. Addams and her colleagues opened a settlement house, offering kindergarten and day care; theater, music, and art programs; classes in English and citizenship; and help with finding jobs. Hull-House grew into a 13-building complex, but only two structures are preserved today: the house where Addams lived and worked, and the Residents' Dining Hall.

Mario's Lemonade draws a line of customers on a summer day.

Continue south. At the southeast corner of Halsted Street and Roosevelt Road, the UIC's Isadore and Sadie Dorin Forum has become one of the area's leading event venues since it opened in 2008. At the southwest corner, a 43-foot-diameter, circular structure looks like a squat silo perched on stilts. Installed in 2006, this is one of artist James Turrell's **10** **Skyspace** pavilions. Enter and gaze up at the 26-foot-high ceiling, where the sky is visible through an eyelike opening.

Continue south on Halsted Street to **11** **Maxwell Street.** In the late 19th century, Jewish immigrants began selling merchandise here, turning Maxwell Street into something akin to a giant flea market on Sundays. Beginning in the 1940s, African American musicians entertained crowds on Maxwell Street by playing the blues. To be heard loud enough, they used electric guitars and amplifiers, forging a new style: Chicago blues. As UIC expanded its campus, the city moved the Maxwell Street Market in 1994 to 800 S. Desplaines St., but it's a shadow of its former self. Meanwhile, the actual Maxwell Street is now a rather ordinary retail strip called University Village Maxwell Street, where sculptures and plaques offer reminders of its more colorful past.

Walk east on Maxwell, then go north on Union Avenue, where you'll find ⓬ **Jim's Original**, a hot dog restaurant that Slavic immigrant Jimmy Stefanovic started nearby in 1939. It's the birthplace of the Maxwell Street Polish: Polish sausage in a hot dog bun, topped with grilled onions and yellow mustard. Jim's Original is on the same block as Express Grill, which his nephew Tom Lazarevski opened in the 1950s, serving a similar menu.

Walk east on Roosevelt, taking the bridge over the Dan Ryan Expressway, then go north on Jefferson Street, where ⓭ **Manny's Coffee Shop & Deli** has been owned by the Rankin family since 1964 (or 1942, if you count an earlier location in the Loop). Serving heaps of corned beef and pastrami alongside latkes and pickles, the cafeteria is popular with cops, businessmen, and politicians. It was Barack Obama's first public stop after his election-night party in 2008.

Continue north to ⓮ **De Koven Street.** The northeast corner was the site of a barn owned by an Irish laborer named Patrick O'Leary, who lived just east of here with his wife, Catherine. Around 9:30 p.m. on October 8, 1871, their barn caught fire, and the flames spread. The Great Chicago Fire decimated 4 square miles, including most of Chicago's downtown, destroying 18,000 buildings, killing about 300 people, and leaving almost 100,000 homeless. It was blamed on a cow kicking over Mrs. O'Leary's lantern, an explanation historians regard as myth. The Chicago Fire Department opened a training academy on the property in 1961, and Egon Weiner's 30-foot-high bronze sculpture *Pillar of Fire* was installed at the spot where the fire started.

To depart, walk back south to Roosevelt and catch a CTA 12 Roosevelt bus—or continue east on Roosevelt 0.5 mile to the Red, Green, and Orange Line station.

Points of Interest

❶ **Louis Pasteur Monument** Northwest of Harrison St. and Wood St.

❷ **West Side Park** Wood St. between Taylor St. and Polk St.

❸ **Pompei Bakery** 1531 W. Taylor St., 312-421-5179, pompeiusa.com

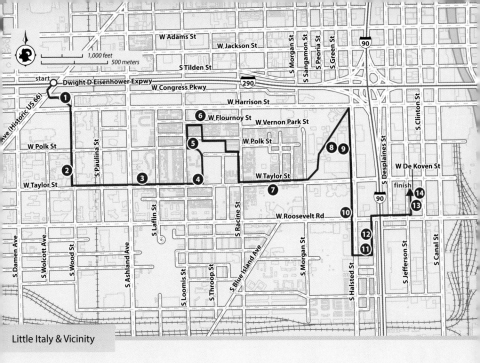

Little Italy & Vicinity

4. **Chicago Public Library's Little Italy Branch** 1336 W. Taylor St., 312-746-5656, chipublib.org /locations/62

5. **Christopher Columbus Monument** Arrigo Park, southeast of Loomis St. and Lexington St., chicagoparkdistrict.com/parks-facilities/christopher-columbus-monument-arrigo

6. **Notre Dame de Chicago** 1334 W. Flournoy St., 312-243-7400, nddc.archchicago.org

7. **Al's No. 1 Italian Beef** 1079 W. Taylor St., 312-226-4017, alsbeef.com

8. **University of Illinois at Chicago** Southwest of Harrison St. and Halsted St., 312-996-7000, uic.edu

9. **Jane Addams Hull-House Museum** 800 S. Halsted St., 312-413-5353, hullhousemuseum.org

10. **Skyspace** Southwest corner of Halsted St. and Roosevelt Rd.

11. **University Village Maxwell Street** Maxwell St. and Halsted St.

12. **Jim's Original Hot Dog** 1250 S. Union Ave., 312-733-7820, jimsoriginal.com

13. **Manny's Coffee Shop & Deli** 1141 S. Jefferson St., 312-939-2855, mannysdeli.com

14. **Origin of the Great Chicago Fire** DeKoven St. and Jefferson St.

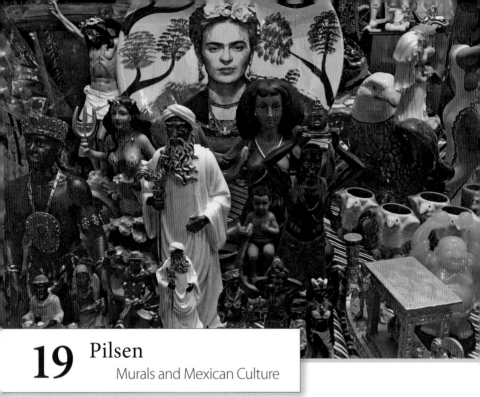

19 Pilsen
Murals and Mexican Culture

BOUNDARIES: Cermak Rd., Halsted St., 16th St., Damen Ave.
DISTANCE: 5 miles
DIFFICULTY: Easy
PARKING: Metered and free street parking
PUBLIC TRANSIT: Red Line to Cermak/Chinatown, then a CTA 21 bus to Cermak and Carpenter

Pilsen has been a hub of Latino life since around 1970. But the neighborhood's moniker offers a clue about its earlier history: Pilsen is named after a city in the Czech Republic's Bohemia region. Bohemians lived in this neighborhood for around a century, working in nearby industrial areas. Residences and businesses stood side by side, in buildings with architectural ornaments evoking Europe. Mexican Americans began moving into the neighborhood in the 1950s and 1960s, transforming those Bohemian-style structures into taquerias and bodegas. With hundreds of murals, the area is like a massive outdoor art exhibit. In the 21st century, Pilsen has attracted a growing number of non-Hispanic white residents, along with hipster record shops and foodie restaurants of varied cuisines. Amid these changes, some longtime Hispanic residents worry about gentrification. Even outsiders—those of us who enjoy visiting Pilsen—are rooting for the survival of its colorful culture.

Walk Description

Begin at the corner of Cermak Road and Carpenter Street. Looking south across Cermak, you'll see the former site of the Fisk Generating Station, which *Electrical World* magazine called "a great cathedral, devoted to the religion of power" in 1908, five years after it opened. A century later, scientists blamed the coal-burning power plant for harming the health of people who lived nearby. Facing economic pressures and protests from activists, the plant shut down in 2012.

The warehouse on Cermak's north side includes 30,000 square feet filled with costumes. ❶ **Broadway Costumes,** which started in 1886 as Fritz Schoultz and Company, calls itself the Midwest's largest costume source for theatrical shows and corporate special events. Visit by pressing the buzzer at 1100 W. Cermak.

Walk west and then north through Dvorak Park. As you reach the park's midpoint, take a look at architect William Carbys Zimmerman's original Prairie-style fieldhouse across the baseball diamond. From the middle of the park, walk east on 21st Street. Then cross Carpenter Street, where ❷ **Lo Rez Brewing and Taproom** lies at the southeast corner. Continuing east, you'll pass a community garden near a railroad crossing, with a mural of an outstretched hand holding dirt. When you reach Canalport Avenue, look south at the ❸ **Lacuna Artist Lofts,** where Lauren Asta's cartoon-style mural covers 5,000 square feet of the walls. A century ago, this was the Chicago Macaroni Company; today, it hosts events and artistic spaces such as Woman Made Gallery.

Walk northeast on Canalport, then north on Halsted Street, entering the ❹ **Chicago Arts District.** Galleries are clustered at 1945 and 1932 S. Halsted, and on Halsted from 21st Street north to 17th Street, with opening receptions on the second Friday of each month. Walk west on 19th Street. At Peoria Street, Zion Evangelical Lutheran—the "Ghost Church"—is on the northeast corner. Built in 1880, it was gutted by a fire in 1979 and a windstorm in 1998, but the 90-foot-tall bell tower survives. The walls now surround a garden, where a burned crucifix hangs on a wall behind a plastic shield.

Walk north on Peoria, then west on 18th Street—the main thoroughfare through Pilsen. Amid countless murals, shops and restaurants line the streets. Mexican dishes dominate the menus, but there's a smattering of other cuisines. Monnie Burke's (at 1163), serving American dishes like

Amish chicken, has earned some of Pilsen's best reviews. Honky Tonk BBQ (at 18th Street and Racine Avenue) serves Memphis-style meat and live roots music.

At the northeast corner of 18th and Allport Streets, St. Procopius Catholic Church originally hosted a Czech congregation, but it changed along with the neighborhood, becoming predominantly Mexican American. Built in 1883, the Romanesque building has brick walls trimmed with Joliet limestone. ❺ **Thalia Hall,** an imposing structure with walls of Bedford limestone, stands like a castle at the southeast corner. Completed in 1892 and designed by Frederick Faber and William Pagels, it was a gathering place for Bohemians, some of whom may have noticed the auditorium's similarities to the opera house in Prague. After closing in the 1960s, the theater sat vacant for decades, finally reopening in 2013 as one of the city's top concert halls. The venue's restaurant, Dusek's Board & Beer—where craft beers and crafty cuisine are served in softly glowing rooms under tin ceilings—has earned stars from the Michelin Guide. Inside Dusek's, you can take the stairs down to the Punch House bar. The complex also includes the Tack Room bar in a space that originally functioned as stables for the horses belonging to Thalia Hall founder John Dusek.

Continue west on 18th. Notable spots in the next few blocks include S.K.Y., a contemporary American restaurant; Shady Rest Vintage & Vinyl; Birrieria Reyes De Ocotlan, a restaurant decorated with goat figurines that specializes in birria, a simmered, spicy goat stew from the Mexican state of Jalisco; and the Chicago Public Library's Lozano Branch.

Turn southwest on Blue Island Avenue, following its diagonal route. La Michoacana Premium Pilsen is a Mexican-style ice creamery with bright neon signs. At 1870, you'll see a Queen Anne–style building that was a Schlitz-tied house (a saloon that exclusively served Schlitz beer) when it opened in 1899. At 19th Street, head east for a block. The *Wall of Hope* mural covers the San Jose Obrero Mission at the northwest corner of 19th and Loomis. Painted by Jesús "Chucho" Rodriguez and members of Yollocalli Arts Reach, it depicts Latino immigrants amid images of butterflies and the words *hope, respect, jobs,* and *dignidad* ("dignity").

Walk two blocks south on Loomis, then go west on 21st Street, where the fields for Benito Juárez Community Academy are on the south side. The high school, built in 1977 with a design meant to evoke Mexico's ancient Aztec monuments, is named after the Mexican president who became a national hero by resisting France's invasion of his country in the 1860s. Walk to the school's west side and go south amid more than a dozen statues—donated by various Mexican state governments and dedicated in 2010—showing revolutionaries and political figures such as Juárez, along with Cuauhtemoc, the last Aztec emperor.

Continue southwest to the intersection of Cermak Road and Ashland Avenue, and then go north on Ashland. Turn east on Cullerton Street, then go back northeast on Blue Island Avenue.

When you've returned to 18th Street, head west, where the *Declaration of Immigration* mural—painted in 2009 by Salvador Jimenez and Yollocalli Arts Reach students—uses the Declaration of Independence as inspiration to make an artistic case for immigrants' rights. Farther west, murals pay homage to Marvel superheroes and James Foley, a journalist killed by the Islamic State. Café Jumping Bean, a coffeehouse, restaurant, and gallery that's been a community anchor since 1994, occupies a storefront that originally housed a photographer's studio in 1907.

Continue west. Recommended restaurants in this stretch include Cantón Regio Steakhouse; Pl-zen; La Mejikana; and the Jibarito Stop. Panaderia Nuevo Leon sells baked goods, while Creperia Nuevo Leon serves Mexican crêpes. Just west of Paulina Street, the ❻ **CTA's 18th Street Pink Line station** is decorated with an array of art. Farther west, notable restaurants include Carnitas Uruapan, which serves street food in a style found in Uruapan, Mexico (including tacos with slow-cooked pork carnitas), and 5 Rabanitos Restaurante & Taqueria, an acclaimed restaurant whose name means "five radishes."

Walk south on Wood Street, where Harrison Park lies on the west side. Along this street, Alejandro Medina's *Powerful Latinas* mural honors women like Guatemalan indigenous rights activist Rigoberta Menchú and Mexican painter Frida Khalo. At the end of the park, continue south two blocks through a residential area. Go west on 21st Street, and then north on Wolcott, where you'll see artist Rahmaan Statik's mural of Mexican revolutionary leaders Pancho Villa and Emiliano Zapata. Continuing north, you'll reach one of Pilsen's most striking works of public art, covering three sides of artist ❼ **Héctor Duarte's home and studio** at the northwest corner of Wolcott and Cullerton. Painted by Duarte in 2005, the 3,000-square-foot *Gulliver in Wonderland* mural shows a Mexican immigrant as the giant Gulliver character, fighting to break free from barbwire.

Continue north. When you reach 19th Street, you'll find the ❽ **National Museum of Mexican Art** at the northeast corner. Open since 1987, it has one of the country's largest collections of Mexican art. In late October, the museum hosts Día de los Muertos Xicágo festivities to commemorate the Day of the Dead, inviting people to create their own *ofrendas* (altars) in Harrison Park.

Walk north on Wolcott, following it as it curves east, turning into 16th Street. Follow 16th, alongside a mural-covered railroad embankment. Some of the paintings are old and fading, while others are freshly painted. You may encounter artists working on new images. When you reach Paulina Street, go south. Then walk east on 17th Street, where ❾ **St. Adalbert Catholic Church** is on the street's north side, with two 185-foot towers encased in protective scaffolding. Built in 1912 for what was then a Polish congregation, architect Henry J. Schlacks's Renaissance Revival–style church closed in 2019. A developer has announced plans to restore the sanctuary while converting other parts of the property into housing.

Continue east on 17th, then head north on Ashland and east on 16th, which is lined by more murals. When you reach Halsted, look at the viaduct north of 16th, where Halsted runs under the tracks. This was the center of a clash in 1877, when many Chicagoans joined in with a national railroad strike. Some 7,500–8,000 people gathered here, some destroying railroad engines. Assisted by federal and state troops, police fired their guns into the crowd on July 25, killing an estimated 30 people.

The walk ends here at 16th and Halsted. To depart, take a CTA Halsted bus.

Zion Evangelical Lutheran, the "Ghost Church" of Pilsen

Pilsen

Points of Interest

① Broadway Costumes 1100 W. Cermak Rd., 312-829-6400, broadwaycostumes.com

② Lo Rez Brewing and Taproom 2101 S. Carpenter St., 888-404-2262, lorezbrewing.com

③ Lacuna Artist Lofts 2150 S. Canalport Ave., 773-609-5638, lacuna2150.com

④ Chicago Arts District 1945 S. Halsted St., 312-738-8000, chicagoartsdistrict.org

⑤ Thalia Hall 1807 S. Allport St., 312-526-3851, thaliahallchicago.com

⑥ 18th Street Pink Line station 18th St. west of Paulina St., transitchicago.com/station/18th

⑦ Héctor Duarte's home and studio 1900 W. Cullerton St., hectorduarte.com

⑧ National Museum of Mexican Art 1852 W. 19th St., 312-738-1503, nationalmuseumofmexicanart.org

⑨ St. Adalbert Catholic Church 1650 W. 17th St.

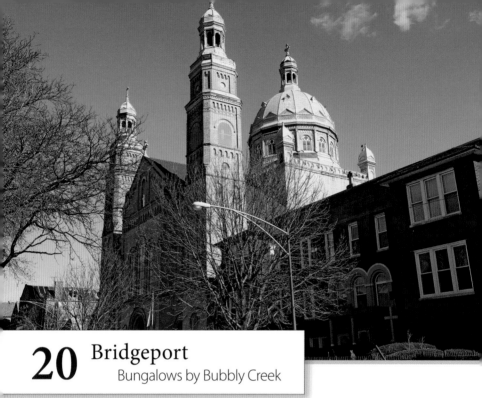

20 Bridgeport
Bungalows by Bubbly Creek

Above: St. Mary of Perpetual Help Catholic Church

BOUNDARIES: 37th St., Dan Ryan Expwy., 27th St., Ashland Ave.
DISTANCE: 4.7 miles
DIFFICULTY: Easy
PARKING: Free and metered street parking
PUBLIC TRANSIT: CTA 8 Halsted bus to 37th Street; or take the Red Line to Sox/35th and head a mile
west, either on foot or on a 35th Street bus

In the working-class neighborhood of Bridgeport, the streets are lined with modest brick bungalows, old warehouses, and mom-and-pop stores—many displaying signs that haven't changed for
half a century. First settled in the 1830s by Irish immigrants who worked digging the Illinois & Michigan Canal, Bridgeport became home turf for Irish, German, Czech, Polish, and Lithuanian laborers
in slaughterhouses and factories. It was also the center of Chicago's Democratic Party machine:

between 1933 and 2011, five men from Bridgeport served as mayor, ruling the city for 68 of those 78 years.

Located just west of the team's ballpark, Bridgeport is a bastion of White Sox fans. In recent decades, the neighborhood has grown more racially diverse, with population spillover from Chinatown and Pilsen. Bridgeport has also seen an influx of art galleries, along with a smattering of new restaurants.

Walk Description

Begin at Halsted and 37th Streets. This corner is where Schaller's Pump opened in 1881, eventually becoming Chicago's oldest tavern. In a sign of changing times, it closed in 2017. At 3659 S. Halsted, the 11th Ward Regular Democratic Organization office was the political base of Richard J. Daley, Chicago's mayor from 1955 to 1976. His son, Richard M. Daley, served in the same office from 1989 to 2011.

Go east on 37th, through the heart of the Daley family's neighborhood, several square blocks known as Hamburg. At the southeast corner of 37th and Union Avenue, Nativity of Our Lord Catholic Church is where Richard J. Daley served as an altar boy and attended elementary school. Walk north on Lowe Avenue. Daley was born in 1902 at the house at 3602 S. Lowe. Farther north, at 3536, there's a one-story, redbrick bungalow built in 1939. That's where Daley lived during his political reign. It's now the home of his grandson Patrick Daley Thompson, elected alderman in 2015.

Continue north. At the southeast corner with 35th Street, there's a police and fire station, which made a cameo in the 1948 Jimmy Stewart movie *Call Northside 777*. At this point, you're 0.5 mile west of ❶ **Guaranteed Rate Field,** where the White Sox play. (Baseball fans may want to take a side trip here, walking east to see the stadium, but it's a rather bland stretch of roadway.)

Turn west on 35th, one of Bridgeport's main streets. At the southeast corner of 35th and Union, ❷ **Morrie O'Malley's Hot Dogs** (open spring–fall) has been a popular spot for three decades. When you reach Halsted Street—where the old-school diner Bridgeport Restaurant is at the southwest corner—look south to see the sign for the Ramova Theater halfway down the block. Considered a sister of the North Side's Music Box Theatre and designed in a similar style, it opened in 1929 and hosted a 1940 appearance by Charlie Chaplin for the local premiere of *The Great Dictator*. Sadly, it closed in 1985, but in 2019 the city approved plans for it to reopen as an entertainment venue.

A massive six-story brick-and-concrete building—constructed in 1936 in the Art Moderne style—fills the north side of 35th west of Morgan. This was the administration building for the Spiegel mail-order company until it closed in 1993. Across the street, the ❸ **Zhou B Art Center** took over an old warehouse in 2004, transforming it into a gallery and studio complex. It's run by the Zhou Brothers, ShanZuo and DaHuang, immigrants from China who collaborate on paintings, performances, and sculpture.

Continue west to another large industrial building, constructed in 1911, at the northwest corner of 35th and Racine. It was Spiegel's warehouse—and before that, it was the home of Albert Pick & Company, the world's largest dealer of hotel and restaurant supplies. Today, its loft spaces are occupied by the ❹ **Bridgeport Art Center,** including art studios, galleries, the Chicago Ceramic Center, and the Fashion Design Center. Walk north on Racine, where sculptures are displayed, then head west through the parking lot, where you'll see the entrance to the ❺ **Chicago Maritime Museum.**

At the parking lot's west end, you'll reach the South Fork of the Chicago River's South Branch, infamously nicknamed Bubbly Creek. In the 19th century, when the Union Stock Yards operated a mile south of here, meatpacking companies dredged this channel, dumping their waste into the water. It's cleaner today, though far from pristine. You may catch a whiff of foul odors or notice a few bubbles in the sluggish stream. A gravel pathway runs south. You can walk the length of the building—as far as the 35th Street bridge—and then return north.

Head back across the parking lot and go north on Racine. Walk west on 33rd Place, through a neighborhood of homes constructed in recent decades. At the street's end, go west through a small park, where you will reach a redbrick path that runs both directions along the creek. Head north on the path, taking in more views of Bubbly Creek. At the path's north end, veer right toward a cul-de-sac. Walk east on 32nd Place, then north on Aberdeen Street.

Go east on 31st Street, passing Ling Shen Ching Tze Buddhist Temple, a brick building with simple triangular geometry. Originally Emmanuel Presbyterian Church, it was designed by John Wellborn Root and completed by his partner, Daniel Burnham, after Root's unexpected death in 1891. The temple has been in the space since 1992, adding Vajrayana Buddhist embellishments and statues.

A block east, ❻ **Maria's Packaged Goods and Community Bar** serves hundreds of craft beers, while the adjoining Kimski is a Korean and Polish street food joint. Ed Marszewski—a Bridgeport entrepreneur who also runs the Co-Prosperity Sphere gallery, *Lumpen* magazine, the WLPN radio station, and Marz Community Brewing—transformed his mother Maria's tavern and liquor store into this cool complex.

Walk south on Morgan Street, amid shops and eateries including Bridgeport Coffeehouse, CROMEgallery, Zaytune Mediterranean Grill, and Soluri & Sons Italian Deli. At 32nd Street, walk half a block west to see St. Mary of Perpetual Help Catholic Church, a 1903 building with a high dome, a Romanesque exterior, and a Byzantine interior. Head back east to Morgan, then continue south, toward ❼ **Co-Prosperity Sphere,** which hosts exhibitions, screenings, presentations, and performances.

Walk east on 33rd Place, then north on Halsted. This stretch of Halsted includes a Chicago Public Library branch named after Richard J. Daley, along with Mitchell's Tap, Let's Boogie Records & Tapes, Bernice's Tavern, Jackalope Coffee & Tea House, a police station, and several Asian restaurants.

After you cross 29th Street, the sloping hills of ❽ **Henry C. Palmisano Nature Park** are on the street's west side. These 26.6 acres were a limestone quarry from 1836 until 1970, leaving a 380-foot hole, which then became a dumping ground for construction debris. It became a park in 2009, named after a Bridgeport fishing enthusiast who ran a local bait shop. Enter just south of 27th Street, near a fountain designed by Ernest Wong, where water rises through a 10-foot metal tube and drips down. Follow the paths up to the park's 33-foot-high peak, "Mount Bridgeport," to see panoramic views of Chicago. Wander down to the catch-and-release fishing pond in the northwest corner, where old quarry walls are visible.

Exit the park to Halsted Street, where the walk ends. To depart, take a CTA 8 Halsted bus.

Henry C. Palmisano Nature Park

Bridgeport

Points of Interest

1. **Guaranteed Rate Field** 333 W. 35th St., 312-674-1000, mlb.com/whitesox

2. **Morrie O'Malley's Hot Dogs** 3501 S. Union Ave., 773-247-2700, morrieomalleys.com

3. **Zhou B Art Center** 1029 W. 35th St., 773-523-0200, zhoubartcenter.com

4. **Bridgeport Art Center** 1200 W. 35th St., 773-247-3000, bridgeportart.com

5. **Chicago Maritime Museum** 1200 W. 35th St., 773-376-1982, chicagomaritimemuseum.org

6. **Maria's Packaged Goods and Community Bar** 960 W. 31st St., 773-890-0588, community-bar.com

7. **Co-Prosperity Sphere** 3219-21 S. Morgan St., 773-823-9702, coprosperity.org

8. **Henry C. Palmisano Nature Park** 2700 S. Halsted St., 312-747-6497, chicagoparkdistrict.com/parks-facilities/palmisano-henry-park

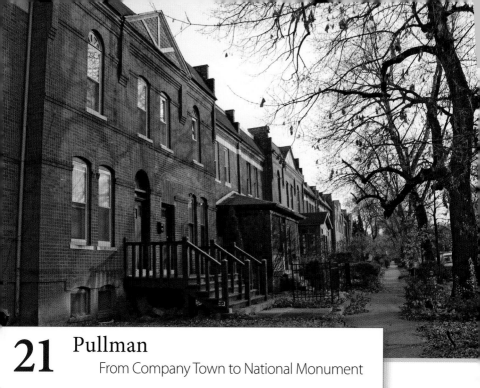

21 Pullman
From Company Town to National Monument

Above: Pullman row houses

BOUNDARIES: Cottage Grove Ave., 109th St., Langley Ave., 115th St.
DISTANCE: 2.5 miles
DIFFICULTY: Easy
PARKING: Free parking in the National Monument Visitor Center lot and on many nearby streets
PUBLIC TRANSIT: Metra Electric District train to 111th St.; Red Line to 95th and Cottage Grove, and
  then 115 CTA bus to Cottage Grove

Pullman is the only national monument in Chicago—or anywhere in Illinois. This enclave of row houses began life in 1881 as a company town. One of Chicago's wealthiest businessmen, George Pullman, built a factory here for Pullman's Palace Car Company—which made luxury sleeping cars for railroads—alongside a town where his employees rented homes. Those workers went on strike in 1894, an action that erupted into a violent nationwide labor conflict. This meticulously planned community for factory laborers was absorbed by Chicago, becoming a city neighborhood and eventually declining into poverty. After a plan to demolish the entire neighborhood south of 111th Street was floated in 1960, local residents rallied to save Pullman, even as the industry continued to decline. The Pullman factory produced its final railroad car in 1981.

But things are looking up in this section of Chicago's Far South Side—thanks, in part, to its designation as a national monument in 2015. With new industrial businesses, as well as artist lofts, opening, the local alderman proclaimed a neighborhood renaissance. Many homes have been spruced up in recent years, while keeping their historical character.

The Pullman name is also closely associated with African American railroad porters, but they did not live in the Pullman town. Rather, they worked on the company's cars around the country. To learn more about *that* part of the Pullman story, consider a side trip to the ❶ **National A. Philip Randolph Pullman Porter Museum** in the north section of Pullman.

Walk Description

Begin at the 111th Street Metra Station. The vibrant *Pullman Legacy* mural covers the walls in the viaduct where 111th Street passes under the tracks. Painted in 2017 by Rahmaan Statik and local high school students, it includes images of George Pullman, the tycoon hailed as a visionary industrial genius and denounced as a cruel overlord; architect Solon Beman, who designed all 1,300 structures in the original company town; Pullman Porters, the African Americans who worked on Pullman cars; and President Barack Obama, who made Pullman a national monument.

Walk east to the northeast corner of 111th and Cottage Grove Avenue. Go north alongside the 12.5-acre grounds of the old Pullman factory. At the time this book was being written, the factory buildings were behind a fence and locked gates. In 2018 the National Park Service began renovating the ❷ **Administration Building,** planning to open it as a visitor center. That building's tall clock tower was originally the center point of a symmetrical factory complex. An artificial lake extended onto the land where the street is today. But all that remains are the Administration Building and the adjoining North Factory Wing. These buildings deteriorated after they shut down in the 1950s, and then they were damaged by arson in 1998. After you've walked along the factory, head back the way you came. As you approach 111th Street, look east to see the Rear Erecting Shops, where the roof was removed in 2001.

Cross to the southeast corner, where you'll enter Pullman Park. Walk south along Forrestville Avenue, the curving drive in front of the ❸ **Hotel Florence,** a "large gingerbread country villa" that George Pullman named after his favorite daughter when it opened in 1881. The trim was painted in Pullman's colors: two shades of greens and a deep red, created by the Sherwin-Williams Company, which had a factory nearby to supply vast quantities of paint for Pullman's railroad cars. The hotel's dining room hosted famous visitors, including President Ulysses S. Grant. Later, the vacant hotel became a movie location, serving as the mansion of an organized crime boss played by Paul Newman in 2002's *Road to Perdition*. Owned by the state, the hotel isn't open to the public as of 2020, but it could be in the future.

Walk to the Pullman 1894 Strike Memorial Rose and Herb Garden on the hotel's south side. Facing south, you'll see Arcade Park, which was lushly landscaped during its heyday. Walk southwest to the block-shaped building with a mural on its north wall. Painted in 1996 by American Academy of Art students, *Visual Interpretations of Pullman* includes images of the massive building that once stood at this spot: the Arcade, a combo of shopping center, library, bank, theater, and meeting place. Sadly, it was demolished in 1926. The building here now, constructed as an American Legion post in 1953, houses the temporary ❹ **Pullman National Monument Visitor Information Center.** Walk southwest to Cottage Grove and 112th Street. The 1885 building at the southeast corner was the Pullman Stables. Wooden horse heads still adorn the facade.

Walk west on 112th, crossing Forrestville. The next block, known as Arcade Row, has some of Pullman's loveliest row houses. These were designed for company officials—or anyone who could afford the higher rent. Some carpenters and a foreman pooled their money and lived together at 535. Note the rare surviving example of an arch over the walkway between the buildings at 531 and 533. At the next corner, the charming ❺ **Pullman Cafe** is to your right.

Cross St. Lawrence Avenue to the east side, where ❻ **Greenstone United Methodist Church** stands. It's covered with serpentine limestone quarried in Pennsylvania. Consecrated in 1881 by Universalist minister James Pullman (George's brother), it stood empty for some time because Pilsen's denominations couldn't agree on a plan to share it. A Presbyterian congregation finally took over, until Methodists bought the church in 1906.

Walk north on St. Lawrence. The five-room cottages between 11145 and 11151 were built in 1880—Beman's first row houses in Pullman. He designed houses in the Queen Anne style, which emphasizes contrasts in color and texture. He avoided monotony in his row houses by changing up the ornamentation and brick patterns.

When you reach 111th, turn east, strolling along Executive Row, where the company's top officials lived. (George Pullman himself didn't live in the town bearing his name; he had a mansion on Chicago's most prestigious street, Prairie Avenue, part of Walk 11.) Go east to 641 E. 111th, a beauty restored by the Bielenberg Historic Pullman Foundation. Thomas Dunbar, a Scottish immigrant who worked his way up from carpenter to factory superintendent, lived here.

Turn back west a short distance, then go south on Champlain Avenue. The two-story buildings at 11146, 11147, 11148, and 11149 are fine examples of the two-flats—two-story buildings with an apartment unit on each floor—that Beman designed for Pullman workers. After another block, you're facing Market Square. Market Hall stood in the middle—with a lunch counter, stalls for selling meat and vegetables, and a meeting hall—until it burned down in 1892. A replacement building was also damaged by fires, in 1931 and 1973. What survives is just the shell. Market Square is encircled by four curved apartment buildings, built circa 1892. The living spaces above their colonnades have been described as "excruciatingly narrow." Turn east and follow the curving sidewalks through these buildings, going around three-quarters of the circle. Then go west on 112th. Turn south on St. Lawrence Avenue. The apartment building just south of Greenstone Church, at 11217, was turned into the Pullman Infirmary in the early 1900s and later converted back into housing. In the 1993 movie *The Fugitive,* this was the home of the one-armed man who killed the wife of Dr. Richard Kimble (Harrison Ford).

When you reach 113th, turn east on the street's north side. As you reach the alley, the handsome brick structure in front of you—at 614—is an apartment building that was converted into a Masonic hall. It's now the ❼ **Florence Lowden Miller Historic Pullman Center,** which the Historic Pullman Foundation uses for offices and meetings. Turn north into the alley. This is another location in *The Fugitive*—a spot where Dr. Kimble sought a place to hide. Follow the alley as it makes an unusual loop around the former Masonic hall until you're back on 113th.

Walk east, then turn south on Champlain. After you cross 114th, look at the first two buildings on the east side (11401 and 11403). This was called Honeymoon Row, because these small apartments were intended for young couples without children, but they ended up crowded with several tenants. Note the trapezoidal bays with three doors. The doors on the left and right sides open directly into apartments, while the middle door leads to a central corridor.

Go back north to the corner, then walk west on 114th. Turn north at St. Lawrence. George M. Pullman Elementary School, built in 1910, will be on your left. At 113th, turn west, crossing Cottage Grove and walking into the viaduct. The walls are covered with *I Welcome Myself to a New Place,* an inspiring but faded mural painted by Olivia Gude, Marcus Akinlana, and Jon Pound in 1988.

As you pass through the viaduct, you exit Pullman, entering a section of the Roseland community called Kensington. Pullman residents often crossed the tracks when they wanted to drink, since their own town was dry (with the exception of an exclusive bar inside the Hotel Florence). Edward Uihlein, an executive at Milwaukee-based Joseph Schlitz Brewing Company, bought 10 acres here and opened a tied house—a saloon exclusively selling beer from one brewery. One bar wasn't enough to meet the demand, so Uihlein opened two more. To see what remains of

Schlitz Row, turn south on Front Avenue, which runs along the railroad embankment. Built in 1906, the former Schlitz Brewery Stable Building at 11314 housed draught horses for Schlitz's delivery wagons. Continue south. A former Schlitz-tied house stands vacant at 11400, with the brewery's globe symbol above the corner door.

Walk west on 114th Street. Reach Martin Luther King Drive, where the New Alpha Progressive Baptist Church sits on the northeast corner. Turn south on King Drive. Schlitz Brewery constructed the brick buildings at 11413, 11419, and 11429 in 1906 as residences for its managers.

Turn east on 115th, walking to the Kensington/115th Street Metra station. This Metra line runs on a track that the Illinois Central Railroad used for its *Panama Limited* passenger train between Chicago and New Orleans 1911–1971. Hobos reportedly hopped off trains in this vicinity, which might explain how Kensington got the nickname Bumtown, though it might have to do with the abundance of drinking establishments. If you're looking for a place to eat before ending your Pullman visit, **❾ Cal-Harbor Restaurant & Lounge**—an old-school diner in business for more than 40 years—is two blocks east from this station. Depart by taking a Metra train, or catch a CTA 4, 111A, or 115 bus on Cottage Grove.

The Pullman Administration Building

Pullman

Points of Interest

1 National A. Philip Randolph Pullman Porter Museum 10406 S. Maryland Ave., 773-850-8580, aphiliprandolphmuseum.com

2 Administration Building (visitor center scheduled to open in 2021) Cottage Grove Ave. north of 111th St.

3 Hotel Florence/Pullman State Historic Site 11111 S. Forrestville Ave., 773-660-2341, pullman-museum.org

4 Pullman National Monument Visitor Information Center (temporary) 11141 S. Cottage Grove Ave., 773-468-9310, nps.gov/pull

5 The Pullman Cafe 11208 S. St. Lawrence Ave., thepullmancafe.com

6 Greenstone United Methodist Church 11211 S. St. Lawrence Ave., 773-785-1492

7 Florence Lowden Miller Historic Pullman Center 614 E. 113th St., 773-785-8181, pullmanil.org

8 Cal-Harbor Restaurant & Lounge 546 E. 115th St., 773-264-5435, facebook.com/calharbor

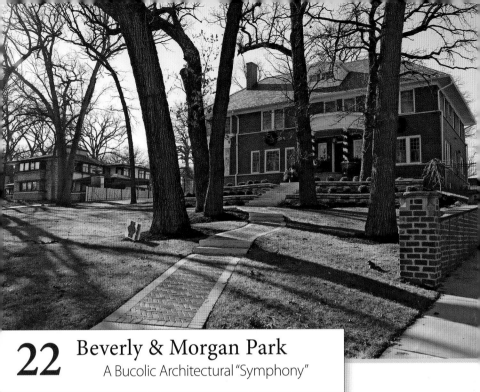

22 Beverly & Morgan Park
A Bucolic Architectural "Symphony"

Above: Houses on the ridge along Longwood Drive

BOUNDARIES: Western Ave., 87th St., Wood St., Prospect Ave.
DISTANCE: 5.4 miles
DIFFICULTY: Easy
PARKING: Free parking in the Dan Ryan Woods lot at Western Ave. and 87th St.
PUBLIC TRANSIT: CTA 95 or 87 bus (both accessible from the Red Line's 95th St. station) to Western Ave. and 87th St.; Metra Rock Island District line to 95th St., then a westbound CTA 95 bus to Western and 87th

Far out on Chicago's Southwest Side, the Beverly and Morgan Park neighborhoods are a trove of beautifully designed houses—ranging from bungalows to mansions—on bucolic, tree-lined streets. There are even some hills, a rarity in Chicago's flat topography. The ridge running through the neighborhoods is a scar left by the melting of glaciers thousands of years ago.

The city annexed the Beverly neighborhood in 1890, but some sections of it remained prairie until the 1940s and 1950s. The racially integrated area is one of Chicago's most stable middle-class neighborhoods. South of Beverly, the Baptist community of Morgan Park became a village in 1882, resembling an English country town. After some resistance, Morgan Park's residents voted to become part of Chicago in 1914.

In 1976 the Ridge Historic District—encompassing more than 3,000 homes on 212 acres of land spanning Beverly and Morgan Park—was added to the National Register of Historic Places. This walk will take you from the forest at Beverly's north end through the heart of that district.

Walk Description

Start at Western Avenue and 87th Street, where the 257-acre **①** **Dan Ryan Woods** extends in three directions. These woodlands and savannas sit atop a glacial ridge called Blue Island—which actually *was* an island 11,000 years ago, surrounded by the waters of prehistoric Lake Chicago. At the northeast corner, go east across the parking lot, then walk up the sledding hill via 63 concrete steps. More than 600 feet above sea level, it's one of Chicago's highest points. Walk south down the hill and look for the pedestrian tunnel under 87th Street, east of the parking lot. Take the tunnel south, emerging into another section of Dan Ryan Woods.

Walk south, looking for a stone pathway that leads southeast into the woods. Follow that, staying on the main path toward the southeast when you see a path forking off to the west. In places, the path runs next to aqueducts made of limestone flagstone—a drainage system from the Great Depression. The path ends at an abandoned street, where you should turn right, walking southeast. You'll emerge on Longwood Drive. Half a block later, turn west on Howland Avenue. This north section of Beverly is hilly, with curving streets lined with lovely houses, many from the 1920s and 1930s. The *AIA Guide to Chicago* calls it "a symphony of architectural styles."

Turn southeast on Pleasant Avenue. Then go west on Hopkins Place, where you'll see the irregular roofline of the Everett Robert Brewer House at 2078 (designed in 1924 by prominent Beverly architect Murray D. Hetherington) and the sprawling Renaissance-style George W. Reed House at 2122 (built in 1929). At the end of the street (at 8918 S. Hamilton Ave.), look at the home Hetherington designed for himself in 1929, which looks like a cottage from England's Cotswolds region.

Walk south on Hamilton, where you'll see another Hetherington design from the 1920s, the Spanish Revival–style James Alex Brough House at 8929. Go east on 90th Street, then south on Damen Avenue, and east on 91st Street. When the street ends at Winchester Avenue, keep going east into the forest, taking a path that emerges at steps just west of the fanciful E. S. Pike House at 1826 W. 91st St. Designed in 1894 by Harry Hale Waterman, who lived in Beverly, it looks like a cottage from a fairy tale—but it now serves as offices for the forest preserve.

Go a short distance west on 91st, then head south on Pleasant Avenue. At 9167, Waterman designed the Hiram H. Belding House in 1894, with a mix of Norman and Tudor styles. At 9203, there's a Colonial Revival house built in 1894 for William M. R. French, the Art Institute's first director. The house at 9326 is attributed to Frank Lloyd Wright, though scholars speculate that its original owner, Williams Adams—who had worked as a contractor for Wright—may have designed it himself in 1900. Either way, it's a fine example of early Prairie School architecture.

Go half a block east on 95th Street, then go south on Longwood Drive, the main scenic route through Beverly. A block south, ❷ **Ridge Park** is on Longwood's east side. The fieldhouse contains the John H. Vanderpoel Memorial Art Gallery, a collection of 500 works by American painters and sculptors. It's named after a Beverly resident who taught at the Art Institute.

As you continue south, a ridge along the street's west side gets higher, with magnificent homes above sloping lawns. The Bryson B. Hill House (at 9800) and Frederick C. Sawyer House (9822) are classical mansions from the 20th century's first decade. The Robert W. Evans House (9914) was created by Frank Lloyd Wright in 1908 with his trademark horizontal lines, but sadly, the architect's original stucco is covered with a faux-stone facade.

The building at the northwest corner of Longwood and 103rd Street is Beverly's most iconic structure: the Givins Irish Castle. Developer Robert C. Givins used Joliet limestone to construct this three-story mansion with round crenellated lookout towers in 1887, modeling it after an Irish castle. Since 1941, it has been the ❸ **Beverly Unitarian Church.**

Walk east on 103rd through a quaint business district, including a Starbucks inside a former Christian Science Reading Room. After crossing the Metra tracks, continue east to Wood Street, where Bethany Union Church (designed in 1927 by Tribune Tower architect Raymond M. Hood) sits at the northeast corner.

Turn south on Wood, then go east on 104th Street, where a couple of homes—at 1632 and 1710—were designed by Walter Burley Griffin, a noted Prairie School architect who had worked for Wright. Turn south on Prospect Avenue, then go west on 104th Place—also known as Walter Burley Griffin Place. Developer Russell L. Blount hired Griffin to design houses on this bucolic street from 1909 to 1913. It's the largest concentration of small-scale Prairie School residences in Chicago. Look for Griffin's rustic wood-and-stucco houses at 1666, 1712, 1724, 1727, 1731, 1736, and 1741, paying attention to the subtle variations in his style. After designing these seven houses, Griffin left for Australia; he had won a competition to design the country's new capital city, Canberra.

Turn south on Wood, then west on 105th Street and south on Longwood. Half a block south of 105th Place, the brick-and-stone Graver-Driscoll House—designed in 1922 by John T. Hetherington in the Tudor Revival style—is occupied by the ❹ **Ridge Historical Society.** (The entrance is on the other side, facing Seeley Avenue.)

Continue south, crossing 107th Street from Beverly into the Morgan Park neighborhood. The whimsical house at 10838 is the one Waterman designed for himself in 1892. Farther south, the beautifully simple Morgan Park United Methodist Church was designed by Waterman in 1913 in the Craftsman style. Just south of it is the Morgan Park Presbyterian Church, built in the 1930s.

Cross to the east side of Longwood, walking east on 110th Place, which leads you to Prospect Avenue. You're at the north end of Bohn Park, a patch of green next to ❺ **Metra's 111th St.–Morgan Park Station.** Like several depots in Beverly and Morgan Park, it was built when this train line was the Chicago, Rock Island & Pacific Railroad, which began offering commuter service to downtown in 1888.

Walk northeast on Prospect Avenue, where colorfully painted houses, including several built in the 1870s and 1880s, line the street's north side. At 10910, the rear portion of the Ingersoll Blackwelder House was built in 1874 for real estate magnate John Ingersoll. A Queen Anne–style annex was added a decade later for the house's new owner, Morgan Park village president Isaac Blackwelder. A century later, artist Jack Simmerling owned the house, and it still contains architectural pieces he salvaged from Chicago mansions. Today, the house leases out its elegant Victorian spaces for special events.

The walk ends at Prospect and Wood Street. To depart, take an eastbound CTA 111 bus to the Red Line. Or take a Metra train. If you parked in the Dan Ryan Woods, head west on Prospect and then go west on 111th Street to Western, where you can catch a Pace 349 bus to 87th Street.

Beverly Unitarian Church,
also known as the Givins Irish Castle

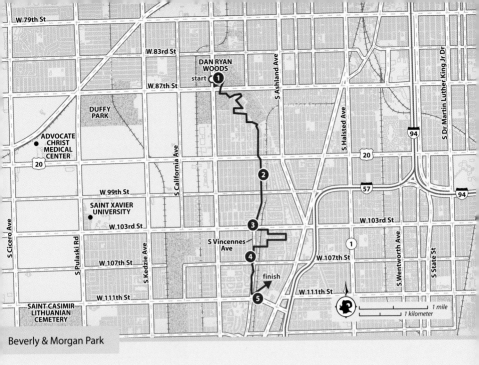

Beverly & Morgan Park

Points of Interest

① **Dan Ryan Woods** Western Ave. and 87th St., 800-870-3666, fpdcc.com/dan-ryan-woods

② **Ridge Park** 9625 S. Longwood Dr., 312-747-6640, chicagoparkdistrict.com/parks-facilities/ridge-park

③ **Beverly Unitarian Church (Givins Irish Castle)** 10244 S. Longwood Dr., 773-233-7080, beverlyunitarian.org

④ **Ridge Historical Society (Graver-Driscoll House)** 10621 S. Seeley Ave., 773-881-1675, ridgehistoricalsociety.org

⑤ **Metra 111th St.–Morgan Park Station** 11046 S. Hale Ave., 888-578-7275, metrarail.com

23 Garfield Park
Country Comes to the City

Above: Garfield Park Lagoon

BOUNDARIES: Garfield Park, Hamlin Ave., Eisenhower Expwy., Homan Ave.
DISTANCE: 2.4 miles
DIFFICULTY: Easy
PARKING: Free parking at Garfield Park Conservatory
PUBLIC TRANSIT: CTA Green Line to Conservatory stop

Garfield Park's major attraction is its century-old botanical conservatory, where visitors can step right into a glass-encased desert and a forest of ferns. But there's much more to this 185-acre park at the heart of Chicago's West Side. Architect William Le Baron Jenney (famous for building the world's first skyscraper) developed the park from 1869 to 1874 as a pastoral place for city dwellers to relax, with a landscape in the English naturalistic style. Another local legend of park design, Danish immigrant Jens Jensen, overhauled Garfield Park in the early 1900s, striving to make the scenery more evocative of Midwestern prairies. "I have always thought, 'If the city cannot come to the country, then the country must come to the city,'" Jensen once wrote.

Walk Description

Begin at the CTA Green Line's Conservatory station. This is one of many places on the Green Line where you can see the tracks extending in a seemingly endless line aiming straight toward the east and west horizons. Stretching for 6 miles on top of Lake Street, this metal structure is one of the city's oldest L tracks, opened in 1893 by the Lake Street Elevated Railway Company.

At the southwest corner, follow the path leading southwest into the park. At the fork in the path, stay left, crossing the roadway to reach Garfield Park Lagoon. Go west on the path along the lagoon, following it as it curves south and then east. You can see the fieldhouse's magnificent dome across the water. When you see a statue south of the lagoon, veer across the grass toward it. This is the Robert Burns Memorial, a 1906 replica of sculptor William Grant Stevenson's monument in Kilmarnock, Scotland, dedicated to that country's most revered poet. Continue southeast across the park toward another sculpture: *Lincoln the Rail-Splitter,* near the northwest corner of Washington Boulevard and Central Park Avenue. Sculpted in 1905 by Irish immigrant Charles J. Mulligan, this bronze figure depicts a youthful Lincoln wielding an ax.

Walk north to the stairs in front of the ❶ **Garfield Park Fieldhouse,** which is topped by a tall gold-leaf dome. This 1928 building was designed by two local Norwegian Americans, Christian S. Michaelsen and Sigurd Anton Rognstad, in the Spanish Baroque style. With its twisty columns, the glazed terra-cotta entrance is decorated with scrolls, pinnacles, niches, human faces, and shapes resembling plants and seashells. A statue of René-Robert Cavelier, Sieur de La Salle, a Frenchman who explored Illinois in the 1680s, stands above the central window. Stop inside to see the two-story rotunda, with its colorful patterned terrazzo floor and sculptural murals by Richard W. Bock.

Exit the building and walk south along Central Park Avenue. Cross Madison Street, then walk west along Madison, turning south along Woodward Drive. Go west along Music Court Circle, where a circular roadway surrounds the Garfield Park Bandstand. With an octagonal roof sheathed in green copper, this structure was designed by Joseph Lyman Silsbe, a mentor of Frank Lloyd Wright. With a platform for a hundred musicians, the bandstand opened for weekly concerts in 1897, attracting several thousand people at some performances, but it has been neglected for decades. Its Georgian marble walls, colored-glass mosaics, and Saracenic motifs are juxtaposed with rusty padlocked doors.

Point yourself south—walking up a small hill covered with trees, one of Garfield Park's most pleasant vistas. On the hill's other side, head east on a path along the north edge of the soccer fields. Then walk north on Central Park Avenue. After passing under the L tracks, head for the ❷ **Garfield Park Conservatory** on the northwest corner. Jens Jensen designed this structure, which opened in 1908, to look like a giant haystack. In addition to 2 acres of indoor greenhouse space filled with specimens of flora from around the globe, the conservatory has 12 acres of outdoor gardens—which you can reach only by going through the building. Enter through the lobby on the east end. Admission is free, but a $5 donation is suggested. Go west through the Palm House, then the Fern Room and the Desert Room, exiting through the doors on the building's west end onto the Bluestone Terrace.

Just north of the terrace, two sculptures known as *Bulls with Maidens* stand guard in front of greenhouses. Daniel Chester French and Edward Clark Potter created the original 12-foot-tall

The Garfield Park Bandstand

Garfield Park

plaster versions of these figures for the 1893 world's fair. One depicts Ceres, the Roman goddess of grain, and the other is supposed to be an American Indian goddess of corn. Six-foot bronze replicas were cast in 1912, but thieves stole one in 1986, while damaging its companion. The stolen statue mysteriously turned up in Virginia in 2010 but remains in storage. What you see on display now is a more recent replica, along with the statue that was damaged in 1986, restored to its beauty.

Take the path that heads northwest into the City Garden, which includes lily pools and a stand of aspen trees. Roam around this space, then return through the conservatory and walk south to the Green Line station. If you're hungry, head two blocks east on Lake Street to ❸ **Inspiration Kitchens,** an eclectic restaurant with a mission of lifting people out of poverty.

Points of Interest

❶ **Garfield Park Fieldhouse** 100 N. Central Park Ave., 773-342-1742, chicagoparkdistrict.com/parks-facilities/garfield-park

❷ **Garfield Park Conservatory** 300 N. Central Park Ave., 773-638-1766, garfieldconservatory.org

❸ **Inspiration Kitchens** 3504 W. Lake St., 773-801-1110, inspirationkitchens.org

24 The 606
A Trail on Old Rails

BOUNDARIES: Ashland Ave., Armitage Ave., North Ave., Ridgeway Ave.
DISTANCE: 3 miles
DIFFICULTY: Easy
PARKING: Street parking
PUBLIC TRANSIT: CTA 9 Ashland and 72 North buses to Ashland and Cortland

Six years after New York City's High Line became a magnet for tourists, a similar elevated trail opened in Chicago in 2015—quickly gaining popularity as a route for walkers, runners, bicyclists, and sightseers. It's known as the 606, a name that comes from the first three digits of all the ZIP codes in Chicago, but some folks prefer to call it the Bloomingdale Trail. When you walk on this 2.7-mile pathway on top of an old freight rail line, you get a chance to see several neighborhoods on Chicago's North and Northwest Sides from a higher-than-usual perspective: 17.5 feet above ground at the trail's highest point.

As the 606 website explains, the trail's embankments "are essentially enormous concrete bathtubs filled with soil, stones, and other drainage material." Seven feet thick at their base, these sturdy walls have stood since 1913, when the Bloomingdale Line was elevated. The 606 path dips and rises in places, revealing portions of those old concrete walls. Along the way, the sights include some 1,400 trees and more than 200 species of plants on the pathway's edges, becoming increasingly lush in the years since the 606 opened, attracting birds, bees, and butterflies.

The 606's galvanized steel railings range from 4.5 feet to 10 feet high—with a grid pattern that lets you look through at the surrounding landscape, with its industrial chimneys, water tanks, and steel girders. Many residential buildings have popped up along the 606, or have taken over old industrial spaces. Real estate prices have jumped, causing some longtime residents to worry that they'll get priced out of their neighborhoods.

The 606 is open daily, 6 a.m.–11 p.m., with curved light fixtures that illuminate the path during darker hours. There are 12 access areas and 17 access ramps, allowing you to ascend onto the trail or descend from it every 0.25 mile or so.

Walk Description

Begin at the trail's eastern end, a curving concrete wall along Ashland Avenue south of Cortland Avenue in the Bucktown neighborhood. Just north of the wall, enter ❶ **Walsh Park** (the former site of Northwestern Yeast Company). Follow the concrete path that rises higher as it circles around, finally pointing to the west. With shrubbery covering its inner side, that concrete wall is designed to muffle the noise from the Kennedy Expressway.

Walk west on the 606. The trail is a 14-foot-wide concrete surface, with 2-foot-wide blue rubberized strips on either side. As you're walking, stay in those side lanes whenever possible. Look out for bicyclists, who are supposed to use the path's middle zone.

As you go, keep an eye on the 606's varied foliage—deciduous trees, flowering shrubs, and perennial flowers and grasses. In spring, the plantings are designed to form a sort of artwork called *Environmental Sentinel,* revealing Lake Michigan's effect on bloom times of temperature-sensitive trees and shrubs. Certain species take up to five days to bloom progressively from west to east along the trail. In summer, the flowers include serviceberries, lilacs, and forsythias.

As you walk west from Ashland, the white dome of St. Mary of the Angels parish looms over Bucktown on your right, north of the trail. Dedicated in 1920, this magnificent Catholic church resembles St. Peter's Basilica in Rome. Slated for demolition in 1988, it escaped the wrecking ball, and now it's fully restored, with 26 angels perched on its roof. After another two blocks, a four-story brick building stands south of the trail (at 1754 N. Wolcott). This was the base of Stenson Brewing, run by mobster Johnny Torrio's silent beer-making partner during the Prohibition era, Joseph Stenson. Today, it's filled with residences.

At Damen Avenue, a ramp leads down to ❷ **Churchill Field Park** (which was the site of a tobacco company called Independent Snuff in the early 1900s). If you're keen on shopping at trendy boutiques, a stroll north or south on Damen could be worth your time. The area also has many restaurants. Where Damen passes under the 606, *CoyWolf,* a psychedelic 2017 mural by Tony Passero, livens up the viaduct's west side.

But don't miss the Damen Arts Plaza on the 606 above the street, a wide space where sculptures are displayed, with a nice view looking south down Damen to the heart of the Wicker Park–Bucktown area (covered in Walk 26).

Continuing west on the trail, you will arrive at one of the coolest green spaces along the 606—the blandly named Park 567, on the trail's north side at Milwaukee Avenue. A serpentine path winds down a hilly slope covered with shrubs and trees. Rectangular limestone boulders work nicely as seats or tables, and the curving lawn seems to attract people reading or chatting with friends. The scene is enlivened by a 42-by-90-foot mural on the adjacent wall, where realistically depicted human faces gaze toward us. Painted in 2016 by Jeff Zimmermann, it's clunkily named after its corporate sponsor: *The ConAgra Brands Mural.* The wall includes ground-floor windows, where you can often see people sitting inside the ❸ **Ipsento 606** coffee shop, looking almost like they're moving figures inside the mural.

After visiting Park 567, follow that snaking walkway back up to the trail, and continue west. The bridge across Milwaukee Avenue includes Luftwerk's art installation ❹ *Turning Sky,* which brightens the night with 800 computer-controlled video pixel lights, mirrors, and video of clouds. Just ahead, the 606 passes beneath a train line that's even higher—the CTA's Blue Line L tracks, a classic steel-girder structure.

As you cross Western Avenue, you pass into another neighborhood: Logan Square. In the next stretch of the 606, hundreds of sumac trees have been planted along the trail. As they grow, they should form a green archway over the path.

As the 606 passes over Humboldt Boulevard, the widened Humboldt Overlook has long wood benches where you can sit to take in the views. Lined by historical houses, the broad green expanse of Humboldt Boulevard presents a beautiful sight in both directions here. (See Walk 25 for Humboldt Park, south of here, or Walk 27 for Logan Square, north of here.)

Continue west. Julia de Burgos Park, featuring a climbing web, a spider sculpture, and a sitting wall, is on the trail's north side at Albany Street. Farther along, after you pass Kimball Avenue, there's a grove with more than 700 poplars. A gravel side path splits off to the trail's south, heading through the midst of this shady wood. Follow that path for the next couple of blocks and then rejoin the main trail.

After crossing Central Park Avenue, you're approaching the end of the 606. As you go over Lawndale Avenue, look to the south. That large brick building with a water tank on top used to be the factory and warehouse of Playskool, which made iconic toys such as Lincoln Logs and the Tyke Bike. Like many old structures along the 606, it was recently renovated. Looking north, you'll see McCormick YMCA, which stands at the site of another old factory. Famed bicycle maker Ignaz Schwinn built what was said to be the world's largest motorcycle factory, Excelsior Motor, at this spot in 1914.

As you go down the slope at the 606's western trailhead, you'll see a pinwheel-shaped ramp spiraling up a small hill. This is the ❺ **Exelon Observatory,** designed by artist Frances Whitehead with guidance from Adler Planetarium. The Chicago Astronomer group hosts a monthly sky-gazing event here on the second Friday of each month—and during daylight hours, it offers a nice vantage point to take in a panoramic view of the city's Northwest Side as well as the distant

The Exelon Observatory at the west end of the 606

The 606

Loop. Just past the trail's end, tar-stained railroad ties are piled up in a yard along a Metra rail line, a reminder of the machinery that makes Chicago run.

You have several options to depart via the CTA: Walk east and catch an 82 bus at Kimball and Bloomingdale. Walk south to the 72 bus at North and Lawndale. Walk northwest to the 53 bus at Pulaski and Cortland. Or go north to the 73 bus at Armitage and Lawndale.

Points of Interest

1. **Walsh Park** 1722 N. Ashland Ave., 312-742-7769, chicagoparkdistrict.com/parks-facilities/walsh-playground-park

2. **Churchill Field Park** 1825 N. Damen Ave., chicagoparkdistrict.com/parks-facilities/churchill-field-park

3. **Ipsento 606** 1813 N. Milwaukee Ave, 872-206-8697, ipsento.com

4. *Turning Sky* 1801–11 N. Milwaukee Ave., chicagoparkdistrict.com/parks-facilities/turning-sky

5. **Exelon Observatory** 1801 N. Ridgeway Ave., chicagoparkdistrict.com/parks-facilities/exelon-observatory

25 Humboldt Park
Prairie Paradise and Little Puerto Rico

Above: The Leif Erikson Monument in Humboldt Park

BOUNDARIES: Kedzie Ave., Bloomingdale Ave., Western Ave., Augusta Blvd.
DISTANCE: 4 miles
DIFFICULTY: Easy
PARKING: Street parking
PUBLIC TRANSIT: CTA 70 Division bus to Division and Humboldt

Alexander Von Humboldt, the famous German explorer and naturalist, never set foot in Chicago. But that didn't stop German Americans from naming a West Side park after him in 1869. Germans no longer dominate the surrounding neighborhood—Humboldt Park is now almost synonymous with Chicago's Puerto Rican community. After exploring the 200-acre park, a delightful oasis of prairie and lagoons, we'll take a stroll down a vibrant stretch of Division Street known as Paseo Boricua, or the Puerto Rican Promenade.

Walk Description

Start at Humboldt Drive and Division Street. Looking west, on the south side of Division, you'll see the ❶ **National Museum of Puerto Rican Arts & Culture.** Built in 1895 as the Humboldt Park Receptory Building and Stable—housing horses, wagons, and landscaping tools—it mixes elements of the Queen Anne architectural style and German country houses. Landscape architect Jens Jensen had his offices here when he was the local park superintendent, reshaping Humboldt Park's scenery in the early 1900s. He demolished other buildings from the park's earliest days but left these structures standing. It's now the nation's only self-standing museum devoted to Puerto Rican arts and cultural exhibitions year-round.

Walk east on Division and turn south on Sacramento Avenue. Walk a few houses south, stopping at Jensen's former home, a handsome greystone at 1141. Jensen emigrated from Denmark in the 1880s and began working as a street sweeper for Chicago's West Park Commission, eventually becoming the boss for this park system—a position he used to develop the Prairie style of landscape design. He said he avoided straight lines because "landscaping must follow the lines of the tree with its thousands of curves."

Head back north to Division and Humboldt, then walk north along the east side of Humboldt Drive. A block north, you'll reach the Fritz Reuter Monument, a bearded figure sculpted by a local German American, Franz Engelsman. Reuter is unknown to most Americans today, but he was an enormously popular author in Germany in the 19th century. When this statue was dedicated on May 14, 1893, more than 50,000 people filled the park.

Cross over to the west side of Humboldt Drive where the *World's Fair Bison* stand, pointing away from the street and toward a circular area known as the Formal Garden. Larger plaster versions were displayed at the 1893 World's Columbian Exposition's livestock exhibit. They were sculpted by Edward Kemeys, who also created the Art Institute's iconic lions. The male figure, *Prairie King,* gazes straight ahead, while the female, *Sound of the Whoop,* has her head tilted down.

Walk west across the Formal Garden. When you reach the pergola (a shaded walkway), follow the path that bends southwest toward a small body of water. This is the south end of a prairie river that Jensen created in 1906. Look for an opening in the fence and take the plank walkway toward the water. Near the water's edge, walk on the large flat rocks, making your way through cattails and broadleaf arrowhead in this swampy patch. After you're back at the main trail, continue west. The trail loops around the water, veering north—where another series of rock steps will take you to a miniature waterfall. Continuing north along the water, you'll reach a clearing, where solar panels and wind turbines supply power for the pumps moving water through the prairie river.

As you walk north, the river widens into a lagoon on your right. Up ahead to your left, you'll see the ❷ **Humboldt Park Beach,** Chicago's only inland beach, with the fieldhouse's towers and arches looming above it.

Walk west, past a baseball diamond called Little Cubs Field. Leave the path and walk up the sledding hill. Even if it isn't toboggan weather, this gentle slope will provide a panoramic view of the park and the adjacent neighborhood. From the top of the hill, walk northwest toward the Illinois National Guard Northwest Armory. Built in 1940, this Art Deco structure has numerous relief images on its walls, depicting wartime figures. The armory played a role in one of Chicago's most haunting tragedies, when it hosted the funeral for 27 young victims of a December 1, 1958, fire at the Our Lady of the Angels School. Nearly 7,000 mourners filled the building.

Walk west along the armory's south wall, then go north on the Kedzie Avenue sidewalk, taking a look at the evocative images covering this wall. Turn east on North Avenue, then go north on Humboldt Park Boulevard, heading up the west side. Like many of the streets in Chicago's historical boulevard system, this is a wide expanse of green space, with a central roadway and a narrower street along each side. Created between 1869 and 1942, the Chicago Park Boulevard System Historic District comprises eight parks, six squares, and 19 boulevards. They're connected, stretching for 26 miles in a half-circle across the city. After you've gone one block north, head east across the boulevard at Wabansia Avenue. The southeast corner of Humboldt and Wabansia is where L. Frank Baum lived in 1899, when he wrote *The Wonderful Wizard of Oz.* Baum's house is long gone, and a generic modern residence sits on the spot now—next to a yellow-brick sidewalk installed in 2019 and an Oz-themed mural by Chicago artist Hector Duarte.

Walk south. When you reach North Avenue, cross over to the southwest corner and continue south into the park. After passing the baseball fields, you'll be facing the ❸ **Humboldt Cultural Center/Fieldhouse,** which was built in 1928, designed by Christian S. Michaelsen and Sigurd A. Rognstad (the same architects responsible for Garfield Park's "Gold Dome Building"). Walk east toward Humboldt Drive, making your way to the Leif Erikson Monument. Sigvald Asbjørnsen, an immigrant from Norway, sculpted this tribute to the Scandinavian explorer, who may have been the first European to set foot on North American soil. When this heroic statue was dedicated on October 12, 1901, tens of thousands of Scandinavian Americans turned out.

Head south, where a walkway on the water's edge takes you underneath Humboldt Drive. As you emerge on the other side, you'll begin making a loop around the Humboldt Park Lagoon. At several places, gravel pathways let you walk closer to the water, the preferred route. As you circle around the lagoon, look for geese, ducks, and other aquatic birds. And you may encounter families out fishing. The lagoon made headlines in 2019 when an alligator was spotted and eventually captured, earning the nickname Chance the Snapper. The Humboldt Park Boathouse Pavilion's elegant arches can be seen across the water. When you turn south and back east along the lagoon, walk out onto the pier that juts out into the water. A little farther along, a bridge will take you onto a small island—a spot popular with wedding photographers.

Return from the island to the path, heading to the Humboldt Park Boathouse Pavilion, where the ❹ **Boathouse Cafe** serves food, with seats on the terrace overlooking the lagoon. Head toward the Alexander Von Humboldt Monument, which stands between the parking lot and roadway. Unveiled on October 16, 1892, the bronze sculpture by Felix Gorling was modeled and cast in Germany. Von Humboldt holds a book representing *Cosmos: Draft of a Physical Description of the World,* his famous five-volume series. At his feet, a globe and lizard symbolize his trips to the Amazon to study plant life and to Siberia, where he studied ocean currents.

Walk southeast through the park. As you approach the corner of the park, you will see one of two Puerto Rican flag sculptures that span Division Street. Erected in 1995, these blue and red steel sculptures are 59 feet tall and weigh some 30 tons. Proposed by then-alderman Billy Ocasio, they were designed by local architectural firm De Stefano & Partners and built by Chicago Ornamental Iron in Melrose Park. The arches mark this stretch of Division Street as Paseo Boricua.

Walk east on Division Street, taking note of the many, many murals and painted doors along the way. You may want to zigzag your way back and forth between the two sides of Division to get a closer look at some of these colorful images, which draw on the rich culture and political

Humboldt Park Lagoon

Humboldt Park

activism of Chicago's Puerto Rican community. This corridor is also a great place to sample the Caribbean island's cuisine. Popular Puerto Rican restaurants along this stretch of Division include La Bruquena, Café Colao, La Plena, Papa's Cache Sabroso, and Nellie's.

This walk ends as you pass under the steel Puerto Rican flag and arrive at Western Avenue, where Robert Clemente High School (named for the iconic Puerto Rican baseball star) is on the east side of the avenue. You may want to head a few blocks south to visit the Empty Bottle rock club (part of Walk 26). Or depart via a CTA 70 Division bus or a 49 Western bus.

Points of Interest

1 **National Museum of Puerto Rican Arts & Culture** 3015 W. Division St., 773-486-8345, nmprac.org

2 **Humboldt Park Beach** 1440 N. Humboldt Blvd., 312-742-3224, chicagoparkdistrict.com/parks-facilities/humboldt-beach

3 **Humboldt Cultural Center/Fieldhouse** 1440 N. Humboldt Blvd., 312-742-7549, chicagoparkdistrict.com/parks-facilities/humboldt-cultural-center-fieldhouse

4 **Boathouse Cafe** 1301 N. Humboldt Dr., 872-817-7000, facebook.com/boathousehumboldtpark

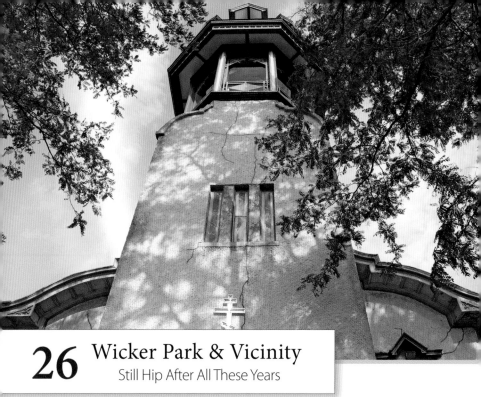

26 Wicker Park & Vicinity
Still Hip After All These Years

Above: Holy Trinity Orthodox Cathedral

BOUNDARIES: Ashland Ave., Wabansia Ave., Western Ave., Augusta Blvd.
DISTANCE: 4.1 miles
DIFFICULTY: Easy
PARKING: Street parking
PUBLIC TRANSIT: CTA 9 Ashland or 72 North Ave. bus to Ashland and Western

Walking in Wicker Park and the surrounding areas, you see traces of how Chicago's neighborhoods continually evolve. At the turn of the 20th century, Germans and Scandinavians lived here. Polish and Ukrainian immigrants established their own communities nearby. Over time, the lines of those enclaves shifted, and by the 1960s, Wicker Park was a working-class neighborhood with a large Hispanic population.

Musicians and artists arrived in the 1980s, when there was still a sense of danger on the streets. By the mid-1990s, media outlets like *Rolling Stone* were describing Wicker Park as an epicenter of cool culture. In the decades since, rents have gone up as a young, predominantly white population has moved in. Amid the patios of trendy restaurants, remnants of Wicker Park's cutting edge persist, including many pieces of street art. And some marvelous buildings from the neighborhood's old, old days are still standing.

Wicker Park lies within a larger area called West Town, and this walk wanders into some of West Town's other neighborhoods: Bucktown (which supposedly gets its name from the goats that roamed its streets circa 1900), Noble Square, and Ukrainian Village.

Walk Description

Starting at Ashland Avenue, walk west on North Avenue, the boundary line between Wicker Park (to the south) and Bucktown (to the north). At 1651, the wall of a house is covered by an image of Vivian Maier, the Chicago street photographer who became famous after her death in 2009. This 2017 painting is by Eduardo Kobra, who also created downtown's Muddy Waters mural.

At 1854, ❶ **Quimby's Bookstore** is one of Chicago's quirkiest emporiums of books, comic books, zines, and peculiar odds and ends. In business since 1991, it's a survivor from the days when Wicker Park was weirder. Farther west, ❷ **Piece Brewery and Pizzeria** is a popular spot co-owned by Cheap Trick guitarist Rick Nielsen.

When North Avenue meets Damen Avenue and diagonal Milwaukee Avenue, you've reached the busy hub of Wicker Park and Bucktown—a spot where pedestrians, cyclists, and autos jostle for space. On the south side of North Avenue, the three-story Flat Iron Arts Building was built in 1913 and designed by Holabird & Roche. Since the 1980s, the top two floors have been filled with art studios and performance spaces. Make your way to the intersection's north point, where a Walgreens occupies the old Noel State Bank, built in 1919. Then cross Milwaukee to the intersection's northwest point and the 12-story ❸ **Robey** hotel. Built in 1928 in the Art Deco style, the limestone-clad skyscraper (with images of swans on its walls) was originally called Northwest Tower. Decades later, local artists supposedly imagined that it looked like a coyote, and for a while—in the 1990s—it was the focal point of the now-defunct Around the Coyote arts festival. In late 2016, it reopened as the Robey (which is named for the former name of the street now called Damen). The hotel includes Café Robey, the sixth-floor Cabana Club, and a rooftop lounge called the Up Room.

Walk northwest on Milwaukee, then turn west on Caton Street, which was originally a gated private avenue called Columbia in the 1890s. The block is still lined with ornate homes from that era, including a row of five houses along the north side (2138–2156), all designed by Faber & Pagels, who boasted, "No two alike!"

Turn south on Leavitt Street, crossing North Avenue. Then turn east on Pierce Avenue, lined with houses from the late 19th century. At 2135, German-immigrant furniture maker Hermann Weinhardt's 1889 home is covered with ornate metal plates, making it look like a gingerbread house. John G. Runge, treasurer of a wood-milling firm, lived across the street at 2138, in a house decorated with wood embellishments. It was designed in 1884 by Frommann & Jebsen, who also designed the North Side's Schubas Tavern and other Schlitz-tied houses, or saloons featuring the Schlitz brewery's globe symbol. In 1902, as more Poles moved into Wicker Park, lawyer-banker-politician John Smulski bought this house, which served for a time as Chicago's Polish Consulate.

Turn north up the west side of Hoyne Avenue, known as Beer Baron Row because German immigrants who had made their fortunes in brewing built mansions along the street in the late 19th century. The imposing three-story house at 1520 with a carved portrait of a woman on its exterior was built in 1886 for Henry Grusendorf, who made his money as a wholesale grocer and lumber dealer.

The Queen Anne–style house at 1558 has a World War I–era Howitzer artillery piece sitting in the front yard, a remnant of the era when the building housed American Legion Pulaski Post 86, 1927–1972. With pressed-metal trim on the towers, cornices, and conservatory, the house was built in 1879 for C. Hermann Plautz, founder of the Chicago Drug and Chemical Company.

At the end of the block, cross to the east side of Hoyne and head back south. The green-painted brick cottage at 1559 is Wicker Park's oldest surviving dwelling, dating back to 1876. The original owner was Albin Greiner, who malted grain, supplying it to brewers, and later started his own brewery. His house has its original wood side porch—and the original address, 732, is above the front door, a remnant of Chicago's pre-1909 street-numbering system.

Cross Pierce and continue south on Hoyne. The street's most impressive mansion stands on a large lot with mulberry trees at the northeast corner of Hoyne and Schiller Street. Built in 1879 for John Raap, this tall Second Empire–style house has a curbed mansard roof, sawtooth window hoods, and cast-iron porch ornamentation. Rapp, a German immigrant in the liquor business, was shot to death in 1897 at his Milwaukee Avenue store by a former employee, who then killed himself.

Go east on Schiller. When you reach Damen, you'll see Wicker Park—the park itself, that is—on the northeast corner. Enter the park, which includes an ornamental garden, athletic fields, a playground, and the cheekily named Gurgoyle Fountain—a 2001 replica of the water-spouting gargoyles installed here back in 1892 but removed in 1908. Near Damen, a 9-foot bronze sculpture depicts Charles Gustave Wicker, the wholesale grocer and railroad official who built many of this neighborhood's homes in partnership with his brother, Joel, and who donated the land for the park. Charles's great-granddaughter Nancy Deborah Wicker-Eilan sculpted this statue, dedicated in

2006, which shows him holding a broom. When Wicker was a state lawmaker, someone asked him why he was sweeping a polling place. "Because it was dirty," he purportedly replied.

Walk south on Damen. The structure at the northwest corner of Damen and Evergreen Avenue obviously looks like a church—and that *was* its purpose, when it was built in 1879 for a Methodist congregation. But in 2014, it was converted into 11 luxury apartments. Go east on Evergreen. Halfway down the block, look for a marker in front of 1958, noting that the third-floor apartment in this brick building was where Nelson Algren, author of *A Walk on the Wild Side* and *The Man with the Golden Arm,* lived in his final years in Chicago, 1958–1976. Algren often wrote about working-class folks from the neighborhood, and he was a regular at local bars.

Continue on Evergreen as the street bends northeast. At the next corner, take a 90-degree turn left onto Wicker Park Avenue, the street along the park's north edge. At the end of that street, turn north on Damen. This stretch includes the ❹ **Violet Hour** (at 1520), the city's first craft cocktail mecca when it opened in 2007; and ❺ **Big Star** (1531), chef Paul Kahan and company's always-crowded taco restaurant and bar.

When you're back at the big intersection of Damen, North, and Milwaukee, take a sharp right, going southeast down Milwaukee, a business corridor some locals call the Hipster Highway. It's filled with restaurants, bars, boutiques, and murals, along with some relics of the era when furniture stores dominated the street. Alas, the Yeti cooler store (at 1572) replaced the Double Door after the 2017 eviction of that concert venue, where the Rolling Stones once played. Another place requiring some retrospective imagination is Rapha (1514), a cycling accessories shop occupying the space that was the fictional Championship Vinyl record store in the 2000 movie *High Fidelity*. Some of the cool spots over the next few blocks include ❻ **Myopic Books** (at 1564); the Wormhole Coffee (1462); Davenport's Piano Bar and Cabaret (1383); ❼ **Reckless Records** (1379); the Emporium Wicker Park arcade bar (1366); the ❽ **Den Theatre** (1331), a complex where a number of acclaimed small theatrical groups perform plays; and Shuga Records (1272).

Cross Ashland Avenue into the Polish Triangle, a plaza frequented by pigeons and people waiting for buses, on the western edge of the Noble Square neighborhood, an old Polish enclave. A wrought-iron fountain named after Algren sits in the center. In 2019 tentative plans surfaced for a plaza redesign. Look south across Division Street to see the ❾ **Chopin Theatre,** which opened in 1918 as a nickelodeon showing silent movies. Since 1990, it has hosted shows by a variety of small theater companies. West of it, Podhalanka restaurant has been serving Polish comfort food like borscht and kielbasa for decades.

Looking west across Ashland, you'll see the six-story Home Bank and Trust Company building from 1926, with its tall arched windows, where the main space is now occupied by a CVS drug store. At the southwest corner of Ashland and Division, the 1611 West Division apartment building was completed in 2013, with gray vertical reflective panels and indented glass windows forming an irregular pattern across its hulking 11-story structure. This was Chicago's first transit-oriented development. Because of its proximity to public transportation, it includes no parking for its tenants.

At the south edge of the plaza, cross Ashland, heading west on Division. The street is filled with restaurants and bars, many of them offering outdoor seating on the wide sidewalk during warm weather. Highlights include Alliance Bakery (at 1736), serving European pastries and desserts, as well as espresso; Caffè Streets (1750); Gold Star Bar (1755), in business since the 1930s; Phyllis Musical Inn (1800), which opened in 1954 as a polka club and has hosted live rock music for decades; Mac's American Food & Drink (1801), notable for the old Schlitz globe on its 1900-era facade; Red Square spa and restaurant (1914), which opened in 1906 as the old Division Street Russian and Turkish Baths; and Jerry's (1938), a restaurant with craft beers and crafty sandwiches.

At Damen Avenue, ❿ **Rainbo Club**—a bar that's been a neighborhood mainstay since 1985, serving as a hangout in the 1990s for local musicians like Liz Phair and the guys in Urge Overkill—lies just south of Division. With its opaque windows, the low-slung brick building feels like a hidden clubhouse.

Continue west on Division, then go south on Leavitt Street into the Ukrainian Village neighborhood. At the southeast corner of Leavitt and Haddon Avenue, ⓫ **Holy Trinity Orthodox Cathedral** is one of only two houses of worship designed by Louis Sullivan. John Kochurov, a priest who emigrated from St. Petersburg, hired Sullivan and raised money for the project, including $4,000 from Czar Nicholas II. (Now regarded by the Russian Orthodox Church as a saint—and often called St. John of Chicago—Kochurov returned to Russia, where he was murdered by Bolsheviks in 1917.) Sullivan modeled this 1903 building after a small wooden church in Tatarskaya, Siberia, but his distinctive abstract designs are carved and painted in the woodwork. Since 2002, the church has been restoring elements of Sullivan's original design that were changed over the previous century.

Turn west on Cortez Street, strolling past St. Volodymyr Ukrainian Orthodox Cathedral. When you reach Western Avenue, you will find ⓬ **The Empty Bottle** at the northeast corner. Open since 1992 (at this site since 1993), it's one of Chicago's leading small venues for indie rock music, where bands including the White Stripes, the Flaming Lips, and Arcade Fire played when they weren't yet famous.

To depart via the CTA, catch a 50 bus on Western Avenue. Or walk a few blocks south for the 66 Chicago Avenue bus.

Wicker Park & Vicinity

Points of Interest

1. **Quimby's Bookstore** 1854 W. North Ave., 773-342-0910, quimbys.com
2. **Piece Brewery and Pizzeria** 1927 W. North Ave., 773-772-4422, piecechicago.com
3. **The Robey** 2018 W. North Ave., 872-315-3050, therobey.com
4. **Violet Hour** 1520 N. Damen Ave., 773-252-1500, theviolethour.com
5. **Big Star** 1531 N. Damen Ave., 773-235-4039, bigstarchicago.com
6. **Myopic Books** 1564 N. Milwaukee Ave., 773-862-4882, myopicbookstore.com
7. **Reckless Records** 1379 N. Milwaukee Ave., 773-235-3727, reckless.com
8. **Den Theatre** 1331 N. Milwaukee Ave., 773-697-3830, thedentheatre.com
9. **Chopin Theatre** 1543 W. Division St., 773-278-1500, facebook.com/chopintheatre
10. **Rainbo Club** 1150 N. Damen Ave., 773-489-5999, instagram.com/real_rainboclub
11. **Holy Trinity Orthodox Cathedral** 1121 N. Leavitt St., 773-486-6064, holytrinitycathedral.net
12. **The Empty Bottle** 1035 N. Western Ave., 773-276-3600, emptybottle.com

27 Logan Square
An Ever-Changing Neighborhood

Above: Houses on Kedzie Avenue

BOUNDARIES: Western Ave., Diversey Blvd., Kimball Ave., Armitage Ave.
DISTANCE: 4.1 miles
DIFFICULTY: Easy
PARKING: Free street parking on Logan Blvd. frontage streets west of I-90
PUBLIC TRANSIT: CTA 50 bus to Western Ave. and Logan Blvd.

Few Chicago neighborhoods have evolved as quickly in recent decades as Logan Square. With a bounty of beautiful old buildings and expansive green space, it was a predominantly Hispanic and working-class area in 1990, when the affordable rents began to attract a growing number of young white tenants. In the early 2000s, hip restaurants began to fill many of the storefronts in this Northwest Side neighborhood. By 2013 *New York Times* travel writers were suggesting Logan Square as the first place tourists should stop in Chicago to find cocktail lounges.

Real estate prices jumped, and many of Logan Square's longtime Hispanic residents moved out. "Logan Square seems like it transitioned from a young, hip neighborhood to yuppie within a couple of years," local historian Paul Durica told the *Chicago Reader* in 2013. Five years after that, *Chicago* magazine declared: "Hipster Logan Square is done. . . . The neighborhood is no longer changing. It's changed."

And yet, in spite of all the hue and cry about gentrification, Logan Square remains a vibrant mix of old and new, both fancy and rough around the edges.

Walk Description

Starting at Western Avenue, walk west on Logan Boulevard, passing through the cavernous space below Kennedy Expressway where skateboarders and BMX bicyclists whirl and crash in the ❶ **Logan Boulevard Skate Park,** amid murals and artist Lucy Slivinski's *Silversurf Gate,* a 2010 sculpture made out of stuff like tailpipes, hubcaps, and traffic signals.

Continue west on Logan Boulevard, a wide corridor with a main roadway down the middle, plus landscaped medians and frontage streets on either side. This is just one segment in a 26-mile Emerald Necklace of boulevards that encircle central Chicago. When construction began on the boulevards in the 1870s, they were on the city's outskirts, but as Chicago expanded outward, this corridor of green space became a focal point of many neighborhoods.

Walk along Logan Boulevard's north edge. Both sides of the boulevard are lined with greystones, constructed in the 1890s and early 20th century. Imported by train from quarries in Indiana, large blocks of durable Bedford limestone cover the front walls of these houses. Some of them are carved with intricate details, while others feature stacks of rocks that look like the rough-hewn walls of a mountain castle. At Talman Avenue, head south across the boulevard, then go west on the sidewalk along the south frontage street. Amid the greystones, note the distinctively Prairie School look and art glass windows of architect George Maher's John Rath House at the southwest corner of Logan and Washtenaw Avenue, built in 1907.

As you approach Logan Square Park—a complicated tangle of streets coming together in a sort of circle—go northwest along Milwaukee Avenue toward ❷ **Comfort Station,** a small Tudor-style building. The local park commission built it in 1926 as a warming station and public restroom for people traveling the boulevard. One of nine such rest stops around Chicago, it's one of only two that still stand today. After storing city lawn equipment for decades, it reopened in 2011 as a multidisciplinary arts space.

Where Milwaukee Avenue runs into the north side of the Logan Boulevard circle, there's a crosswalk to your left. Follow that west, heading into the park, where locals sit for relaxation or gather for events including a farmers' market and occasional concerts. A 70-foot-tall marble column topped by an eagle sculpture stands at the center of a plaza. Built in 1918 to commemorate 100 years of statehood, the ❸ **Illinois Centennial Monument** was designed by architect Henry Bacon, famed for creating the Lincoln Memorial. Images at the column's base show explorers, American Indians, farmers, and laborers. These are the handiwork of Evelyn Beatrice Longman, the first woman sculptor elected as a full member of the National Academy of Design. Walk in a circle around the monument—shaped like the columns of the Parthenon in Greece—taking in views of the surrounding neighborhood.

Return back across Milwaukee Avenue on the same crosswalk. Following Milwaukee northwest, walk across Logan Boulevard, then head north on Kedzie Avenue. A block north, ❹ **Longman & Eagle,** praised by the *Michelin Guide Chicago* and renowned for its cocktails and inventive cuisine, is a popular spot for foodies. Open since 2010 (and named after the sculptor of Logan Square's monument), it includes a boutique hotel with six quirkily decorated rooms.

Continue north to Diversey Avenue, where at the northwest corner lies Bric-a-Brac Records and Collectibles, a record store with an indie-rock vibe, colorful pop-culture-drenched decor, and frequent musical performances by garage bands—always free and always loud. Next door, just to the east, a bland storefront conceals the ❺ **Lost Lake** tiki bar, famous for its tropical drinks (with names like Saturn in the House of Saturday Forever and Hula Hips of Heaven). In 2018 it was named America's best cocktail bar at the Spirited Awards.

Walk west on Diversey until you reach the big intersection where Diversey, Milwaukee, and Kimball Avenues meet. Across the street to the west, Crown Liquors is an old-school bar and liquor store, where the specials include a mystery drink determined by a roll of dice.

Walk southeast on Milwaukee Avenue, Logan Square's main street for restaurants, bars, and shops, along with a colorful array of murals and street art. This stretch is anchored by the ❻ **Logan Theatre,** which opened in 1915 as Paramount Theatre, a single-screen cinema, before a decades-long run as the multiscreen Logan. Renovations in 2012 added a bar and lounge, while revealing a stained glass arch and Art Deco details that had been hidden behind bland plaster walls. In addition to first-run movies, the Logan hosts occasional festivals and special events.

As you approach the intersection with Kedzie Boulevard—with the Illinois Centennial Monument looming up ahead—turn south, walking past an entrance for the Blue Line subway, as well as the Paseo Prairie Community Garden. As you continue south, you'll see the Norwegian Lutheran Memorial Church, known as Minnekirken or The Red Church, where the services are bilingual, alternating between English and Norwegian. Built in 1912—when the neighborhood had a large Scandinavian population—the Gothic Revival structure has superb acoustics.

Cross Wrightwood Avenue and head south down the western edge of Kedzie—another leg in the system of boulevards that form a ring across the city's neighborhoods. Like Logan Boulevard, Kedzie is lined with magnificent old houses. Noteworthy buildings in this stretch include the Stan Mansion (at 2434), a Masonic lodge designed by John Ahlchlager in the 1910s, which was restored in 2018 and turned into a wedding venue. Also check out the William Nowaczewski House (2410), an ornate 1897 fortress with a crenellated tower.

When you reach Fullerton Avenue, turn east, walking across the boulevard, then head north up the boulevard's eastern sidewalk. As you cross Albany Avenue, note the bulky rectangular structure of Armitage Baptist Church at the northeast corner; it was the Logan Square Masonic Temple when it opened in 1921. **7 City Lit Books,** an independent shop that opened in 2012, sits just north of the church. The big building north of that is Logan Square Auditorium, constructed in 1915, which now hosts rock concerts in the upstairs ballroom. The ground floor includes **8 Lula Cafe,** which serves a farm-to-table and vegetarian-friendly menu. It's been one of Logan Square's most popular restaurants since it opened in 2000—years before other trendy dining spots arrived.

As you return to the traffic circle with the big monument, turn east, walking a block along Logan Boulevard, and then veer southeast down Milwaukee Avenue. The seven-story building

Logan Square Auditorium

stretching along the southwest side of Milwaukee here is a potent emblem of how Logan Square has evolved. This land was filled with auto dealerships and repair shops from the 1920s until the 1960s. In 1995 Discount Megamall, running an indoor flea market, took over a big chunk of the street. That mall was demolished in 2017 to make way for this complex: 220 pricey apartments, plus 62,000 square feet of retail space, including a small Target. The opposite side of the street is more interesting, filled with spots like New Wave Coffee and the Owl bar.

At Sacramento Avenue, take a little detour to see some of the prime spots where street artists paint walls with an ever-changing array of murals. Go south down the east side of Sacramento. About a block later, take the diagonal alley that runs toward the southeast under the L tracks—where the walls are always colorful. Go south across Fullerton Avenue. (Jog a bit west to use the walk signal to cross.) Half a block east of Sacramento, take the alley running south from Fullerton. Half a block later, walk east along the wall where mural painting is encouraged. You may even see some painting in progress. At the end of the wall, take the alley that runs southeast under the L tracks. Turn east on Medill Avenue, where more murals cover the back walls of a building that houses the East Room bar.

Rejoin Milwaukee Avenue, heading southeast down a mural-packed corridor. Dining and drinking spots along this stretch include Cole's Bar, ❾ Revolution Brewing's brewpub, Cafe Mustache, Logan Bar, Cozy Corner Restaurant and Pancake House, and the Boiler Room.

At the northeast corner of Milwaukee and Rockwell Street, the Congress Theater, constructed in 1926 with a four-story facade featuring columns, looks something like a Greek temple. After many years of hosting rock concerts (as well roller derby games and wrestling matches), the decrepit building closed in 2013. Renovations began a few years later. Farther southeast, there's another concert venue: ❿ Concord Music Hall, which opened in 2013. A giant image of Robin Williams's face, painted in 2018 by artists Jerkface and Owen Dippie, watches passersby from the building's north wall.

When you reach Armitage Avenue, cross over to the south side of the street, then walk east one block. At the southwest corner of Armitage and Western Avenues, ⓫ Margie's Candies has been a popular ice cream parlor and confectionery since 1921, owned all that time by the Poulos family and crammed with kitschy knickknacks. (Originally called the Security Sweet Shop, it became Margie's Candies in 1933, when Margie Michaels married into the family.) According to the Poulos family, the Beatles visited Margie's in 1965, ordering six-scoop Atomic Sundaes.

The walk ends at Armitage and Western. To depart via the CTA, you can take the 50 bus on Western or the 73 bus on Armitage—or go two blocks south to the Blue Line station on Western.

Points of Interest

1 **Logan Boulevard Skate Park** Western Ave. and Logan Blvd., chicagoparkdistrict.com/parks-facilities/logan-boulevard-skate-park-0

2 **Comfort Station** 2579 N. Milwaukee Ave., comfortstationlogansquare.org

3 **Illinois Centennial Monument** 3150 W. Logan Blvd.

4 **Longman & Eagle** 2657 N. Kedzie Ave., 773-276-7110, longmanandeagle.com

5 **Lost Lake** 3154 W. Diversey Ave., 773-293-6048, lostlaketiki.com

6 **Logan Theatre** 2646 N. Milwaukee Ave., 773-342-5555, thelogantheatre.com

7 **City Lit Books** 2523 N. Kedzie Blvd., 773-235-2523, citylitbooks.com

8 **Lula Cafe** 2537 N. Kedzie Ave., 773-489-9554, lulacafe.com

9 **Revolution Brewing** 2323 N. Milwaukee Ave., 773-227-2739, revbrew.com

10 **Concord Music Hall** 2051 N. Milwaukee Ave., 773-570-4000, concordmusichall.com

11 **Margie's Candies** 1960 N. Western Ave., 773-384-1035, margiesfinecandies.com

28 The Gold Coast & Old Town
Rich Territory

Above: Looking south across South Pond

BOUNDARIES: Oak St., Lake Michigan, Armitage Ave., Cleveland Ave.
DISTANCE: 4.3 miles
DIFFICULTY: Easy
PARKING: Metered street parking and paid lots
PUBLIC TRANSIT: CTA buses 143,146, 147, 148, and 151 stop at Michigan Ave. and Delaware Pl., two
blocks south of the starting point for this walk; or walk 0.5 mile from the CTA Red Line's Chicago
Ave. station (go east on Chicago and north on Michigan)

As its name suggests, the Gold Coast is one of Chicago's wealthiest neighborhoods. Potter Palmer, who founded the Palmer House Hotel, was the pioneer, constructing a castle along the lakeshore in the 1880s. Other rich Chicagoans soon followed.

The neighborhood west of the Gold Coast started calling itself Old Town after World War II, when some residents fought to preserve the area's historic architecture from urban planners eyeing it as a blighted zone ready for demolition. It was an early battle in Chicago's ongoing neighborhood wars over gentrification.

The Gold Coast and Old Town are both picturesque, with boutiques and restaurants nestled among many awe-inspiring buildings. Walking through these neighborhoods, you'll also see Rush Street—a name once synonymous with drinking and sex—and stroll through the green fields at Lincoln Park's south end.

Walk Description

Starting at Michigan Avenue, walk west on Oak Street. High-end fashion boutiques line the street, including showcases for designers like Christian Louboutin and Tom Ford. Amid these pricey shops, a tall sign spells out ESQUIRE, the name of a theater that showed movies here 1938–2006. Turn north on Rush Street, which was famous—or infamous—for decades as the spot where men and women came to drink, dance, and hook up. At the southwest corner of Rush and Bellevue Place, ❶ **Gibsons Bar & Steakhouse** sits where Mister Kelly's nightclub was 1957–1975, featuring performances by everyone from Barbra Streisand to Lenny Bruce. Rush Street's nightlife may be tamer today, but it's still a popular spot after dark.

Go north across Bellevue, entering Mariano Park, a plaza on the west side of Rush with a fountain, chairs, and a coffee kiosk. Acquired by the city in 1848 and transferred to the Chicago Park District in 1959, this sliver of open space was named in 1970 after *Chicago Daily News* reporter Louis Mariano. Exiting the park's north end, you're at the point where Rush Street merges into State Street. Walk north up State. When you reach Division Street, a few famous drinking spots will be to your west, including the Original Mother's, Mother's Too, and Butch McGuire's. But head east on Division, then go north up Astor Street.

The street is named for John Jacob Astor, America's richest person when he died in 1848. He never lived in Chicago, but many of the city's wealthiest citizens resided on this street. At 1210, a redbrick apartment building with prominent bays was designed by Holabird & Roche in 1897. At 1260 and 1301, two Art Moderne apartment towers were among the Gold Coast's first high-rises west of Lake Shore Drive when Philip B. Maher designed them in the early 1930s. The row houses at 1308, 1310, and 1312 are the survivors from a set of four—built in the late 1880s and designed by John Wellborn Root. At 1355, a Georgian Revival building (designed in 1914 by Howard Van Doren Shaw) has details like animal heads and skulls topped by fruit baskets. At 1365, the ❷ **Charnley-Persky House Museum** was designed by Louis Sullivan in 1882, when Frank Lloyd Wright was a draftsman at his firm. Today, it houses the Society of Architectural Historians, which offers guided tours at noon, Wednesday and Saturday.

When you reach Schiller Street, jog a bit to the east and continue north on Astor. At 1406, David Adler designed a French-style mansion for stainless steel tycoon Joseph T. Ryerson Jr. in 1922, then added a fourth floor several years later to accommodate Ryerson's collection of Chicago memorabilia, which was later donated to the Chicago Historical Society. At the northwest corner of Astor and Burton Place, an Italian Renaissance–inspired palazzo was designed by Stanford White in 1893 for *Chicago Tribune* editor Robert Patterson and his wife, Elinor (daughter of the newspaper's longtime publisher, Joseph Medill). Cyrus H. McCormick Jr. bought it in 1914, and Adler more than doubled its size in 1927. The 90-room mansion was converted into condominiums after it was saved from demolition in the 1970s.

Half a block north of Burton, turn west into the alley—a rare example of an alley made with wooden blocks. Chicago used such blocks for some street surfaces starting in 1856. The chemically treated wood didn't burn easily, so most wooden thoroughfares survived the Great Chicago Fire of 1871. This alley, constructed in 1909 and restored in 2011, is just south of the Residence of the Roman Catholic Archbishop of Chicago, a Queen Anne–style mansion from 1880 with a multifaceted roof and 19 chimneys. After becoming archbishop in 2014, Cardinal Blase Cupich opted against living in this ostentatious mansion.

At the alley's end, go north on State Parkway. Cross North Avenue into Lincoln Park, following the paths north toward *Fountain Girl.* Sculpted by English artist George Wade, the original version of this bronze was displayed near the Woman's Christian Temperance Union booth at the 1893 world's fair, providing "pure drinking water" as an alternative to booze. It was later installed at downtown's Chicago Woman's Temple, then moved to Lincoln Park when that building was demolished. The statue was stolen in the late 1950s and never found, but this replica was installed in 2011. Head northwest toward *Abraham Lincoln: The Man* or "Standing Lincoln," a larger-than-life bronze from 1887 by Augustus Saint-Gaudens, who also sculpted Grant Park's "Seated Lincoln."

Go southwest to the corner of North Avenue and Clark Street, then walk north on Clark, alongside the ❸ **Chicago History Museum.** Founded in 1856—and known as the Chicago Historical Society until a rebranding in 2006—the museum has been here since 1932. A permanent show called *Chicago: Crossroads of America* is a marvelous introduction to the city and its story. Visitors can peruse rare books and documents in the research center. Look across Clark to see the Moody Church, named after evangelist Dwight L. Moody. Built in 1925, it is one of America's grandest Romanesque Revival churches, with 36 stained glass windows and a 3,700-seat sanctuary—Chicago's largest column-free auditorium. Continue north, looking east into the park to see Couch Tomb. This limestone mausoleum, where hotel owner Ira Couch was buried in 1857, is a reminder of the fact that this used to be the City Cemetery. Graves were moved elsewhere as the land was transformed into a park in the 1860s, but it was a haphazard effort, so many bodies—thousands, according to some estimates—likely remain beneath the park.

Walk north across La Salle Drive. Belgian sculptor Count Jacques de la Laing's 1889 bronze figure of explorer René-Robert Cavelier, Sieur de La Salle, stands at the northeast corner. Walk east, crossing Stockton Drive toward Richard Henry Park's 1895 sculpture of Benjamin Franklin. Look north at the Ulysses S. Grant Monument in the distance. Sculpted in 1891 by Italian immigrant Louis T. Rebisso, this 18-foot-tall bronze depicts Grant riding a horse. Follow the paths toward the monument, then walk through the stone passageway underneath Grant. Turn right and go down the steps. Turn right again, entering a tunnel below the monument and heading west toward South Pond.

Follow the paths northwest along the pond, walking under the arches of the Peoples Gas Education Pavilion. (At this point, you could leave our route and visit Lincoln Park Zoo, part of Walk 29.) Go west on the bridge over the pond, pausing to look at the downtown skyline. After crossing, go south on the path between the pond and Lincoln Park Zoo's Farm-in-the-Zoo, where cows, goats, chickens, pigs, rabbits, and ponies live amid a red barn, farmhouse, dairy barn, and garden. Take the South Pond Nature Walk's boardwalks (installed in 2010 and designed by Studio Gang Architects) out over the water, getting a close look at the aquatic flora and fauna.

Once you've reached the pond's southwest corner, go west through the park, heading toward the 12-story ❹ Hotel Lincoln, which opened in 1928 as the Park View Hotel. Playwright David Mamet lived here in the early 1970s and often wrote in the ground-floor restaurant. Today's hotel includes the J. Parker Rooftop Bar.

Cross Clark Street and walk one short block west on Lincoln Avenue, then go south on Wells Street. Turn into a pedestrian-only entrance on the street's west side, going west on Menomonee Street into the Old Town Triangle. Turn north on Lincoln Park West, where many of the houses were built shortly after the fire of 1871. Adler & Sullivan designed the row of four rental houses at 1826, 1828, 1830, and 1834 in the mid-1880s. The namesake of downtown's Wacker Drive—Charles Wacker, a German immigrant who made his fortune in brewing and later promoted urban planning—lived at 1836. His son Frederick lived in the Swiss chalet–style cottage at 1838.

Go west on Wisconsin Street, where the south side is filled with octagon-front Italianate houses from the late 1870s. Then go south on Orleans Street and west on Menomonee, where the cottages lining the street's south side (325–345) give you an idea of what this neighborhood looked like before the 1871 fire. Half a block west of Orleans, look for the tiny building at the northwest corner with the alley. It's a rare example of the one-room "relief cottages" that the Relief & Aid Society constructed after the 1871 fire.

Turn north on Sedgwick Street. Halfway up the block on Sedgwick's west side, enter Ogden Mall Park, a plaza with a playground, chess tables, and *Horsepower I*—two horse sculptures that John Kearney created in the 1970s by welding together steel bumpers from automobiles. Looking southwest, you can see the corridor where Ogden Avenue once cut through, until the diagonal street was removed from this neighborhood in 1967. Walk south through the park, just east of the Midwest Buddhist Temple, founded in 1944 by Japanese Americans who came to Chicago after being released from US prison camps during World War II.

Cross Menomonee and go south on Fern Court. Then walk west on Willow Street and south on Hudson Avenue. The fortress at 1700 is the home that modernist architect Walter A. Netsch Jr. designed for himself in 1974. Hidden from the street, it has a 33-foot-high central loft under skylights and solar panels. When you reach Eugenie Street, you'll see St. Michael Catholic Church, a German parish founded in 1852. The building includes stone walls that survived the 1871 fire. It's said that if you can hear the bells of St. Michael's, you're in Old Town.

Head east on Eugenie. At the corner with Sedgwick, **❺ Twin Anchors Restaurant & Tavern,** famed for its barbecue ribs, has been in business since 1932. It was a tavern as far back as 1910. During Prohibition, it was a speakeasy called Tante Lee Soft Drinks. And starting in the 1950s, it was one of Frank Sinatra's favorite spots.

Continue east on Eugenie. From 215 to 225, four wooden Italianate cottages with gabled roofs were built in 1874, just before a new law (prompted by Chicago's devastating fires) banned wooden construction inside city limits. Turn south on Wells Street, where the **❻ Second City,** the legendary improvisational comedy company, resides inside the Piper's Alley building. The entrance is a terra-cotta frieze salvaged from Alder & Sullivan's demolished Schiller Theatre, decorated with busts of German writers and philosophers. Founded in 1959 and located here since 1967, the Second City is where many of America's most famous comedic actors, including stars of *Saturday Night Live* and countless movies, got their start. The complex includes seven performance spaces, as well as a training center.

When you reach North Avenue, you may want to stop into the **❼ Old Town Ale House—** one block west on the south side of North. Open at this spot since 1971, it's a legendary hangout for eccentrics and Second City stars. Nearly every square inch of wall is covered with paintings by owner Bruce Elliott, some depicting the tavern's regular customers and others showing politicians in provocative poses.

Continue south on Wells, Old Town's main corridor of restaurants and shops, as well as **❽ Zanies Comedy Night Club.** When you reach Division, you've arrived at this walk's end. To

The Gold Coast & Old Town

depart via CTA, go one block west for entrances to the Red Line's Clark/Division subway station—or catch a 70 bus on Division.

Points of Interest

1. **Gibsons Bar & Steakhouse** 1028 N. Rush St., 312-266-8999, gibsonssteakhouse.com
2. **Charnley-Persky House Museum** 1365 N. Astor St., 312-573-1365, sah.org
3. **Chicago History Museum** 1601 N. Clark St., 312-642-4600, chicagohistory.org
4. **Hotel Lincoln** 1816 N. Clark St., 312-254-4700, jdvhotels.com/hotels/illinois/chicago/hotel-lincoln
5. **Twin Anchors Restaurant & Tavern** 1655 N. Sedgwick St., 312-266-1616, twinanchorsribs.com
6. **The Second City** 1616 N. Wells St., 312-337-3992, secondcity.com
7. **Old Town Ale House** 219 W. North Ave., 312-944-7020, theoldtownalehouse.com
8. **Zanies Comedy Night Club** 1548 N. Wells St., 312-337-4027, chicago.zanies.com

29 Lincoln Park
From DePaul to the Zoo

Above: The Victory Gardens Biograph Theatre

BOUNDARIES: Sheffield Ave., Willow St., Diversey Pkwy., Cannon Dr.
DISTANCE: 5 miles
DIFFICULTY: Easy
PARKING: Metered street parking
PUBLIC TRANSIT: CTA Red, Brown, or Purple lines to Fullerton

Shortly after President Abraham Lincoln was assassinated in 1865, Chicago named a park in his honor. Or rather, it was a cemetery being turned into a park. Today, it's the Chicago Park District's largest park, sprawling for 1,189 acres along the North Side's lakefront. But when most people talk about Lincoln Park, they probably mean the section of the park near Fullerton Avenue. Or they might be referring to the nearby Lincoln Park *neighborhood*.

In Chicago's early years, German truck farmers lived in this area. The Great Chicago Fire of 1871 destroyed swaths of the neighborhood, but Lincoln Park is also where the flames finally died out. In the following years, mansions went up on some of Lincoln Park's streets, especially near the park. By the late 1940s, some residents worried that the neighborhood was headed toward becoming a slum. Decades of zoning and development battles followed, transforming Lincoln Park from a working-class area into a gentrified zone with high property values.

As you walk through the Lincoln Park neighborhood, you'll see pieces of all that history, along with the youthful presence of the DePaul University campus and the artistic spirit of theaters and music venues. And no visit to the neighborhood is complete without a stroll through the park itself. (You can shorten this walk by 0.5 mile or so if you leave out the concluding stroll through Lincoln Park Zoo.)

Walk Description

Walk east from the CTA station, and immediately arrive at the ❶ **DePaul Art Museum,** which has been open since 2011. Fullerton Avenue's south side is lined with Queen Anne–style row houses built in the 1880s, originally used by the McCormick Theological Seminary to generate rental income. The seminary (named after its founding benefactor, mechanical reaper tycoon Cyrus H. McCormick) moved to Hyde Park in 1975. The 56 historical homes it left behind are now part of the McCormick Row House District. At the corner with Fremont Street (where a gate blocks auto traffic), walk south into this landmark area. After a block or so, you'll see DePaul's Cortelyou Commons building on the west side of the street. Walk west and south around that building to see the university's athletic field, then go back east, crossing Fremont. Continue east on Chalmers Place, a secluded horseshoe-shaped street with a park in the middle. You'll reach the entrance of the DePaul University's School of Music's Holtschneider Performance Center—the campus's biggest structure, completed in 2018. If the building is open, walk east through its three-story atrium, then go north on Halsted Street. (If not, head north on Chalmers Place and east on Fullerton.)

When you reach the intersection where Fullerton hits Halsted and Lincoln Avenue, go north across Fullerton. Then go half a block west and north through an alley, where strings of lights hang overhead. A Peter Max–style mural, painted in 2018 by Chicago artist Mac Blackout, covers the walls of ❷ **Lincoln Hall,** one of Chicago's leading venues for indie rock music, which opened in 2009 with a capacity of about 500. Movies were shown in the same building from 1912, when it opened as the Lincoln Theatre nickelodeon, until 2006, when it was called the 3 Penny.

When the alley ends at Lincoln Avenue, look across the street at Julia Porter Park. It's named after the woman who created an eight-bed cottage for the free care and treatment of sick children in 1882, about a block south of here—naming it after her son, Maurice, who died when he was 13. Maurice Porter Memorial Hospital later became Children's Memorial Hospital. This park is on the spot where fugitive bank robber John Dillinger stayed in an apartment, hiding with his girlfriend Polly Hamilton and brothel owner Anna Sage. On July 22, 1934, the three of them went up the street to the Biograph Theater—which you can see just a bit to the northwest—to see *Manhattan Melodrama* starring Clark Gable. As they came out of the movie, FBI agents, led by Melvin Purvis, shot Dillinger. He died near the alley you can see in between the Biograph and the park. The Biograph showed movies from 1914 to 2004. After extensive renovations, ❸ **Victory Gardens Theater** moved into the space in 2006, presenting plays.

Walk northwest on Lincoln. The building at 2438 was Lounge Ax, where indie rock musicians played in front of sweaty crowds from 1987 to 2000. Regular performers included Wilco, whose front man, Jeff Tweedy, married the venue's co-owner Sue Miller in a ceremony inside the club. Lounge Ax makes a cameo in the 2000 film *High Fidelity*. It's now Millie's Supper Club. Two buildings farther north, the ❹ **Red Lion Pub** has the authentic look of an English pub, along with the appropriate drinks and food—and supposedly some ghosts. The building has been there since 1882, but it didn't become the Red Lion until 1984. After it closed for several years, a new owner reopened it in 2014, adding shelves filled with books about British history and literature. Look across the street at the oral surgery clinic at 2449. From the late 1970s until 1993, it was a hot spot for punks, the Wax Trax! record store—which launched a label in 1981, pioneering noisy industrial music by bands like Ministry.

Turn west on Montana Street. At the northeast corner with Sheffield Avenue, an apartment building is engraved with the curious name of its original occupant: The Common Sense Novelty Company. Go south on Sheffield, then walk west on Fullerton's south side, turning south through DePaul's Quad. Go east on Belden Avenue. At the southwest corner of Sheffield and Belden, a 9.5-foot bronze statue of Roman Catholic priest and human rights activist John J. Egan stands in front of DePaul's Student Center. Sculpted by Margot McMahon, it stands on a pedestal engraved with a question Egan asked: "What are you doing for justice?" Go south on Sheffield, where the grand Romanesque structure of St. Vincent de Paul Roman Catholic Church is on the west side.

Turn west on Webster Avenue through a short stretch of dining and drinking spots, then go south on Bissell Street. Twenty buildings on this block—from the alley south to the next corner—were all designed by Iver C. Zarbell and constructed together in 1883, giving them a unified look. Go east on Dickens Avenue, where St. James Lutheran Church was built in 1916. Then turn north on Fremont Street, where the Italianate brick houses on the west side north to the alley were all designed by Edward J. Burling and built in 1875.

Turn east on Webster. A room on the second floor at 851 is where a reclusive janitor named Henry Darger lived from 1930 to 1973. Just before Darger's death in 1973, his landlord discovered that his apartment contained a stash of large, peculiar paintings, illustrating a 15,145-page fantasy Darger had written, *The Story of the Vivian Girls.* Darger posthumously became one of the best known outsider artists. (A replica of his room, including items preserved from it, can be found at Chicago's Intuit gallery.)

Cross Halsted, continuing east on Webster, where Oz Park is along the street's south side. The park is named after *The Wonderful Wizard of Oz,* written by Chicagoan L. Frank Baum in 1900. Baum didn't actually reside in this neighborhood—he was in Humboldt Park (see Walk 25)—but this park stars his beloved characters. When you see Dorothy and Toto—one of four sculptures in the park by John Kearney—walk southeast alongside Dorothy's Playground. Head down to Oz Park's southeast corner to see the Cowardly Lion, then walk north on Larabee Street. The Tin Man occupies the next corner, with the Scarecrow standing just a bit west of him in the Emerald City Garden.

Go north across Webster, then walk northwest up Lincoln Avenue, through a stretch filled with bars and restaurants, including ❺ **Bacino's,** where the stuffed pizza is among Chicago's best. Halfway up the block, the ❻ **Greenhouse Theater Center** hosts plays by various small companies. This was the home of Victory Gardens before it moved up the street into the Biograph.

Turn east on Belden for three blocks, amid well-tended historical homes, then go north on Cleveland Avenue and west on Fullerton, where Church of Our Savior, built in 1888 with a Romanesque facade, is on the north side, with five stained glass windows from the 19th century, including one by Tiffany. Another block west, several houses from the 1880s are on either side of Fullerton, along with Lincoln Park Presbyterian Church, an impressive 1888 structure made with greenish Michigan buff sandstone.

When you reach Orchard Street, look southeast to see Lincoln Commons, a pair of 20-story apartment towers that opened in 2019 on the land where Children's Memorial Hospital was from 1904 until 2012, when it moved to the Streeterville neighborhood and became Lurie Children's Hospital. Turn north on Orchard, then go east on Deming Place, which bends slightly north amid a row of 1890s mansions.

Turn north on Clark Street, then go east on Wrightwood. One of the city's most grandiose residences stands at the southwest corner with Hamden Court, with two statues that appear to be holding up its front balcony. Adolph Cudell and Arthur Hercz designed the imposing mansion in 1896 for Francis J. Dewes, a Prussian immigrant who made his fortune as a brewer.

On the next block east, the Second Church of Christ, Scientist, was designed by Pullman architect Solon Beman, who patterned it after the Merchant Tailors' Building he created for the 1893 world's fair. Completed in 1901, the limestone-and-granite church went up for sale in 2017, prompting calls for the building to be preserved.

Continue east, crossing Lakeview Avenue and Stockton Drive to enter Lincoln Park. Look north to see sculptor John Angel's gilded figure of Alexander Hamilton, installed here in 1952. The original 78-foot-tall granite pedestal was demolished in 1993, and Hamilton has been more down-to-earth ever since. Go east across Cannon Drive to the John Peter Altgeld Monument, a tribute to the controversial liberal Illinois governor who pardoned three anarchists imprisoned for inciting the Haymarket Square bombing. This 1915 sculpture by Gutzon Borglum—most famous for creating the Mount Rushmore National Memorial in South Dakota—includes a man, woman, and child crouched next to the governor, apparently under his protection. Walk northwest toward Munich sculptor Herman Hahn's 1913 monument to Johann Wolfgang von Goethe: an 18-foot-tall, 80-ton bronze figure of a Greek god–like man holding an eagle on his knee that symbolizes the German writer's Olympian achievements.

Now go south through the park, crossing back to the west side of Cannon Drive and heading toward the North Pond, where ❼ **North Pond** restaurant occupies a 1912 structure originally built as a warming shelter for ice skaters. Go south along the pond's east side, using the North Pond Nature Sanctuary's trails, which lead toward the ❽ **Peggy Notebaert Nature Museum.** Founded in 1857 as the Chicago Academy of Sciences, it changed names when this building opened in 1999. Its most popular attraction is the Judy Istock Butterfly Haven, a 2,700-square-foot greenhouse with more than 1,000 butterflies of 40 species.

Go south across Fullerton. Near the southwest corner, the Alfred Caldwell Lily Pool, built in 1889, was reimagined as a prairie river in the 1930s under the guidance of landscape architect Alfred Caldwell. After decades of neglect, the 3-acre natural area was restored in 2002, with stonework and paths resembling limestone bluffs. Enter through the gate near Fullerton and walk around the lily pool, listening to birdsongs and the trickle of the waterfall.

You may choose to end the walk here, returning to Fullerton to catch a bus. Or walk a bit west to visit the ❾ **Lincoln Park Conservatory** (constructed in the 1890s), which showcases plants in its greenhouses. Or continue south to ❿ **Lincoln Park Zoo.** Founded in 1868, it's the fourth-oldest zoo in North America—and one of the few where admission is free. Entrances on all four sides make it easy to pop in for a short jaunt among the animals. You could also spend hours watching lions, bears, penguins, gorillas, and the rest of the 1,100 animals representing 200 species. (Walk 28 includes the area of the park south of the zoo.) Past the zoo, with Café Brauer and South Pond

Lincoln Park

to your left, make your way southwest to Stockton Drive, go north on Stockton, and then head west on Dickens Avenue to Clark Street, where this walk ends. Depart by taking a CTA 22 or 36 bus.

Points of Interest

① **DePaul Art Museum** 935 W. Fullerton Ave., 773-325-7506, resources.depaul.edu/art-museum

② **Lincoln Hall** 2424 N. Lincoln Ave., 773-525-2501, lh-st.com

③ **Victory Gardens Theater** 2433 N. Lincoln Ave., 773-871-3000, victorygardens.org

④ **Red Lion Pub** 2446 N. Lincoln Ave., 773-883-2422, redlionchicago.com

⑤ **Bacino's** 2204 N. Lincoln Ave., 773-472-7400, bacinosoflincolnpark.com

⑥ **Greenhouse Theater Center** 2257 N. Lincoln Ave., 773-404-7336, greenhousetheater.org

⑦ **North Pond** 2610 N. Cannon Dr., 773-477-5845, northpondrestaurant.com

⑧ **Peggy Notebaert Nature Museum** 2430 N. Cannon Dr., 773-755-5100, naturemuseum.org

⑨ **Lincoln Park Conservatory** 2391 N. Stockton Dr., 312-742-7736, chicagoparkdistrict.com/parks-facilities/lincoln-park-conservatory

⑩ **Lincoln Park Zoo** 2001 N. Clark St., 312-742-2000, lpzoo.org

30 Lake View
Wrigleyville, Boystown, and In Between

Above: Lake Willowmere in Graceland Cemetery

BOUNDARIES: Southport Ave., Byron St., Lake Shore Dr., Wrightwood Ave.
DISTANCE: 3.9 miles
DIFFICULTY: Easy
PARKING: Metered street parking on Southport Ave. and nearby
PUBLIC TRANSIT: CTA Brown Line to Southport

Lake View began as a rural township north of Chicago, where German immigrants grew vegetables. It was said to be the country's largest producer of celery. As the Lake View name suggests, the area included scenic spots along the lakefront, where well-to-do Chicagoans built homes. Lake View Township was swallowed up by the city in an 1889 annexation, and that original, sprawling area is now divided up into various smaller neighborhoods.

Today's Lake View neighborhood—or Lakeview, as it's often spelled—includes Wrigleyville, where the streets are filled every summer with Cubs fans, merchants selling baseball hats, and barhops tippling at the many drinking establishments. Another noteworthy enclave within Lake View is Boystown, which became the nation's first officially designated gay village with a Chicago City Council declaration in 1997. There's no shortage of restaurants and shops on Lake View's major streets, and the side streets offer pleasant walks through leafy residential areas.

Walk Description

Starting at the Brown Line station on Roscoe Street, walk north up Southport Avenue, which is filled with boutiques and restaurants, including Crosby's Kitchen, Corridor Brewery & Provisions, Julius Meinl, Cafe Tola, and Coalfire pizza. This corridor is anchored by the ❶ **Music Box Theatre,** which has shown movies since 1929. A tall sign spells out the theater's name in lights, beckoning cinema fans to events like 70 mm screenings of classic films, an annual weekend of free *Looney Tunes* cartoons, or appearances by filmmakers. With a smaller second screening room, plus a cool lounge and a back-door patio, the Music Box is one of Chicago's main gathering places for people who love movies.

A bit farther north, ❷ **Mercury Theater Chicago** is in a building that opened as the Blaine Theatre, a nickelodeon, in 1912. Today, it presents plays, including long runs of popular musicals. Nearby restaurants include Argentine steakhouse Tango Sur, along with its sister stores El Mercado Food Mart and Bodega Sur wine shop.

Turn east on Grace Street. At the southwest corner of Clark Street is ❸ **Uncommon Ground.** Since its opening in 1991 as a coffeehouse with live music—including a legendary concert in February 1994 by Jeff Buckley, celebrated with an annual tribute show—it has expanded into a restaurant and added Greenstar Brewing, the state's first certified organic brewery.

Head south on Clark, entering Wrigleyville. As you cross Racine Street, you'll see the marquee for Metro up ahead. But before you get there, note the ❹ **GMan Tavern,** formerly the Gingerman Tavern, which Metro took over in 2012. Paul Newman and Tom Cruise played pool here in 1986's *The Color of Money.* Continue south to ❺ **Metro,** one of Chicago's top rock venues. Smartbar, a nightclub where DJs play electronic dance music until the wee hours of the morning, is in the basement. They're both inside the Northside Auditorium Building, constructed in 1928 and designed in the Spanish Baroque Revival style by Christian Michaelsen and Sigurd Rognstad (who also designed many of Chinatown's buildings and the Garfield Park Fieldhouse). Joe Shanahan opened Metro on July 25, 1982, charging $5 for a show by R.E.M., which hadn't yet released a full album.

Walk south across Waveland Avenue, entering the block of Clark Street where ❻ **Wrigley Field** looms to the east. The second-oldest Major League Baseball stadium, it was Weeghman

Park when it opened in 1914, home of the Federal League's Chi-Feds, later renamed the Whales. The Cubs took over the park in 1916, renaming it Wrigley Field in 1927, after chewing gum magnate William Wrigley had become the team's owner. In 2016 the Cubs won their first World Series since 1908, finally earning the right to display WORLD CHAMPIONS on the electronic sign facing Clark and Addison Streets. As you head south toward that corner, you're walking through a section of Wrigleyville almost completely transformed in the decade after the Ricketts family bought the Cubs in 2009. The owners spent nearly $1 billion renovating the ballpark—restoring some of its old decorative touches—and constructing Gallagher Way, a plaza along the east side of Clark, plus the seven-story ❼ **Hotel Zachary** across the street. With a variety of restaurants and bars, this corridor looks classier than Wrigleyville once did, but also more generic.

Look for the statue of "Mr. Cub" Ernie Banks on the east side of Clark. When you reach Addison, you're at Wrigleyville's busiest corner, where fans congregate on game days and crowds head to the bars on pretty much every day. Head east on Addison, where sculptures of Cubs players Ron Santo and Billy Williams stand near the next corner. Go north on Sheffield Avenue, where the houses across the street offer seating on their roofs during games. At the next corner, there's a statue of the legendary Cubs TV and radio announcer Harry Caray.

Turn west on Waveland Avenue, lined with more rooftop clubs. Farther along, there's a red-brick Chicago Fire Department station, built in 1915. Cubs fans often stop to chat with the firefighters in Engine Company 78 or take photos of the Cubs logo on the fire truck's grille. Next to the station, turn north on Seminary Avenue. When you reach Grace, take a slight jog to your right, then go north up Alta Vista Terrace. Built from 1900 to 1904, this Street of Forty Doors was one of the final projects of Samuel Eberly Gross, who built thousands of Chicago's homes. The cozy block has 20 different architectural designs for its 40 row houses—each townhouse on one side is duplicated at the diagonally opposite end of the block.

Turn east on Byron Street, continuing east as it becomes Sheridan Road, then go south on Broadway. A block south, when Broadway veers to the southeast, stay on the west edge, going straight south onto Halsted Street. This is the main corridor through Boystown, where many gay Chicagoans began living in the 1960s and '70s—and the focal point of the city's Pride Parade each June. Over the next 0.5 mile, 20 steel rainbow pylons feature the Legacy Walk's bronze plaques, commemorating important people and events from the history of the LGBTQ+ community.

Popular nightspots on Halsted include ❽ **Kit Kat Lounge & Supper Club** (at 3700), where drag queens perform nightly, and ❾ **Sidetrack** (3349), where raucous crowds sing along with videos of show tunes. Popular restaurants include Chicago Diner (3411), which has been serving a meat-free menu since 1983, and Yoshi's Cafe (3257), serving French-Japanese fusion cuisine.

Halsted's storefronts are packed with colorful, quirky, and sexy merchandise. The clothing shops include Egoist Underwear (3739) and Men's Room (3420). ❿ **Center on Halsted** (3656) is the largest comprehensive community center in the Midwest focusing on LGBTQ+ community health and wellness—and it also hosts special events like the annual Chicago Alternative Comics Expo.

At the northwest corner of Halsted and Addison, notice the words 42ND PRECINCT above the doorway of an old building. That's Town Hall Station, a police building constructed in 1907—at the same spot where the Town Hall had been earlier, back when Lake View was a separate town. After the station closed in 2010, it was incorporated into the new Town Hall Apartments, a complex for LGBTQ+ residents age 55 or older.

Continue south several blocks, then turn east on Belmont Avenue, where the street is dominated by the Indiana limestone steeples of Our Lady of Mount Carmel Roman Catholic Church, built in 1914. Beyond that, on the south side of Belmont, note the bright red doors and battlemented tower of the medieval-looking St. Peter's Episcopal Church, built in 1895.

Turn south on Broadway, the main business street in this part of Lake View. This stretch includes the ⓫ **Laugh Factory** (3175), a comedy club in a former movie theater built in 1915; the Bagel Restaurant (3107), a deli with a busy takeout counter; and ⓬ **Stella's Diner** (3042), a family-owned diner open since 1962 under various names.

The corner of Clark Street and Addison Avenue, next to Wrigley Field

After walking several blocks south on Broadway, go east on Surf Street, which has a few classic high-rises: the Commodore Apartments (at 550–568), built in 1897; the Green Briar Apartments (559–561), built in 1904; and the Willows Hotel (555), a 1925 structure with an ornate terra-cotta facade and an unusual footprint: The building is only 36 feet wide, but it extends back 216 feet from the street.

Turn south on Pine Grove Avenue, where the east side is lined with row houses built in 1891. On the west side, the Pine Grove Apartments (2828) were constructed in 1924 as a luxury apartment hotel with an ornate octagonal entry pavilion. South of that is the Brewster Building, architect Enoch Hill Turnock's 1893 masterpiece. The Jasper stone exterior resembles a towering fortress, but each apartment opens onto a gabled, skylighted court.

Turn east on Diversey Parkway. When you reach Lakeview Avenue, you're just north of the life-size bronze elks (sculpted by Chicago native Laura Gardin Fraser) standing next to the Elks National Memorial Headquarters, a 1926 Beaux Arts–style landmark—dedicated as a memorial to Benevolent and Protective Order of Elks members who died serving in World War I.

This is where the walk ends. (Walk 29 explores Lincoln Park just south of here.) To depart by CTA, use the 76 Diversey bus or one of several buses running on Sheridan Road.

Another Nearby Walk: Graceland Cemetery

Established in 1860, ⓭ **Graceland Cemetery** is the resting place for a who's who of famous Chicagoans, ranging from architects, tycoons, and mayors to artists, boxers, and baseball players. And many of its grave markers and mausoleums are incredible works of design and architecture, making a stroll through the cemetery grounds something like walking through a museum of sculpture. It's also a marvelous example of a planned landscape, featuring a wide variety of trees across its 121 acres. Don't be too surprised if you notice a coyote lurking on the fringes of the graveyard, or see turtles in Lake Willowmere's water around Burnham Island, where architect Daniel Burnham and his family are buried.

Enter through the gates at Irving Park Road and Clark Street. Stop into the nearby office for a map showing the locations of burial plots for Graceland's most famous residents. Choose your own route, but we suggest making a counterclockwise loop of about 2 miles through the cemetery, beginning with a walk east toward the grave of Dexter Graves, where Lorado Taft's haunting sculpture *Eternal Silence*—an eerie cloaked and hooded figure—stands sentinel. From there, head north toward Lake Willowmere, a pond surrounded by burial places for Chicago's elite. Then wander south through Graceland's west side, making your way back toward the entrance.

Lake View

Points of Interest

1 Music Box Theatre 3733 N. Southport Ave., 773-871-6604, musicboxtheatre.com

2 Mercury Theater Chicago 3745 N. Southport Ave., 773-325-1700, mercurytheaterchicago.com

3 Uncommon Ground 3800 N. Clark St., 773-929-3680, uncommonground.com

4 GMan Tavern 3740 N. Clark St., 773-549-2050, gmantavern.com

5 Metro 3730 N. Clark St., 773-549-4140, metrochicago.com

6 Wrigley Field 1060 W. Addison St., 800-THE-CUBS (843-2827), mlb.com/cubs

7 Hotel Zachary 3630 N. Clark St., 773-302-2300, hotelzachary.com

8 Kit Kat Lounge & Supper Club 3700 N. Halsted St., 773-525-1111, kitkatchicago.com

9 Sidetrack 3349 N. Halsted St., 773-477-9189, sidetrackchicago.com

10 Center on Halsted 3656 N. Halsted St., 773-472-6469, centeronhalsted.org

11 Laugh Factory 3175 N. Broadway, 773-327-3175, laughfactory.com/clubs/chicago

12 Stella's Diner 3042 N. Broadway, 773-472-9040

13 Another Nearby Walk: Graceland Cemetery 4001 N. Clark St., 773-525-1105, gracelandcemetery.org

31 The Lakefront from Addison to Foster
Bird Sanctuaries and Beaches

Above: A boat sails into Montrose Harbor.

BOUNDARIES: Addison St., Foster Ave., Lake Shore Dr., Lake Michigan
DISTANCE: 3.9 miles
DIFFICULTY: Easy
PARKING: Chicago Park District lots or metered parking on nearby streets
PUBLIC TRANSIT: CTA 135, 146, 151, or 152 bus to Lake Shore and Waveland; or the Red Line to Addison, and walk 0.7 mile east

With blue waters stretching beyond the horizon, Lake Michigan looks like an ocean. "In its every aspect it is a living thing, delighting man's eye and refreshing his spirit," Daniel Burnham and Edward Bennett wrote in their 1909 *Plan of Chicago*. Chicago's lakefront offers many opportunities—including many parks, beaches, harbors, and piers—to experience that sense of delight. In 2019 the city completed a project to separate the 18-mile Lakefront Trail into two separate trails—one for bicyclists and one for pedestrians—both stretching from Ardmore Avenue on the north to 71st Street on the south.

Walking anywhere on that trail is nice, but many of the most scenic spots are a little ways off the path. This walk covers one stretch of the North Side's shoreline, passing through two bird sanctuaries, some dunes, and two beaches, following a route near the water. If you plan to go in or near the water, pay heed to city and Chicago Park District alerts about water quality and dangerous waves. As Burnham and Bennett also observed: "The Lake is living water, ever in motion."

Walk Description

Begin on Lake Shore Drive—that is, the smaller street west of the Lake Shore Drive expressway. South of Waveland Avenue and north of Addison Street, look for ramps to a pedestrian tunnel. Take the tunnel under the expressway. On the other side, cross Recreation Drive and head for *Kwa-Ma-Rolas,* a replica of a circa 1900 totem pole by Vancouver Island's Kwakiutl Indians. Kraft Foods founder James L. Kraft bought the original and donated it for display here in 1929, but it was returned to Canada in the 1980s and replaced with this copy, carved by Tony Hunt, a Kwagulth Indian.

Just east of the totem pole, the 10-acre ❶ **Bill Jarvis Migratory Bird Sanctuary** attracts more than 150 different species of birds. Like much of Chicago's lakefront, the sanctuary is man-made land. Created in the 1920s—and later named after a local bird-watcher who helped save it from demolition in the 1960s—the sanctuary mimics landscapes that were common along Lake Michigan's shores, with undulating wooded ridges and wet swales. A fence surrounds the core area, protecting it from humans.

Walk south along the fence, where a marsh is visible. Follow the path as it curves east and then veers north along the fence, where the wood-chip trail is surrounded by wildflowers, sedges, woodland grasses, oaks, and hackberry trees. As the path continues north, you can walk up onto a platform to get an elevated view. The sanctuary often attracts black-crowned night herons, most noticeable when they roost in tall trees during early spring. Other birds seen here include wood ducks, hawks, yellow-billed cuckoos, hummingbirds, thrushes, 18 species of sparrow, and 34 species of warbler. Dragonflies and butterflies, along with chipmunks and other small critters darting through the underbrush, are a regular sight.

Exit north from the woods, heading northeast toward the lake. The nine-hole ❷ **Sydney R. Marovitz Golf Course** is along the lake here, anchored by the Waveland Fieldhouse, a Collegiate Gothic–style building from 1931 with a four-story clock and carillon tower. The Clock Tower Café and its outdoor patios are next door.

Walk north along the lake, where the waves lap up against revetments—blocks arranged in a formation similar to giant steps. For the next 0.75 mile, the golf course is to your west and Lake Michigan is to your east. When the stepped structure ends, continue north on the gravel road along the boulder-lined shoreline. Farther north, a pier extends out to a small lighthouse-like beacon. A short distance across the water, there's a peninsula with another pier and beacon. The opening between these piers is the mouth of ❸ Montrose Harbor.

Continue north along the harbor, which has 711 slips. As you reach the harbor's northwest corner, you come upon an area of prairie grass and wildflowers to your west, along with a housing complex for purple martins. This is one of four spots along the lake where the Chicago Park District provides nesting for these migratory birds, which arrive each spring after spending the winter in South America. Martins can often be seen darting in and out of the holes in these miniature white buildings, which are elevated atop poles.

Walk east along the harbor's north edge, passing the Corinthian Yacht Club in a stretch frequented by boaters, fishermen, ducks, geese, and gulls. At the harbor's east end, continue east across the roadway toward the ❹ Montrose Point Bird Sanctuary. Before exploring the woods, head southeast across a grassy area until you reach stone steps leading down to Lake Michigan. This is the south shore of Montrose Harbor's peninsula, a popular spot for fishing—and for gazing south toward downtown's skyline.

Head north into the bird sanctuary's 15 acres of woods and meadows, where bird-watchers have spotted more than 340 species over the years, including some rare ones. In winter, you might see owls. The way Montrose Point juts out into Lake Michigan makes it a natural stopping place for migratory birds heading north in the spring or south in the fall, and many of them are drawn to a clump of shrubs and trees. Popularly known as The Magic Hedge, it grew out of honeysuckle that the U.S. Army planted to shield barracks from public view when the military leased land here from the 1950s through the 1970s.

You can take any number of routes through the woods—do a little exploring. Just stay on the paths, which are lined by ropes. Eventually, make your way northeast, emerging onto the Montrose Beach Dunes. This 13-acre area used to be part of the beach, but the park district stopped fighting plant growth amid the sands in 2001. Sea rockets, willows, and cottonwoods grew, trapping the sand and forming dunes. Plants like bog arrow-grass grow in the watery space between the dune ridges. The dunes made headlines in 2019, when two birds nicknamed Monty and Rose became the first piping plovers ever seen nesting in the city of Chicago. The dunes were temporarily closed to protect their newly hatched chicks, while photographers with big lenses stood watch every day, keeping an eye out for this endangered species. You may want to take a walk out on the long fishhook-shaped pier east of the dunes. Or look for minnows swimming in the shallow water just west of the pier. When you're ready to move on, go north on the path between the woods and the dunes, heading toward the main area of ❺ **Montrose Beach.**

Restrooms and a concession stand are in the buildings along the beach, along with the ❻ **Dock at Montrose Beach,** which serves drinks and bar food on an outdoor deck May–October, with live music every evening. As you continue north, you can either walk on the sand along the lake's edge—even dipping your toes into the water—or follow the stone embankment and grassy area above the sand. Water often covers large patches of Montrose Beach when Lake Michigan's levels are high (as they were in 2019, measuring 6 feet higher than they'd been in 2013).

When you reach the Montrose Dog Beach, you'll need to walk around its walled-in zone. North of that, go up the hill and continue north, following a well-worn rut in the grass or the nearby rocky embankment overlooking the water. Go north 0.75 mile, then follow the lakefront as it curves west, with another pier jutting out into the lake. As you go around the bend, you'll arrive at ❼ **Foster Beach.** Looking north across the sand, you'll see Edgewater's high-rises, including the pink Edgewater Beach Apartments. Restrooms and concession stands are in the building overlooking the beach. The field south of Foster Beach hosts the Full Moon Jam, a family-friendly celebration of fire dancing and music, on one night each month May–September.

The fields northwest of Montrose Harbor

The Lakefront from Addison to Foster

Walk south from the beach and then west on Foster Avenue, where this walk concludes. At Foster and Marine Drive, you can take a CTA 136, 146, or 147 bus. Or continue west to the Red Line's Berwyn stop.

Points of Interest

1 **Bill Jarvis Migratory Bird Sanctuary** 3550 N. Lake Shore Dr., 312-742-7529, chicagoparkdistrict .com/parks-facilities/lincoln-park-bill-jarvis-migratory-bird-sanctuary

2 **Sydney R. Marovitz Golf Course** 3600 N. Recreation Dr., 312-742-7930, sydneymarovitz.cpdgolf.com

3 **Montrose Harbor** 601 W. Montrose Ave., 312-742-7527, chicagoharbors.info/harbors/montrose

4 **Montrose Point Bird Sanctuary** 4400 N. Simonds Ave., chicagoparkdistrict.com/parks-facilities /lincoln-park-montrose-point-bird-sanctuary

5 **Montrose Beach** 4400 N. Lake Shore Dr., 312-742-3224, chicagoparkdistrict.com/parks-facilities /montrose-beach

6 **The Dock at Montrose Beach** 200 W. Montrose Harbor Dr., 773-704-8435, thedockatmontrosebeach.com

7 **Foster Beach** 5200 N. Lake Shore Dr., 312-742-3224, chicagoparkdistrict.com/parks-facilities /foster-beach

32 Andersonville & Uptown
From Sweden to Saigon

Above: The Green Mill

BOUNDARIES: Bryn Mawr Ave., Lake Shore Dr., Wilson Ave., Ashland Ave.
DISTANCE: 2.9 miles
DIFFICULTY: Easy
PARKING: Metered street parking on Clark St. and nearby
PUBLIC TRANSIT: CTA's 22 Clark bus to Bryn Mawr; or the Red Line to Bryn Mawr, then walk 0.5 mile
west on Bryn Mawr

Uptown, one of Chicago's most diverse neighborhoods, was a hot spot for watching movies and dancing in the 1920s, thanks to its cluster of big theaters—which explains why a street called Evanston Avenue was renamed Broadway. But Uptown lost its glamour over the next half century, as poor whites from Appalachia, American Indians, African Americans, and other ethnic groups made their homes in the neighborhood's low-rent apartments.

Over the years Uptown gained a reputation for crime and homelessness, but more recently that reputation has improved due to gentrification. Cheap single-room occupancy hotels became pricey apartments, causing some residents to worry that Uptown could become less diverse. It remains something of an entertainment district, with a few important music venues.

Just north of Uptown, Andersonville is a charming pocket of the larger Edgewater area. It's one of those places where the big city feels more like a small town, with a main street (Clark) lined by locally owned shops, restaurants, and bars. Swedish immigrants began settling here in the mid-19th century, when this was farmland. Andersonville was originally the name of a school, located at Clark and Foster, but it gradually came to represent the neighborhood itself. In the late 1980s, many lesbians and gay men moved to the area, making it feel like something of a sister city to Lake View's Boystown. The blue-and-yellow Swedish flag can still be seen all over Andersonville, even if the neighborhood isn't quite as Swedish as it used to be.

Walk Description

Begin at Clark Street and Bryn Mawr, just south of the lighted sign for Philadelphia Church, its big letters declaring JESUS SAVES. The sign was placed on the building in 1940, transforming what had been the Capital State Savings Bank. (The church's name refers to brotherly love, not the city of Philadelphia.) The congregation originally held its services in Swedish, calling itself Filadelfiaforsamlingen.

Walk south on Clark, which is filled with stores and restaurants over the next 0.75 mile. At 5404, the Calo Theater's name is still at the top of a building with lovely terra-cotta details. Movies were shown here from 1915 until the 1950s, but today the old theater space serves as the Brown Elephant resale shop. Calo Restaurant, an Italian eatery, opened in this building in 1963, before moving down the street in 1979 to its current location (5343).

At the northwest corner of Clark and Balmoral Avenue, Hamburger Mary's restaurant and Andersonville Brewing are in a building that opened in 1913 as the Swedish American State Bank, with terra-cotta details including fruit-filled cornucopias, an eagle, and Chicago's Y symbol (which represents the Chicago River and its two branches). Farther south, Svea (5236) is Andersonville's only remaining Swedish restaurant. Open for breakfast and lunch, the cozy diner has been in business since 1971.

❶ **Women & Children First** (5233), one of the country's largest feminist bookstores, hosts many appearances by authors. A Dala horse—a carved, painted wooden statue symbolic of Sweden—stands at the southeast corner of Clark and Farragut Avenue, next to the Candyality sweets shop. Installed in 2005 and painted by Lars Gillis, the horse is blue with a yellow cross on its head. Scenes of Stockholm are on one side, Chicago on the other. On the next block south, the ❷ **Swedish American Museum,** featuring exhibits, special events, a gift shop, and the Children's Museum of Immigration, is the heart of Chicago's Swedish community. On top of the building—which was originally Lind Hardware Store—a water tank was painted with the Swedish flag, becoming a beloved symbol of Andersonville. After cold weather damaged the original tank, it was removed in 2014, but a replica was lofted onto the roof three years later. Made of fiberglass and steel, it's purely decorative.

Across the street, Swedish and US flags wave at ❸ **Simon's Tavern,** near a neon sign depicting a fish wearing a Viking helmet and holding a martini glass. Simon's has been open since 1934, but the basement was reportedly a speakeasy called No Name Club during Prohibition. Inside, a mural called *The Deer Hunters Ball* is faded, peeling, and supposedly haunted—because of a face that was cut out of the painting. Environmentalist author Sigurd F. Olson painted it in 1956, based on a photo of Simon's regulars on a hunting trip, including the bar's original owner, Simon Lundberg. Glögg, a Swedish mulled wine, is a specialty at Simon's, where great local musicians play on Sundays and Wednesdays.

On the same block, Transistor, Transit Tees, and Strange Cargo sell T-shirts, gifts, and various quirky items. Half a block west of Clark on Foster Avenue, the Woolly Mammoth antiques store offers some truly weird curios, including animal skulls and obsolete medical devices. (A short distance from this walking route, the ❹ **Neo-Futurists** perform shows including *The Infinite Wrench*—a barrage of 2-minute plays—on Ashland Avenue south of Foster.)

Continue south on Clark. On the next block, ❺ **Hopleaf** is often called one of Chicago's best bars, offering a huge selection of craft beers since 1992. Farther south, Uncharted Books is stocked with a smart selection of used books. And the ❻ **Chicago Magic Lounge** presents magic shows in a lounge hidden behind the facade of a 1940s-era commercial laundry building.

Continue south until you see St. Boniface Catholic Cemetery on the east side of Clark. Go through the cemetery gates and head for the tallest monument in this corner of the graveyard—a pillar topped by a statue of a soldier. Dedicated in 1887, it's a monument to German immigrants who fought for the Union in the Civil War. Head toward an exit on the cemetery's north wall, a block east of Clark. Walk north on Janssen Avenue, then go east on Argyle Street. St. Augustine College lies on the street's south side. Look for a pair of doors framed by glazed white terra-cotta, under the name ESSANAY and flanked by two images of American Indian heads. That was the trademark of Essanay Studios, which made silent movies here from 1908 to 1918 with stars such as Gloria Swanson, Ben Turpin, and Wallace Beery. Charlie Chaplin arrived in December 1914 but made just one short film—*His New Job*—before deciding that Chicago's winters were too cold for him and heading west to Hollywood. Today's college campus includes portions of the old studio buildings, including an auditorium named after Chaplin.

Go south on Magnolia Avenue, then east on Ainslie Street. Turn south on Broadway, where Uptown's post office stands, with two large sculptures outside the 1939 Works Progress Administration building. Henry Varnum Poor's murals, installed inside the building in 1942, depict architect Louis Sullivan and poets Vachel Lindsay and Carl Sandburg. On the next block south, the massive Uptown Theatre has been mothballed for nearly four decades. But as of 2020, a $75 million restoration is being planned for the 4,381-seat theater, which has a luxurious, six-story-high lobby. The biggest cinema ever built in Chicago—and one of America's most opulent movie palaces—it was designed for the Balaban and Katz company by brothers Cornelius and George Rapp, the same architects responsible for downtown's Chicago Theatre as well as 1918's Riviera Theatre, which is just down the block. In later years, Uptown hosted concerts by Bruce Springsteen, Bob Marley, Prince, and the Grateful Dead.

A few doors farther south, blinking lights and a vintage neon sign mark the entrance of Chicago's most famous jazz club, the ❼ **Green Mill.** Starting in 1914, it was Green Mill Gardens, with a green windmill atop a building surrounded by a sunken garden for dancing. That outdoor area closed in the early 1920s as the Green Mill became a smaller venue; the garden's L-shaped land is where the Uptown Theatre now stands. By the 1970s, when Uptown was a rough neighborhood, the Green Mill was nicknamed Slime Corner. Current owner Dave Jemilo rejuvenated the place as a music venue in 1986, the same year it began hosting Marc Kelly Smith's Uptown Poetry Slam on Sunday evenings—the original event that popularized this format of live poetry performance. More than a dozen movies have been filmed in the club, including *Ocean's 12, High Fidelity,* and *Thief.* There's live music every night, including top touring artists and locals with weekly gigs. Just don't talk during the music—and don't ask for a tour of the Prohibition-era tunnels that supposedly connected the Green Mill with other nearby buildings.

At the southeast corner of Broadway and Foster, the Sheridan Trust and Savings Bank Building rises up 12 stories, all clad in white terra-cotta. The first eight floors were designed by Marshall and Fox and built in 1924; another four stories were added in 1928. *Public Enemies,* a 2009 movie starring Johnny Depp as John Dillinger, includes scenes filmed inside the bank. A residential developer bought the building from Bridgeview Bank in 2019. On the opposite side of Broadway, the ❽ **Riviera Theatre** has been a major concert venue since 1986, often attracting lines of music fans. A multicolored ring-shaped sculpture designed by Uptown artist Lowell Dennis Thompson was installed in 2019 on an adjacent plaza, symbolizing diversity.

Looking south, you'll see a building that once housed a Goldblatt's department store. Walk southeast on Broadway, along the building's east side. Over on the other side of Broadway, the Uptown Broadway Building—designed by Walter W. Ahlschlager in 1926—has an incredibly ornate terra-cotta facade populated with gods, rams' heads, birds, and fruits. The ❾ **Baton Show Lounge,** a drag club that operated in the River North neighborhood for 49 years, moved into the basement in 2019. After you walk under the L tracks, the Wilson station for the Red and Purple Lines will be on Broadway's west side. The large new station was completed in 2018, while the 1923 Gerber Building at street level was restored.

Turn east on Wilson Avenue, where the Wilson Avenue Theater (at 1050) started hosting vaudeville shows in 1909 before becoming a bank in later decades. Turn north on Sheridan Road, where the Sheridan Plaza Hotel at the northeast corner is another fine example of Walter Ahlschlager's architecture. Completed in 1921, it was where the Chicago Cubs and visiting baseball teams often stayed. It's now an apartment building. After two blocks, go west on Lawrence Avenue. On the street's north side, the Lawrence House opened as a glamorous hotel in 1928. It was in dilapidated shape, catering to low-income residents, when developer Cedar Street bought it in 2013,

Deer in Rosehill Cemetery

converting it into small studio apartments marketed to millennials—and rediscovering an Art Deco skylight in the lobby. That space now doubles as a seating area for the Heritage Outpost coffee shop and ⑩ **Larry's** bar.

Continue west to Winthrop Avenue, where the ⑪ **Aragon Ballroom** is at the northwest corner. Built in 1926 and designed in the Moorish style by Huszagh & Hill—the same architects who designed Lawrence House—the Aragon was popular in its early decades as a dance hall. Since the 1960s, it has been a rock concert venue with a capacity of 5,000. Head north on Winthrop, then go east on Ainslie Street and north on Kenmore Avenue, walking past St. Thomas of Canterbury Church and the Aragon Arms Hotel.

Turn west on Argyle Street, a fragrant corridor filled with Asian restaurants and shops, along with some colorful murals. Restaurateur Jimmy Wong bought up property here in the 1960s, planning to create a new Chinatown. Over the years, however, the street attracted many Vietnamese and Thai businesses, turning it into more of a Pan-Asian enclave. The Red Line bridge over the street identifies the area as Asia on Argyle. The most popular restaurants on Argyle and nearby blocks of Broadway include ⑫ **Tank Noodle,** Sun Wah BBQ, Ba Le, Furama, Pho 777, Miss Saigon, and Nha Hang Viet Nam, to name just a few. In 2016 this three-block stretch of Argyle was designated as a shared street, where pedestrians supposedly have the right-of-way even in the middle of the street, but the concept seems to confuse most people, who generally treat it like any other street. It's safest to stick to the sidewalks.

Continue west to Broadway, where this walk ends. Depart by a Red Line train or CTA 36 Broadway bus.

Another Nearby Walk: Rosehill Cemetery

Covering 350 acres, ⑬ **Rosehill** is Chicago's largest nonsectarian cemetery—as well as one of the most scenic and historic. Founded in 1859, it includes the burial places for more than a dozen 19th-century Chicago mayors and many other prominent citizens. Enter through the gate on the cemetery's east side, at Rosehill and Ravenswood Avenues, where the entrance structure resembles a Gothic castle. Constructed with Joliet limestone in 1864, it was designed by William W. Boyington, who also created the iconic Chicago Water Tower. Choose your own route through Rosehill, but plan to walk about 2 miles. Several historical monuments, including the Civil War Soldiers Memorial, lie just west of the entrance. Farther west, the area around Rosehill's lake is especially scenic. Deer are a common sight in Roseland; during one of my visits, I encountered a herd of 10 deer, including a couple of bucks with large antlers, wandering amid the headstones. Over toward the cemetery's west side—near Western and Bryn Mawr Avenues—you can walk

Andersonville & Uptown

through the quiet, marble-lined hallways of the massive Rosehill Mausoleum, where many of the family crypts are decorated with stained glass windows.

Points of Interest

1 **Women & Children First** 5233 N. Clark St., 773-769-9299, womenandchildrenfirst.com

2 **Swedish American Museum** 5211 N. Clark St., 773-728-8111, swedishamericanmuseum.org

3 **Simon's Tavern** 5210 N. Clark St., 773-878-0894, facebook.com/simonstavern

4 **The Neo-Futurists** 5153 N. Ashland Ave., 773-878-4557, neofuturists.org

5 **Hopleaf** 5148 N. Clark St., 773-334-985, hopleafbar.com

6 **Chicago Magic Lounge** 5050 N. Clark St., 312-366-4500, chicagomagiclounge.com

7 **The Green Mill** 4802 N. Broadway, 773-878-5552, greenmilljazz.com

8 **Riviera Theatre** 4746 N. Racine Ave., 773-275-6800, rivieratheatre.com

9 **The Baton Show Lounge** 4713 N. Broadway, 312-644-5269, thebatonshowlounge.com

10 **Larry's** 1020 W. Lawrence Ave., 872-999-3905, larryschicago.com

11 **Byline Bank Aragon Ballroom** 1106 W. Lawrence Ave., 773-561-9500, aragonballroom.org

12 **Tank Noodle** 4953 N. Broadway, 773-878-2253, tank-noodle.com

13 **Another Nearby Walk: Rosehill Cemetery** 5800 N. Ravenswood Ave., 773-561-5940, dignitymemorial.com/funeral-homes/chicago-il/rosehill-cemetery/0306

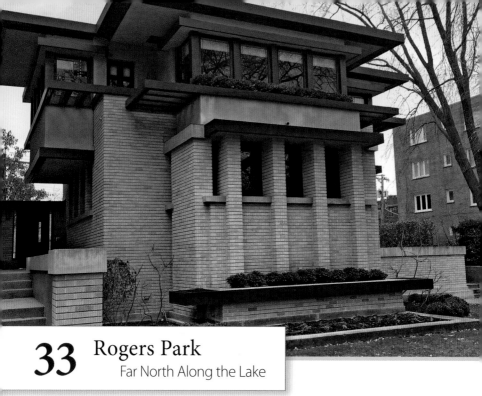

33 Rogers Park
Far North Along the Lake

Above: Frank Lloyd Wright's Emil Bach House

BOUNDARIES: Devon Ave., Lake Michigan, Juneway Terrace, Paulina St.
DISTANCE: 4.5 miles
DIFFICULTY: Easy
PARKING: Free street parking near Sheridan Road on Winthrop Ave. and Rosemont Ave., or paid garage at Loyola University
PUBLIC TRANSIT: CTA 136, 147 or 151 bus to Sheridan and Kenmore; or the Red Line's Granville or Loyola, and walk to Sheridan and Kenmore

Hugging the lakeshore at Chicago's far north end, the Rogers Park neighborhood is known for its racial and ethnic diversity, as well as its collection of small beaches. Unlike the beaches in other parts of Chicago, these spots are at the ends of residential streets. Much of the neighborhood sits on 1,600 acres of government land that Irishman Phillip Rogers purchased between the late 1830s and his death in 1856. After Chicago annexed Rogers Park in 1893, mansions were built along Sheridan Road. But within a few decades, many were torn down to make way for tall apartment buildings. Today, Rogers Park includes a mix of those architectural styles. It's also home to the beautiful campus of Loyola University Chicago.

Walk Description

Starting around Kenmore Avenue, walk east on the north side of Sheridan Road, where the ❶ **Mundelein Center for the Fine and Performing Arts,** built in 1930 with a zigzagging Art Deco design by Nairne W. Fisher and Joseph W. McCarthy, soars 15 stories high. Two mammoth archangels flank the entrance: Uriel holds a holy book and points to the sky, while Jophiel holds the torch of knowledge and a celestial globe. Originally housing Mundelein College, this was the world's first self-contained "skyscraper college" for women. It's now part of Loyola University, including an auditorium, atrium, theaters, and several classrooms.

At the next corner, where Sheridan curves south, continue walking east toward a green-roofed white house. Now Loyola's Piper Hall, a venue for special events, this 1909 building was the home of Albert G. Wheeler, president of the Illinois Tunnel Company (which built downtown's freight tunnels in the early 1900s without proper permission from the city—the same tunnels that caused 1992's Great Chicago Flood; see Walk 8).

Take the sidewalk that bends south of Piper Hall, past a figure of Jesus with outstretched arms, then head north along the lake's edge toward Madonna della Strada Chapel. This Art Deco–style house of worship was built in the late 1930s, when Chicago planned to extend Lake Shore Drive along this stretch of the lakefront. But Lake Shore Drive was never extended north of Hollywood Avenue, leaving Lake Michigan right on this chapel's front doorstep. Architect Andrew N. Rebori's design includes elements by Edgar Miller, a renowned Chicago artist. Look above the entrance at the rose window, which is surrounded by symbols of the Four Evangelists. Just north of the chapel, walk west through a colonnade—and then look back for a beautiful view of the lake through the archways.

Continue west into Loyola's East Quad (which is really more of an oval). Walk north along the Loyola Information Commons' wall of glass windows toward the ❷ **Elizabeth M. Cudahy Memorial Library,** an Art Deco gem from 1930 with a steeple and ornate green metal doors. Like the chapel, it was designed by Rebori, but a 1968 addition on the library's west end is decidedly more modern. Inside, the Donovan Reading Room, a churchlike space, features a high ceiling, tall arched windows, and a John Warner Norton mural depicting French explorers on a map of the Great Lakes.

Go west from the library, crossing the quad and following the sidewalk south of Dumbach Hall. The oldest building on campus, this 1909 structure was originally Loyola Academy high school, which moved to its current location in north suburban Wilmette in 1957. Just south of the sidewalk, Michael Cudahy Science Hall was designed three years later by the same architects responsible for Dumbach Hall (Worthmann & Steinbach) in the same Spanish Mission style. Its copper-clad dome was intended to serve as an astronomical observatory, but it was never used.

After passing between these buildings, you'll emerge onto the West Quad. Head north, taking a pathway west of Dumbach Hall. Just west of the path are the Norville Athletics Center and the ❸ **Joseph J. Gentile Arena,** nicknamed The Joe, where the Loyola Ramblers play basketball. Mexican sculptor Pancho Cardenas's 8-foot-high *Los Lobos de Loyola,* which depicts two wolves and a kettle—a symbol from the family shield of Jesuit founder St. Ignatius of Loyola)—was installed near the entrance in 2012. (Legend has it that the Loyola family in Spain's Basque country showed generosity by feeding wolves.) The statue is the focal point for the university's annual Wolf and Kettle Day, when students collect money for charity.

Make your way north until you reach Loyola Avenue, then head west. Turn north on Sheridan Road. When you reach 6560, look up at the frieze along the top of the Art Deco Kirchbaum Building. The Northwestern Terra Cotta Company, which supplied much of that decorative material for Chicago's buildings, created this scene in 1922, showing what the city looked like at that time—plus one image from much earlier in Chicago's history, Fort Dearborn, over on the left. The picture isn't painted. Rather, the colors were fired into the ornamental clay as the company was molding it. In 1956 the building became Bruno and Tim's Lounge, now simply Bruno's Lounge. Continue north on Sheridan past the ❹ **New 400 Theater,** which started showing movies in 1912 as the Regent Theater. In 1930 it was renamed the 400—a now-forgotten catchphrase for high society's most fashionable people.

Turn west on Pratt Boulevard. At the southeast corner of Pratt and Lakewood Avenue, the nine-story Seville Apartments, built in 1927, represent a lovely example of that era's high-rises. Continue west. Several of the houses along Pratt's south side were built in the 1890s. After crossing under the viaduct, turn north on Glenwood Avenue. Note that Glenwood is divided, with one half on either side of the Red and Purple Lines; look for the sidewalk west of the tracks. Since 2007, artists have been painting the railroad's concrete walls with scenes that often reflect on the history and character of the Rogers Park neighborhood, a project called the Mile of Murals. Amid the bars, restaurants, and galleries along Glenwood, an artsy enclave is anchored by ❺ **Lifeline Theatre** (6912), acclaimed for staging ambitious literary adaptations in an intimate space. When Glenwood ends at Estes Avenue, go east through the viaduct, and then south down Glenwood's other half.

Turn east on Farwell Avenue, crossing Sheridan and continuing east. At the street's end, veer southeast into Tobey Prinz Beach Park, named after the Rogers Park Tenants Committee's founder, who fought in the 1950s to save a dozen beaches at the end of local streets. Look for the pier leading out to the Lighthouse at Loyola Beach, and walk out to its tip for views of the lake and the city, then return to land. North of this pier, stroll through the grassy sands of the 6-acre Loyola Dune Habitat, staying on the pathways with rope railings as you keep an eye out for nesting shorebirds. Make your way back west, then go north through Loyola Park Beach along a 600-foot-long step-shaped seawall. Since 1993, it has been painted—and repainted each spring—with dozens of images, as part of a project called the Artists of the Wall Festival.

Continue north on the beach or the nearby grass until you reach Leone Beach Park, where the open land along the lakefront is interrupted by some private property. Go west through the park, then turn north on Sheridan, on a stretch that includes the Lighthouse Tavern (7301). At 7415, check out the classic Prairie School shape of the ❻ **Emil Bach House,** built in 1915—the only Chicago building designed by Frank Lloyd Wright that's available as a vacation and event rental.

Loyola University's Madonna della Strada Chapel

Turn east on Howard Street, which leads to Howard Beach Park, then go north on Eastlake Terrace. When you reach Rogers Beach Park, look southwest down Rogers Avenue. This diagonal street follows the Indian Boundary, a line drawn in the Treaty of St. Louis of 1816, when American Indian tribes signed away a 20-mile corridor south of here to the United States government, setting the stage for the creation of the city of Chicago. American Indians lost the land on the line's other side in an 1833 treaty.

Continue north on Eastlake to Juneway Beach Park, where Davis McCarty's 2019 sculpture *Quantum Dee*—a 20-foot-high curved pyramid with a shiny sphere at its core—reflects and refracts sunlight in rainbow patterns that shift throughout the day. This park was one of the spots where Vivian Maier often sat when she lived on Eastlake Terrace near the end of her life. Some of her neighbors regarded her as a bag lady. It was only after her death in 2009 that she became famous for her photography. Like other beaches on the Far North Side, this park has suffered erosion in recent years, as Lake Michigan has swallowed up chunks of land.

You're at the city limits. Looking north across Sheridan Road, you'll see the suburb of Evanston and Calvary Catholic Cemetery. Walk west on Sheridan, following the sidewalk as the street curves south. Turn southwest on Rogers Avenue, and then go west on Howard Street. The Red Line Howard station, the end of this walk, will be on your left.

Another Nearby Walk: Edgewater

The ❼ **Edgewater** neighborhood, south of Rogers Park and north of Uptown, is filled with wonderful buildings in a variety of architectural styles. Here's a simple 1.3-mile route that hits a few of the highlights. Begin at the Red Line's Bryn Mawr station, walking east on Bryn Mawr Avenue along a line of early-20th-century gems, including the Art Deco Belle Shore Apartment Hotel at the northwest corner with Winthrop Avenue. The remarkable Edgewater Beach Apartments—a massive pink building, the surviving half of a complex that once included a sister hotel, designed in 1928 by Benjamin Marshall—stands at the southeast corner with Sheridan Road. Go north on Sheridan Road, the area's main lakefront thoroughfare, which has many high-rises. Scenic Berger Park is at the northeast corner with Granville Avenue, with a couple of historical mansions sitting near a rocky beach. After visiting the park, go west on Granville, a street with businesses such as Metropolis Coffee Company and old buildings including the Sovereign Hotel from 1923, which is now the Edgewater Athletic Club. The walk ends at the Granville station for the Red Line.

(See tinyurl.com/chicagoedgewaterwalk for a map.)

Rogers Park

Points of Interest

1 Mundelein Center for the Fine and Performing Arts 1020 W. Sheridan Rd., 773-508-8400, artsevents.luc.edu

2 Elizabeth M. Cudahy Memorial Library 1032 W. Sheridan Rd., 773-508-2632, libraries.luc.edu/cudahy

3 Joseph J. Gentile Arena 6525 N. Sheridan Rd., 773-508-2610, loyolaramblers.com

4 New 400 Theater 6746 N. Sheridan Rd., 773-856-5977, thenew400.com

5 Lifeline Theatre 6912 N. Glenwood Ave., 773-761-4477, lifelinetheatre.com

6 Emil Bach House 7415 N. Sheridan Rd., 773-654-3959, emilbachhouse.com

7 Another Nearby Walk: Edgewater *Start:* Bryn Mawr Red Line station, 1119 W. Bryn Mawr Ave., transitchicago.com/station/bryn; *finish:* Granville Red Line station, 1119 W. Granville Ave., transitchicago.com/station/gran

34 Lincoln Square & Nearby
Riverbanks and Main Streets

Above: Riverbank Neighbors Park

BOUNDARIES: California Ave., Irving Park Rd., Leavitt St., Gunnison St.
DISTANCE: 3 miles
DIFFICULTY: Easy
PARKING: Free and metered street parking
PUBLIC TRANSIT: Brown Line to Rockwell

Chicagoans argue about what their neighborhoods are called—and where to draw the boundary lines. Take Lincoln Square as an example. If you look at the quasi-official maps of "community areas" drawn up in the 1920s, Lincoln Square covers a large chunk of the North Side. But it seems to overlap with a vaguely defined place called Ravenswood. As the *Chicago Reader* once remarked, "What's unique about Ravenswood is that even people who live there hardly know where it is."

For most people, Lincoln Square means the area along Lincoln Avenue from Montrose north to Lawrence, a neighborhood where German used to be spoken almost as much as English.

Today, the sidewalks are filled with parents pushing baby strollers, and music students carrying guitar and violin cases. Many of the shops and restaurants in this cozy corridor are locally owned.

This walk ranges beyond Lincoln Square's core, going through the bungalows of the nearby Ravenswood Gardens subdivision and two pathways through natural areas along the North Branch of the Chicago River. And if you really want to get technical about boundaries, you may notice that this route touches on the adjacent community areas of Albany Park, Irving Park, and North Center. But there's no need to worry about those borders as you enjoy the scenery.

Walk Description

Begin on Rockwell Street, where crossing signals stand next to the Brown Line tracks. This is a rare example of CTA trains running at ground level. As the Brown Line's elevated trains head northwest, they descend in the stretch just east of here. There were no streets on this land when the rail line was extended in 1907, so no elevation was required. With a few shops north and south of the tracks, Rockwell resembles a sleepy small-town business strip. ❶ **Beans & Bagels** café lies at the block's north end, and Rockwell's Neighborhood Grill is south of the tracks.

Walk south on Rockwell. At the next intersection, notice the square brick pillars on the southeast and southwest corners, marking the north edge of Ravenswood Gardens—a subdivision of single-family homes founded in 1911, when it was marketed as a "suburb beautiful." Similar pillars stand at other corners in the neighborhood, with street names emblazoned on each side, along with an RG logo. Walk another block south, then go west on Wilson Avenue, following it to a bridge, constructed in 1914, over the North Branch of the Chicago River. In 2017 local artists JoAnne Conroy and Thomas Melvin painted murals on the bridge, covering its four concrete gateway walls with scenes that evoke the surrounding landscape. Walk out onto the bridge, taking in views of the tree-lined river, then return east.

Just east of the river, go south across the grass to reach a cul-de-sac, then walk south on Virginia Avenue. Go east on Sunnyside Avenue, then south on Rockwell. Pause at the corner with Agatite Avenue to look at the pillars, where the street's short-lived original name, Potwyne Place, is still carved in stone. Continue south, crossing Montrose Avenue and turning west.

Take the bridge over the river, then turn south into ❷ **Horner Park.** Like a lot of land along the North Branch, this 58-acre park used to be a brick factory, where clay was excavated from the ground and baked into building blocks for the growing city. After the factory closed and left gaping holes in the ground, it became a garbage dump. Today, the site is filled with athletic fields. Between 2014 and 2018, invasive plants were removed and native trees and shrubs were planted in Horner Park near the river. Follow the path through this natural area—but before you go too far, take the stone staircase leading down to the water. Climb back up, then continue south, veering down to the wood-chip trail near the water—a tranquil path amid prairie plants, birds, and insects like grasshoppers.

At the trail's south end, go up the bank, then head east on the Irving Park Road bridge over the river. On the other side, turn north on Rockwell Street, entering an area of industrial buildings that contain some interesting places, like Delmark Records' office and studio, CHIRP Radio, and Albany Auto Repair & Auto Body, where vintage cars are often visible. Turn west on Berteau Avenue. At the end of the street, take the path into ❸ **Riverbank Neighbors Park,** which an organization of local residents created in 1994, adding native plants like bottlebrush grass, columbine, and wild rye. Head north on the trail along the river, where some of the neighbors have their boats docked. Continue half a block north of Pensacola Avenue, then turn east into the alley. Cut north across a parking lot and continue east on Montrose, where you'll see Lutz Café & Pastry Shop, in business since 1948.

After crossing Western Avenue, enter ❹ **Welles Park** on the north side of Montrose. The Welles Park Nature Play Space opened in this corner of the park in 2018, with small hills, a tree circle council ring, a climbing stone, and other elements designed to get kids interested in exploring nature. Head northeast through the 16-acre park, which has playgrounds, athletic fields, and an indoor swimming pool. Near Sunnyside and Lincoln Avenues, Crepes in the Park stand is open April–October. Looking east across the park, you'll see the ❺ **Sulzer Regional Library.** One of three regional libraries in the Chicago Public Library's system, it's an important gathering place for the surrounding neighborhoods. Exiting the park, walk northwest on Lincoln Avenue, where the dining spots include Bistro Campagne, a French restaurant, and the Grafton, an Irish-style pub.

At almost any given time, some of the people walking on Lincoln Avenue are carrying guitars or other instruments. This block is dominated by the ❻ **Old Town School of Folk Music,** which was founded in 1957 in the Old Town neighborhood, attracting students such as Steve Goodman, John Prine, and the Byrds' Roger McGuinn. In 1998 the school took over the Art Deco building at 4544 N. Lincoln, which has a sculpted owl above its entrance. It had been the Hild Regional Library 1931–1985, when the Sulzer Regional Library opened down the street. Now, it houses a concert hall and a shop selling instruments, sheet music, and assorted musical gear. And of course, there are many classrooms where musicians of all ages and skill levels gather to learn and play together. The interior features two beautiful Works Progress Administration murals by Francis F. Coan. In 2012 the school added another building across the street, which has a smaller concert room.

Continue northwest, entering a stretch of Lincoln where the restaurants include the Daily Bar & Grill, Fork, and Luella's Southern Kitchen. On the east side of Lincoln, a few doors north of Wilson Avenue, you'll see a stunningly ornate green terra-cotta facade. Built in 1922, this was the Krause Music Store, one of the final buildings designed by Louis Sullivan—a project he took on when he was sickly and insolvent. A miniature masterpiece of Sullivan's organic and geometric shapes, the lovingly restored building now contains offices.

On the west side of Lincoln, the ❼ **Davis Theater** has been showing movies since 1918, when it opened as the Pershing Theater, designed by architect Walter W. Ahlschlager. Renovations in 2016 restored some lovely old details and modernized the movie house, adding the Carbon Arc Bar. A bit farther north, ❽ **Laurie's Planet of Sound,** which occasionally hosts special events like musical performances, is a favorite spot for many of Chicago's record collectors.

Continue northwest on Lincoln. When the street seems to be curving west, don't be deceived—Lincoln actually continues straight here, becoming a one-way street with wide sidewalks, a mall

Looking north up the North Branch of the Chicago River from the Wilson Avenue bridge

created in 1978 to boost local businesses. Keep walking northwest on the same trajectory, entering a stretch of Lincoln where notable spots include Merz Apothecary, an upscale drugstore in business since 1875 (at this location since 1982); **❾ Huettenbar,** a "cottage bar" serving German beers on draft; Café Selmarie, inside a building where the Bertha Theatre showed movies 1914–1951; Giddings Plaza, an open area with a fountain and benches where live music is often heard; the **❿ Book Cellar,** an independent bookstore with a café and frequent author events; and **⓫ Gene's Sausage Shop and Delicatessen,** which serves beer and sausages during the summer in a friendly rooftop space featuring a life-size fiberglass cow.

When you reach Lawrence Avenue, walk a short distance west, then go north across Lawrence, where *Chicago Lincoln,* a 1956 statue designed by Lloyd Ostendorf for a city contest and modeled by sculptor Avard Fairbanks, stands in a small plaza. Alas, the backdrop includes the uninspiring sight of a Walgreens store. The monument depicts President Abraham Lincoln holding books and his hat in his left hand, while resting his right hand on a podium. An inscription quotes Lincoln: "Free society is not, and shall not be, a failure."

To depart via the CTA, take an 81 Lawrence or 49 Western bus, or head a few blocks south to catch a Brown Line train at the Western station. Or if you feel like walking farther, you could wander southeast from here through more of the Ravenswood neighborhood.

Another Nearby Walk: Ravenswood Avenue

As it stretches across several North Side neighborhoods, **⓬ Ravenswood Avenue** is lined with old factories and warehouses. Many of those buildings have been converted to new uses over the decades—including condominiums and apartments as well as art galleries, restaurants, and breweries—which makes it interesting to stroll down this generally quiet street, observing all of these adaptations of old architecture. Ravenswood is adjacent to the railroad tracks for the Metra commuter service's Union Pacific North Line, which was originally built in 1854 by the Chicago & Milwaukee Railroad. Begin at Peterson Avenue, walking south on Ravenswood near Rosehill Cemetery. South of Lawrence Avenue, Ravenswood Avenue is split into two one-way roads, with one half on either side of the railroad embankment. For a 2.8-mile walk, go as far south as Grace Street. And then if you feel up for it, head back north up the other side, ending at Lawrence, for a total distance of 4 miles.

(See tinyurl.com/ravenswoodavenuewalk for a map.)

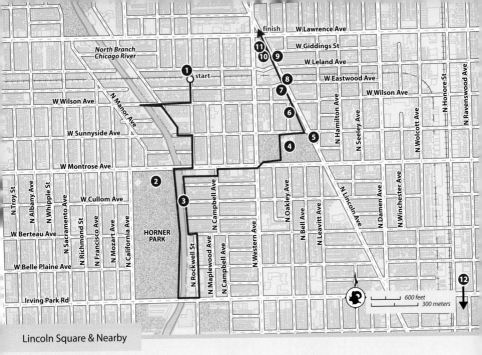

Lincoln Square & Nearby

Points of Interest

1. **Beans & Bagels** 2601 W. Leland Ave., facebook.com/beansandbagels

2. **Horner Park** 2741 W. Montrose Ave., 773-478-3499, chicagoparkdistrict.com/parks-facilities/horner-henry-park

3. **Riverbank Neighbors Park** East bank of Chicago River's North Branch between Berteau Ave. and Montrose Ave., riverbankneighbors.org

4. **Welles Park** 2333 W. Sunnyside Ave., 312-742-7511, tinyurl.com/wellesparkchicago

5. **Sulzer Regional Library** 4455 N. Lincoln Ave., 312-744-7616, chipublib.org/locations/67

6. **Old Town School of Folk Music** 4544 N. Lincoln Ave., 773-728-6000, oldtownschool.org

7. **Davis Theater** 4614 N. Lincoln Ave., 773-769-3999, davistheater.com

8. **Laurie's Planet of Sound** 4639 N. Lincoln Ave., 773-271-3569, lauriesplanetofsound.com

9. **Huettenbar** 4721 N. Lincoln Ave., 773-561-2507

10. **The Book Cellar** 4736 N. Lincoln Ave., 773-293-2665, bookcellarinc.com

11. **Gene's Sausage Shop and Delicatessen** 4750 N. Lincoln Ave., 773-728-7243, genessausage.com

12. **Another Nearby Walk: Ravenswood Avenue** *Start:* N. Ravenswood and W. Peterson Aves.; *finish:* N. Ravenswood Ave. and W. Grace St. *or* N. Ravenswood and W. Lawrence Aves.

35 North Branch Trail
Into the Woods on the Far Northwest Side

Above: The North Branch Trail

BOUNDARIES: Foster Ave., Pulaski Rd., Pratt Ave., Nagle Ave.
DISTANCE: 4.8 miles
DIFFICULTY: Moderate
PARKING: Free street parking on Keeler Ave., Tripp Ave., and other streets south of Foster Ave.
PUBLIC TRANSIT: CTA's 92 Foster bus to Tripp Ave.

This is where the North Branch of the Chicago River meanders into the city limits: way out on the Far Northwest Side. The river is surrounded by woods and wetlands where American Indians lived and hunted centuries ago. In 1829 the US government granted much of this property to Billy Caldwell, also known as Sauganash, a Potawatomi Indian chief who reportedly saved John Kinzie's life during the Battle of Fort Dearborn. Acquired a century ago by the Forest Preserves of Cook County, the land includes an area named after Caldwell. Walking through it today, you'll get a glimpse of what Illinois was like before the arrival of white men—if you can ignore the noise of traffic on nearby roads.

Walk Description

Begin your walk near the ❶ **Gompers Park Fieldhouse,** on the north side of Foster Avenue near Tripp Avenue. Walk west through the park. Look for the opening in the fence at the park's northwest corner, near the river, and walk into LaBagh Woods, following a dirt path along the river's south edge. (Taking this next portion of the route requires a little dexterity. If you'd rather take a paved trail, go west on the North Branch Trail at the park's southwest corner, connecting with our suggested route after a mile or so.)

As you walk amid the oaks, maples, and cottonwoods, listen and look for birds such as spring warblers, tanagers, sparrows, ducks, Cooper's hawks, and red-tailed hawks. And keep an eye out for forest mammals. During one of my walks here, I saw several deer, which kept on grazing even when I was standing a few yards away. Some people have seen American minks near the river, but it may be hard to catch a glimpse of those mostly nocturnal creatures. Other inhabitants of LaBagh Woods include snakes, turtles, and muskrats.

After a while, you'll run into a spot where an old railroad bridge crosses the river. Walk up the bank, and go out onto the bridge, which has a gravel surface. This was a Union Pacific Railroad line called the ❷ **Weber Spur,** but the tracks were removed in 2009 after service ended. Looking north, you'll see a corridor where the rails cut through the woods. Return to the river's south side and walk down the bank west of the bridge. Continue walking northwest along the river. In this area of low bottomlands, there's a slough—a type of wetland that forms where an old channel of a river once flowed—a short distance south of the trail. Depending on how high the water is, the landscape here may look like a Southern swamp.

As you approach Cicero Avenue—with the William G. Edens Expressway roaring nearby—your suggested route connects with the paved North Branch Trail. An American Indian village was located around here centuries ago. Turn right (northwest) onto the paved pathway. From this point on, follow the North Branch Trail as it winds along the river, generally heading northwest.

Follow the path as it crosses Cicero Avenue and passes below the Edens Expressway. Cross Forest Glen Avenue and follow the trail as it turns left, heading southwest along the avenue. Stay on the trail as it veers off from the road, heading northwest into the woods, later passing on a high bridge over railroad tracks. A metal structure lined with chain-link fencing, this bridge, constructed in 2016, created a vital link on this trail, and it offers panoramic views.

The trail bends north, arriving at a meadow in Thaddeus S. "Ted" Lechowicz Woods, where you can get a drink of well water by cranking a metal pump. Walk west along the roadway and parking lot. The trail begins again before you reach Central Avenue. Follow it, heading north along Central Avenue—continuing on it as it crosses over to the street's west side, on the edge of a forest preserve called Edgebrook Woods.

When you reach the forest's north edge, you'll see an area where several streets intersect: Central, Devon, Caldwell, and Lehigh Avenues. (If you'd like to take a short break from your walk through the woods, go east on Devon Avenue to visit some of the ❸ **Edgebrook** neighborhood's shops and restaurants.) To continue west on the North Branch Trail, look for the paved path on the north side of Devon Avenue just west of Caldwell Avenue.

Continue on the trail as it veers northwest from Devon, with the waters of the North Branch of the Chicago River running on your left side amid pin oaks and bottlebrush grass. You're now in an area called Sidney Yates Flatwoods. Look for a savanna east of the path, where the flora include blazing stars, prairie sundrops, big bluestems, mountain blue-eyed grass, and fringed gentians, and the fauna include swallowtail butterflies, song sparrows, and woodcocks.

The trail emerges on a large meadow at the ❹ **Bunker Hill Forest Preserve.** Continue on the trail as it turns south. When you arrive at a fork, take the trail to your left, heading south toward the bridge. (If you turn right here, you'll remain on the main North Branch Trail, which goes north into the suburbs, leading to the Skokie Lagoon and the Chicago Botanic Garden in Glencoe; the entire route is 33.5 miles.) Although there's no sign marking the city limits here, you're near the line where Chicago ends and the suburb of Niles begins.

Crossing the bridge, follow this branch of the trail south into ❺ **Caldwell Woods.** It will lead you to a hill with a parking lot. Walk south through the lot until you reach Devon Avenue. This is the end of this walk—but if you're hungry, you may want to stop at one of Chicago's most legendary hot dog restaurants, the ❻ **Superdawg Drive-In,** which has been open since 1948. It's one block west on Devon and one block south on Milwaukee Avenue. Just look for the roof with two figures of anthropomorphized hot dogs standing on top of it: a demure female in a skirt and a boastful male showing off his muscles. To depart via public transit, use a Pace 270 bus on Milwaukee Avenue.

Another Nearby Walk: North Park Village Nature Center

The 58-acre ❼ **North Park Village Nature Center** is part of the North Park Village campus, which was the grounds of the Chicago Municipal Tuberculosis Sanitarium from 1915 until it closed in 1974. The nature area lies in the northwest corner of the overall campus. Enter from Pulaski Road south of Peterson Avenue, walking a short distance west, then follow the signs for the nature

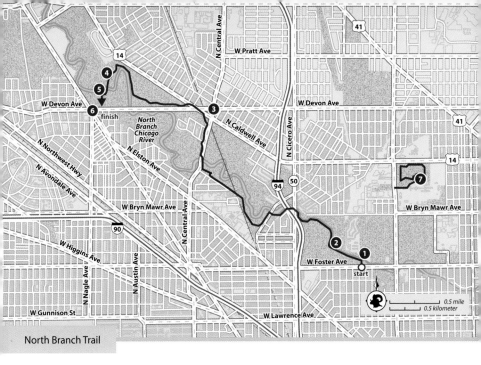

North Branch Trail

area, where you can follow trails for 1 mile or longer amid the woodlands, wetlands, prairies, and savannas. Be on the lookout for deer and other wildlife.

Points of Interest

1 **Gompers Park** 4222 W. Foster Ave., 773-685-3270, chicagoparkdistrict.com/parks-facilities/gompers-samuel-park

2 **Weber Spur** North of the Irene C. Hernandez Family Picnic Grove, 4498 W. Foster Ave.

3 **Edgebrook shops and restaurants** Devon Ave. and Central Ave., escc60646.com

4 **Bunker Hill Forest Preserve** Caldwell Ave. and Touhy Ave., 800-870-3666, fpdcc.com/places/locations/bunker-hill

5 **Caldwell Woods** Devon Ave. and Milwaukee Ave., 800-870-3666, fpdcc.com/places/locations/caldwell-woods

6 **Superdawg Drive-In** 6363 N. Milwaukee Ave., 773-763-0660, superdawg.com

7 **Another Nearby Walk: North Park Village Nature Center** 5801 N. Pulaski Rd., 312-744-5472, chicagoparkdistrict.com/parks-facilities/north-park-village-nature-center-park

Appendix: Walks by Theme

Architecture

Arts & Culture

Dining

Lakes & Rivers

Appendix: Walks by Theme *(continued)*

Lakes & Rivers *(continued)*

Wolf Lake (Walk 16)
Bridgeport (Walk 20)
Humboldt Park (Walk 25)
Lincoln Park (Walk 29)
The Lakefront from Addison to Foster (Walk 31)
Rogers Park (Walk 33)
Lincoln Square & Nearby (Walk 34)
North Branch Trail (Walk 35)

History

Michigan Avenue at the Chicago River (Walk 1)
The Loop, Part 1 (Walk 2)
The Loop, Part 2 (Walk 3)
The Loop, Part 3 (Walk 4)
Grant Park (Walk 6)
The Museum Campus & Northerly Island (Walk 7)
River North (Walk 9)
The Magnificent Mile (Walk 10)
Chinatown (Walk 12)
Bronzeville (Walk 13)
Hyde Park & Kenwood (Walk 14)
Jackson Park & South Shore (Walk 15)
West Loop (Walk 17)
Little Italy & Vicinity (Walk 18)
Pilsen (Walk 19)
Pullman (Walk 21)
Beverly & Morgan Park (Walk 22)
Wicker Park & Vicinity (Walk 26)
Logan Square (Walk 27)
The Gold Coast & Old Town (Walk 28)
Lincoln Park (Walk 29)

Shopping

Parks & Nature

Index

About the Author

Robert Loerzel, a freelance reporter, copy editor, and photographer, has lived in the Chicago area since 1988, when he graduated from the University of Illinois in Urbana-Champaign. He currently resides in the city's Uptown neighborhood.

photographed by Karen Kring

Robert's first book, *Alchemy of Bones: Chicago's Luetgert Murder Case of 1897,* was published in 2003. He has written about news, the arts, and local history for publications including the *Chicago Tribune* and *Chicago* magazine, and he has reported on-air for WBEZ Chicago Public Radio. His concert photography has appeared in many online and print publications.

In 2016 Robert won the *Chicago Reader*'s poll for Best Chicagoan to Follow on Twitter (@robertloerzel). To learn more about him, visit robertloerzel.com.